The new British politi...
Government and society

Ian Budge, David McKay, David Marsh, Edward Page, Roderick Rhodes, David Robertson, Martin Slater, Graham Wilson

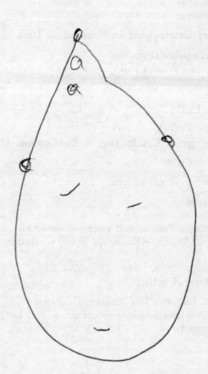

LONGMAN
London and New York

Longman Group Limited
Longman House, Burnt Mill, Harlow
Essex CM20 2JE, England
Associated companies throughout the world

Published in the United States of America
by Longman Inc., New York

First published 1983
Second impression 1984
Revised edition 1985

British Library Cataloguing in Publication Data

The New British political system.
   1.Great Britain—Politics and government
   —1964—
   I. Budge, Ian
   320.941   JN234

   ISBN 0–582–29553–X

Library of Congress Cataloging in Publication Data

Main entry under title:

The New British political system

   Bibliography: p.
   Includes index.
   1. Great Britain—Politics and government—20th
century. 2. Great Britain—Economic policy. I. Budge,
Ian.
JN231.N4   1983   320.941   82-12675
ISBN 0-582-29553-X (pbk.)

Set in 10/12pt Linotron 202 Baskerville Roman
Produced by Longman Singapore Publishers (Pte) Ltd.
Printed in Singapore

Contents

Preface

The economic difficulties and social problems which increasingly confront British governments set up strong pressures for change. These make it unlikely that political processes and institutions will continue unaltered over the next decade. Adjustments in the party system and in the relationships of central and local government are already evident, and the courts (to take only one example) have assumed a more prominent political role than in the past.

As a result, analyses of British politics cannot now, as they used to, concentrate on the major features of the central political institutions in the confidence that they will remain largely as they are. The forces for change are too powerful and pervasive to leave such a description applicable for long. What we have done here is to provide a self-contained and comprehensive account of contemporary British politics and of their relations with economy and society, which is as up to date as possible while identifying tendencies likely to alter the present situation quite radically. We have deliberately devoted attention to neglected institutions such as the European Community, quangos, and the police, who hardly figure at all in traditional analyses. This is because their power and influence, extensive at the moment, is almost bound to increase further and to alter the established balance.

Political changes in post-war Britain have followed economic developments. As a practical recognition of their importance, we start with the major challenges which have faced governments in the economic sphere over the last fifty years, and the various attempts to meet them. In explaining the relative failure of government strategies, we consider the internal dynamics and philosophy of government and Civil Service in Chapter 2, and the relevance of Parliament to policy-making in Chapter 3. Parliamentary procedures inevitably involve the political parties, both at the level of leaders and activists and of their relationships with electors (Ch. 4). An important question from the viewpoint of representative democracy in Britain is what electors want and how they relate this to voting decisions in favour of one party or another. This also involves some consideration of the influence of the media – the press, radio and television.

Of course the central government is not the only elected authority – even less the only administrative authority – in Britain. There is an incredibly diverse range of local and regional governments of various kinds active both in servicing their constituents and supporting or opposing central government, which we consider in Chapter 5. There are also the European bodies exercising authority in Britain by virtue of various treaties – most important, those setting up the European Community. Community institutions increasingly affect daily life in Britain, so we examine their activities in Chapter 6. As political disputes become more difficult to resolve, the only bodies left in many cases to make even interim decisions are the courts: we analyse their possibly increasing and certainly independent powers in Chapter 7. While authorities in Britain usually rely on persuasion and compromise to get people to do what they want, they must, like other political bodies, ultimately resort to physical coercion in the face of riots and disorder. As these become more frequent in response to economic and social hardship, the role of the police and military assumes greater prominence and political significance. Usually ignored in discussions of British politics because of the traditional law-abidingness of the population, the question of the autonomy and attitudes of the coercive forces is considered in Chapter 8. Chapter 9 draws together our conclusions on the nature of British policy-making, its prospects for overcoming current economic and social problems (which are intimately related to the ways it can adapt and change) and its ability to meet the desires and needs of the population. We end with a brief assessment of the features which distinguish the new politics of the 1980s.

Each chapter in the book has been prepared by a specialist. However, owing to the authors' daily association, the overall themes have been considered as a whole and each chapter closely related both to these and to the other chapters. The result is an analysis which combines an authoritative and detailed treatment of each topic with a clear development of overall conclusions. We hope that this avoids the weaknesses and combines the strengths of single-author treatments on the one hand, and collections of specialised papers on the other. If it does, this is due in large part to the congenial atmosphere of the Essex Department of Government, and the frequent opportunities it provides for the meeting of like, and sometimes unlike, minds!

Obviously the book draws on a vast range of discussions and analyses of British politics. The use we make of them is our own and we retain responsibility for any errors of interpretation or fact. (However, we trust these are limited!) Bearing in mind the need for a free-running and uncluttered discussion we have forborne the use of footnotes except where discussion has relied exclusively on one source for a particular area or where sources for detailed figures are being cited. The References and Bibliography lists major references and makes suggestions for further reading.

List of figures and tables

Chapter 1

Economic difficulties and government response 1931–1985

Wherever we look in contemporary Britain, evidence of increasing political and administrative activity is manifest. From social security to aid for industry to land-use planning to police surveillance, no one would dispute that governments are more active now than at almost any other time in history.

The extent and nature of government involvement in society and economy has been the dominant issue of British politics in the post-war period. To understand why this is so, and to appreciate why all governments, whether they wanted to or not, have been forced to expand their economic role, requires some appreciation of economic developments and political reactions to them over the modern period, which from this perspective starts in 1931.

British politics and government intervention 1931–85

1931–45 The rise of intervention

Contrary to usual belief, central economic management became firmly established not during the Second World War but following the world economic crisis of 1931. World economic dislocation exposed the weakness of the major established British industries such as steel-making, coal-mining, shipbuilding and textile manufacture; radically increased the numbers of unemployed to a quarter or a third of the workforce in many regions; and forced the abandonment of the gold standard, that is, the link between the value of the pound and the price of gold, symbolic of the unquestioned integrity and value of the currency.

The National (basically Conservative) Government of the ensuing eight years reacted to these alarming developments with a new economic strategy. Although this fell short of modern economic planning, it did represent a fundamental break from the essentially liberal traditions which had dominated policies until then. The new policy was inspired by the need to protect weak British industry and agriculture from foreign competition. To achieve this it was necessary both to raise tariffs on imports and to encourage the reconstruction of ailing industries. A contemporary comment by Neville Chamberlain on the introduction of the Import Duties Bill shows how interventionist the new policy was:

[The Bill] does provide us with such a lever as has never been possessed before by any government for inducing, or if you like, forcing industry to set its house in order. I have in my mind particularly iron and steel and cotton; and my belief in the advantages of protection is not so fanatical as to close my eyes to the vital importance of a thorough reorganisation of such industries as these, if they are even to keep their heads above water in the future. (Beer 1965: 293)

During the 1930s the National Governments encouraged reorganisation in the basic industries (mainly through the creation of cartels), provided central marketing schemes for agricultural products (the marketing boards) and began a policy of regional revival (via the Special Areas Acts of 1935, 1936 and 1937). The Government also pursued a low interest rate policy of monetary expansionism – although the motivations here were probably as much a desire to reduce the national debt as to fuel economic expansion. However, it would be misleading to characterise the National Government as benevolent in relation either to industrial recovery or to social policy. By modern standards it was neither, and on the social side cut welfare and unemployment benefits and applied means tests, but the protection of industry from foreign competition combined with reorganisation was a radical change. There was no indicative planning in the sense of pointing the general direction in which economic and social change should go, and administrative innovations were few and far between (the marketing boards being the main exception). But a regulative framework for unsystematic, special purpose developments was laid down, and for the first time applied to industrial protection.

Towards the end of the decade, support for more comprehensive regulation and planning was mounting steadily and manifested itself in a number of policy areas. In land use, the Government legislated to control the urban sprawl which was occurring in the still prosperous Midlands and South East. More significantly, in 1937 the Barlow Commission on the Distribution of the Industrial Population was instituted. When it reported in 1940 the Barlow Report recommended a two-pronged attack on the twin problems of regional unemployment and the continuing sprawl caused by rapid population drift to London and the Midlands. Growth in the prosperous cities should be contained with rigid controls on industrial location, while industry should be given incentives to locate in the distressed North and West. These were radical proposals indeed, and clearly demanded some central coordinating authority if they were to be effectively implemented.

Between 1937 and 1942 a number of other commissions were initiated to provide recommendations on New Towns (Reith Report), land values (Uthwatt Report), land utilisation in rural areas and national parks (Dower and Hobhouse Report) and social security (Beveridge Report). Many of the commissions were concerned with the physical environment – a fact reflecting the growing influence of the town-planning lobby during the 1930s. Beveridge was given a very wide brief – all income maintenance (unemployment benefit, pensions, national assistance), welfare services and health – as was Barlow. But it is notable that no commission on the reorganisation of industry or industrial relations was created. We can sum up the growth of state intervention in the 1930s in terms of two major developments. First, an acceptance by the Government of a role in regulating industrial and agricultural production, and second the beginnings of a planning movement with some recognition that the problems of society and economy could be solved only through increased government action. There is no doubt that these changes came about in response to the near collapse of international capitalism in the 1930s. But, crucially, recovery was seen in terms of reviving old industries (iron and steel, mining, textiles, shipbuilding) and regions which were assumed to be victims of international forces. Little thought was devoted to the restructuring of industry or to channelling investment into high productivity, high growth industries. Physical planning apart, the enhanced state role was perceived solely in terms of how to help declining traditional industries and, in embryo form at least, how to ameliorate the social evils of industrial decline. Within the Labour Party the same issues dominated – although the more draconian solutions were adopted of government ownership and control of industry, together with state support of comprehensive welfare and health services.

Between 1936 and 1945 attitudes towards state intervention among political leaders and public alike were transformed by two events – the acceptance of Keynesian economics and the total modification of the economy during the Second World War. The monetarist orthodoxy accepted by the National Governments of the 1930s held that industrial development could take place only if there were general confidence in the currency, maintained by government budgets in which revenues equalled or surpassed expenditures. Keynes showed that the economy could function for long periods well below the level of production it might potentially attain with full use of available resources. Since one underused resource was labour, this implied long-term unemployment for large sections of the workforce. Governments could, however, raise the equilibrium to nearly full capacity by increasing government expenditure and therefore stimulating demand. The war seemed to confirm the validity of this assumption. Massively increased expenditure on armaments started during the late 1930s; by June 1943 only 60,000 people were registered as unemployed. By 1945 few political leaders disputed the need for at least partial acceptance of Keynesian demand management. The war also gave planning an enormous boost – both in theory and in practice. Prices, incomes, industrial relations and production were all strictly controlled by central committees. Not before or since has the British economy been so rigidly disciplined.

Being both authoritarian and comprehensive, wartime controls were always seen by civil servants and many politicians as temporary – a fact reflected by the *ad hoc* nature of the administrative reforms of the period. The old pre-war ministries remained intact ready to resume their traditional roles once hostilities ceased. Labour politicians were much less antipathetic to controls, but as the post-war period was to confirm, even they were highly ambivalent about centralised planning of the positive variety, where the state took all important economic decisions leaving only a residual role to the market.

The Keynesian Revolution and the war destroyed for ever the minimal state spending policies of the previous eras. Towards the war's end the major earlier Reports plus further White Papers on employment and education laid foundations for greatly increased state spending in social and economic policy. This accepted, state planning through a central planning agency was rejected by the Conservatives and had won little sympathy among Labour politicians. Moreover, neither party had devoted much intellectual energy to the question of industrial reorganisation and planned industrial investment.

Labour and the new order, 1945–51

Between 1945 and 1950 the Labour Government elected in 1945 passed a remarkable volume of legislation. Basic industries were nationalised, the welfare state created, regional policy strengthened dramatically and physical planning by local authorities established as mandatory. All these policies remain with us today – indeed they still constitute the core of state intervention in British society. Conservative Governments have tinkered with the basic framework but they have rarely dismantled an essential part of it.

Post-war policy was dominated by a driving desire to re-establish full employment. Keynesian demand management, nationalisation and regional policy were either primarily or partly designed to achieve this end, and in combination with a favourable international trading position after 1945, successfully produced full employment until 1951. Industry readapted to peacetime conditions very efficiently and Britain's share of world trade actually increased during these years. If full employment and industrial recovery were achieved quickly, little progress was made in the field of economic policy. Various wartime reports had, in fact, pleaded for a close co-ordination of industrial location and industrial policy (Barlow) and for full-blown positive economic planning (Beveridge 1944, in his 'unofficial' report on employment). Neither were to transpire, however, in part because of opposition from established bureaucracies – and in particular the Treasury – to a new central planning agency. (There was even opposition to calling the new Ministry of Town and Country Planning just plain 'planning' for fear it might assume a more comprehensive planning role.)

But probably more important was the absence of a coherent policy towards economic policy within the Labour Government. In the first year after the war there was much talk about the need for a national plan plus all the administrative machinery necessary to implement it, but instead the Government opted to retain the wartime planning machinery. The 1947 fuel crisis came as a rude shock to the new Government, bringing severe shortages of coal and other raw materials. In response, the Government created a Central Economic Planning Staff (CEPS) who would implement an annual economic survey or short-term plan for manpower resources and economic growth.

Under the guidance of Stafford Cripps a limited and short-term form of planning actually prevailed during 1947 and 1948. Some reassertion of direct control over labour, and an effective wage freeze were part of the strategy, as was voluntary restraint on prices by manufacturers. From late 1948 onwards, however, enthusiasm for planning slowly declined and was effectively abandoned by the Labour Government by 1950. Reasons for its demise are varied. The unions objected to wage restraint, the new austerity of 1947/8 was electorally unpopular. Perhaps more important, the administrative innovations were never more than *ad hoc* in nature. Existing departments continued much as before, the economic surveys were for one year only, and opposition to yet more controls and planning from within the Cabinet was mounting.

But we should be wary of underestimating the scope of Labour's efforts during these years. In social policy a truly comprehensive welfare state had been created providing free health care and secondary education, public housing, and a wide range of income maintenance payments for the disadvantaged. Similarly in land-use planning a comprehensive approach had been adopted – although there was no attempt to co-ordinate physical with economic planning. In the economic area, indeed, Labour's efforts depended more on improvisation and persuasion than on radical reforms:

. . . Labour leaders quite failed to see the possibilities of using the new public sector as a way of steering the whole economy in the direction they desired. They behaved as if, while carrying through their plans for nationalisation, they had no understanding of the real meaning of what they had done. Ownership changed; power did not. It had long since ceased to be true, if indeed it ever was, that the shareholders in industries like the mines and railways exercised any real power over them. (Leruez 1975: 76)

And in economic affairs, nationalisation was the only legacy left by Labour to successive governments. Keynesian demand management had already been accepted by the late 1930s, and was continued through to the late 1970s. When the Conservatives came to power in 1951, the basic relationships between government and unions and government and industry were almost unchanged from the pre-war years. The unions played no integrated role in economic or industrial policy and although big business was quite happy to accept a regulative government role, especially in foreign trade, they too were largely excluded from central economic policy-making. Administrative changes were largely confined to the creation of new bureaucracies to implement the programmes of a burgeoning welfare state. So while the public sector had been expanded enormously, the basic tools available to governments to guide and control the public sector had changed very little.

The Conservatives and the state, 1951–64

The Conservatives fought the 1951 election on the twin themes of preservation of the welfare state and the decontrol of the economy. Decontrol meant lower income and purchase taxes (in 1951 they remained very high), an end to rationing (especially of building and other materials), abolition of the prohibitive tax (100 per cent) on land development profits, relaxation of exchange controls and the denationalisation of certain industries (notably road transport and steel). All of these were achieved by 1959, and decontrol almost certainly contributed to the growing prosperity of the 1950s.

The Conservatives also preserved the essentials of the welfare state for which there was considerable public support throughout the 1950s. Some small changes were made, mainly by tinkering with some services (notably housing and charges for health services) so as to make their free availability somewhat more selective. But the changes were quite small.

If the Conservatives did not dismantle the welfare state or the other by then fairly substantial parts of the public sector, what part did they play in controlling or guiding the public role? To answer this we have to divide the period into two parts. Until about 1960, government intervention in industry was minimal but Keynesian demand management was continued. After 1960 Keynesian methods were combined with incomes policy and some embryonic planning devices both to control inflation and to achieve a higher rate of economic growth. The transition from the minimalist role to something approaching indicative planning, with government stipulation of general goals and priorities, was inspired by an increasing disenchantment with Britain's economic performance, which was falling behind that of its main competitors.

Using fiscal and monetary policy to stimulate or depress economic activity in the Keynesian fashion, the Government soon found itself in a vicious 'stop-go' cycle. The fundamental problem was perceived as a need to defend the value of sterling by avoiding recurring balance of payments deficits (an imbalance of imports over exports which affected confidence in sterling). As the economy expanded, so imports increased, the trade deficit widened and the Bank of England was forced to buy more pounds with its foreign currency reserves to maintain exchange rates at their declared values. With reserves falling and the deficit continuing, governments felt obliged to depress economic activity by raising taxes and restricting credit in order to reduce imports and solve the balance of payments crises. But this brought a rise in unemployment and a fall in output causing governments once more to inflate the economy thus precipitating yet another sterling crisis. Such 'stop-go' tactics became common between 1953 and 1970. A related problem was inflation which accelerated during 'go' periods and declined during 'stop' periods. In today's terms both the inflation and unemployment rates were very low (Table 1.1); but, crucially, Britain was losing out to her main economic competitors.

Indeed, as the decade wore on the fundamental problem with the economy was increasingly defined as a failure to achieve a rate of economic growth comparable to other major industrial countries. Measured by almost any criteria – industrial investment, productivity, gross national product *per capita* – Britain was being outstripped by other countries and in particular by Germany, Japan and France.

By the late 1950s sympathy for more state intervention in industry and the economy generally was mounting within the Conservative Government and, infatuated with the French experience, Selwyn Lloyd, the Chancellor of the Exchequer and Harold Macmillan, the Prime Minister, launched a limited form of indicative planning in 1961. Their main planning device was the National Economic Development Council (NEDC or Neddy) which comprised members of government, industry and the unions and whose main function would be to identify the obstacles to faster growth and then recommend ways in which these could be removed.

Table 1.1 Unemployment and inflation, UK, 1956–84

Year	Unemployment %[*]	Change in retail prices[†]
1956	1.0	2.0
1957	1.3	3.7
1958	1.9	3.0
1959	2.0	0.6
1960	1.5	1.0
1961	1.3	3.4
1962	1.8	2.6
1963	2.2	2.1
1964	1.6	3.3
1965	1.3	4.8
1966	1.4	3.9
1967	2.2	2.5
1968	2.3	4.7
1969	2.3	5.4
1970	2.5	6.4
1971	3.3	9.4
1972	3.6	7.1
1973	2.6	9.2
1974	2.5	16.1
1975	3.9	24.2
1976	5.2	16.5
1977	5.7	15.8
1978	5.6	8.2
1979	5.3	13.4
1980	7.1	15.0
1981	10.1	12.0
1982	12.3	8.6
1983	13.1	4.6
1984	13.2	4.7 (to Sept)

Sources: *British Labour Statistics, Historical Abstract*, HMSO; *Department of Employment Gazette*, HMSO.

[*] Wholly unemployed, Great Britain, excluding school-leavers and adult students.

[†] Twelve-monthly change in weekly rates from December of previous year.

In its first report, Neddy estimated that an annual growth rate of 4 per cent per annum between 1961 and 1966 was possible *if* there was a change in the relationship between government and industry, *if* public expenditure could be projected ahead accurately over the five years, and *if* prices and incomes could be held down and thus balance of payments crises avoided. There is little doubt that Neddy's recommendations in this and in subsequent reports were both sensible and carefully worked out. However, in spite of the fact that the Government accepted the 4 per cent target, few of the recommendations were implemented in full. Relations with industry were to be fostered via a number of Economic Development Councils or 'little Neddies', whose job was to improve the flow of information between a range of key industries and the Government. However, as with similar experiments under Cripps in 1945, these were more talking shops dominated by industry spokesmen than genuine policy instruments designed to fix targets and then set about meeting them.

Neddy also had to compete with the Treasury – a key government department largely antipathetic to planning and eager to defend sterling and pursue monetary orthodoxy. To be fair, the Government did go so far as to reorganise the Treasury in 1962 and create a new section on the National Economy, whose job would be to liaise with Neddy. Also, for a short period between 1962 and 1964, Neddy did constitute a real rival to the Treasury and with the Chancellor (by then Reginald Maudling) on its side, led the way towards economic expansion. What Neddy and the Chancellor were unable to do was to control prices, wages and, perhaps most importantly, public expenditure. Failure with prices and incomes was understandable given the absence of a long-term legislative framework to control either (although Selwyn Lloyd had introduced a 'pay pause' during the sterling crisis in 1961). As the economy expanded so labour became scarcer and unions were better able to bargain for higher wages and to oppose more efficient, but disruptive, work practices.

Public expenditure was viewed in a way dramatically different from today. As pointed out earlier, the growth of the welfare state and nationalisation had been accompanied by remarkably few administrative reforms. The system of control over expenditure in the 1950s was largely unchanged since the mid nineteenth century. In sum it was approved annually in the budget, never surveyed systematically and never planned more than one year ahead. With the publication of the Plowden Report in 1961 (*Control of Public Expenditure*, Cmnd 1432) and Neddy's call for five-year expenditure planning, the Government at last accepted the need for expenditure surveys which eventually became a regular annual affair in 1969 (known as the Public Expenditure Survey Committee or PESC). But in the early 1960s, when the prevailing view was that the Government could spend its way out of trouble, very few systematic controls on expenditure existed.

In sum then, the later Tory years were characterised by a new enthusiasm for economic planning, by some quite ambitious experiments in planning, but also by a failure to institute the detailed changes needed to make planning work. On the production side, targets were of the broadest macro variety, planning within specific sectors of industry being quite primitive. Incomes, prices and expenditure were at least partly beyond the Government's control: thus as expansion set in, so inflation and trade deficits were aggravated yet again.

Labour and planning 1964–70

Serious overheating of the economy together with the usual sterling crisis appeared before the 1964 general election, so on coming to power Labour inherited a difficult economic position. As a Labour government emerging from thirteen years in Opposition, Harold Wilson and his Cabinet were eager to pursue reforms in social policy (mainly in housing, pensions, education and transport) all of which were expensive; to renationalise steel (also expensive) as well as to continue the Conservative policy of rapid economic growth.

Significantly, however, Labour's ideas about how to produce growth had developed very little in opposition. Their main innovation, the creation of the

Department of Economic Affairs (DEA) in 1965, was inspired by a deep mistrust of the Treasury and a perception that Neddy's role was by necessity limited because it was outside the main machinery of government. Hence the DEA was a full-blown government department assigned the job of long-term economic planning, the Treasury being confined to its traditional role as short-term expenditure controller. The DEA's brief was extensive: to devise a longer-term national plan, to revitalise industry and improve efficiency (working partly through the 'little Neddies'); to work out a prices and incomes policy and to reorganise regional policy. As it turned out this most radical administrative change lasted just four years, and as an effective policy institution the DEA was operational for less than two. Two major reasons for its failure can be identified. First and foremost was the accelerating rate of economic crisis during the 1965–67 period. Britain's competitive position had been deteriorating for some years, balance of payments deficits were slowly increasing, and sterling was clearly overvalued. Committed as it was to economic growth and the expansion of public services, the Labour government found it impossible to reconcile its policy objectives with economic reality. In historical perspective it is clear that a bad situation was aggravated by the Government's deference to the official Treasury line of giving priority to the value of sterling. So when in 1966 a serious payments' crisis and a crippling seamen's strike coincided to induce investors to sell pounds, the Government opted to abandon national planning and safeguard the currency by restricting credit. Indeed, the second reason for the DEA's demise was precisely its organisational isolation from that institution, the Treasury, responsible for providing immediate advice in crisis situations.

... The structure (of the DEA) was such as to reinforce the Treasury's traditional weaknesses: a low concern for growth among economic priorities, a lack of knowledge of and interest in the working of industry (including the impact on industry of fiscal and monetary policies), and an overriding concern for the defence of sterling. Thus as the balance of power within Whitehall tilted away from the DEA and towards the Treasury, the ills which Labour in Opposition had diagnosed and sought to cure became embedded deeper and deeper in the structure of government (Shanks 1977: 34–5).

It is crucial to understand that deflation in order to defend sterling was not the only policy option open to Harold Wilson in 1966. He could have devalued and solved the immediate crisis – an option actually taken a year later in 1967. He could have cut public expenditure, but with Keynesian economics still very much alive and a host of election commitments to honour, this was never a realistic alternative. Finally, he could have frozen prices and incomes in order to cut costs, improve industry's productivity and reduce inflation. In fact prices and incomes policy was gaining in popularity as a possible solution to the country's problems. In 1965 a new independent body, the National Board for Prices and Incomes (NBPI), had been created to investigate income and price increases and arbitrate on their fairness. But a total wage and price freeze would have been unpopular with the unions as well as with industry and was avoided, at least for the time being.

Economic planning was effectively laid to rest after 1967. The DEA together with the institutions it fostered fell into disuse. So the Industrial Reorganisation Corporation, which had been set up to provide loans to industry to speed efficiency, found it could not operate in the absence of a secure and predictable economic climate. The NBPI and an incomes policy were also effectively abandoned. Instead, under the guidance of the new Chancellor, Roy Jenkins, economic policy reverted almost to a pre-Keynesian strategy: some government expenditure was cut (mainly in defence), foreign loans repaid and taxes increased. Interestingly, the Jenkins deflation was not so damaging to employment as might have been expected (Table 1.1), largely because the 1967 devaluation did produce something of an investment boom.

Labour's six years in office were characterised by continual economic crises. The reconstruction of industry and achievement of a high growth rate eluded the Government. In fact, Britain's share of world trade fell from 13.9 per cent to 10.8 per cent during these years. In spite of this, some important reforms and election pledges were carried through. Comprehensive education was launched, and public transport and physical planning reorganised. Public expenditure also increased, notably in education, health and local government; but in comparison with the 1945–50 period, Labour had hardly been a radical reforming government. Taxation increased quite dramatically from 32 per cent of gross domestic product in 1965 to 43 per cent in 1970. Moreover, within the Labour movement the seeds of disquiet at the Government's failure to redistribute income and wealth had been sown. It was clear that the failure of economic planning had prevented the government from instituting major reforms in social planning.

The 1970s: plus ça change . . .?

If the 1960s were years of periodic economic crises, the 1970s were years of unremitting crisis. For present purposes we can divide the decade into five quite distinct periods, each representing a sharp change in the role of the state in economy and society.

1970–72: Conservative expansionism The first thing the new Conservative Government of Edward Heath did on coming unexpectedly to office in 1970 was to dismantle the NBPI and the Industrial Reorganisation Corporation, therefore apparently disavowing both income policy and a strong state role in guiding industry. The Government was also intent on reforming industrial relations (primarily to render the introduction of more efficient working practices easier) by imposing a more rigid framework of law on union activity. What transpired was the 1971 Industrial Relations Act which sought to make unions accept certain legal restrictions on their activities, notably on their right to strike, and to submit themselves to a special court. From its inception this inspired the fiercest hostility from the unions.

In the absence of an incomes policy and industrial strategy, how were inflation and payments crises to be solved? Strangely, and in spite of some reforms in the control of public expenditure, *not* by reducing expenditure. Instead, a policy of economic expansion via reduced taxation and increased public expenditure was followed. With no controls on income and expenditure, inflation took off, soaring from 6.4 per cent in 1970 to 9.4 per cent in 1971 – easily the highest figure since 1950 (Table 1.1). This situation could not last long as the rapid increase in prices and expenditure was bound to undermine the balance of payments and Britain's trading position. In a famous about-turn in November 1972, Edward Heath, the Prime Minister, announced a prices and incomes freeze.

1972–74: incomes policy and confrontation Phase I of the Heath freeze lasted until March 1973 when under phase II all employees were to be subject to an annual increase of £1.00 a week plus 4 per cent *per annum*. The new system was to be policed by a Pay Board, and price increases were also to be carefully controlled by a newly established Price Commission. Phase II represented a highly significant break with past Conservative principles. Machinery was created to control prices and incomes for a minimum of three years, implying the acceptance of a permanent incomes policy. This indicated Conservative endorsement of a highly interventionist economic policy.

Although opposed by the unions, phase II was generally adhered to. Not so with phase III, however, which provoked confrontation by the unions and eventually brought down the Government. In fact phase III was really quite flexible, permitting a maximum of 7 per cent increase plus extra amounts for productivity payments and working unsocial hours. The miners demanded more than the norm on the grounds that they were a special case. Faced with extensive picketing not only of collieries but of power stations and other energy supplies, hardship and short-term working throughout the country, with the addition of a railway strike and public disenchantment with statutory wages policy (by October 1973, only 37 per cent of the public considered phase III fair – *Financial Times*, 16 November 1973), Heath decided to call a general election.

The Government's 'U-turn' on incomes policy in 1972 was accompanied by another *volte face* on industrial policy. In spite of the liberalism and minimal state intervention which apparently prevailed in 1970, Heath very soon began to indulge in a range of policies to aid, succour and guide industrial recovery. Bankrupt companies (Rolls Royce, Upper Clyde Shipbuilders) were bailed out, regional incentives and development grants were strengthened, a Minister for Industrial Development attached to the new Department of Trade and Industry, and manpower retraining reorganised and greatly strengthened. All this did not amount to planning in the sense of economic targets being set over a fixed time period, but it did represent a new corporatism involving close liaison between government and industry.

Finally, the Government was pledged after 1972 to cut public expenditure.

Table 1.2 Total government expenditure as a percentage of GNP, 1970–82

Year	1970	1971	1972	1973	1974	1975	1976	1977	1978	1979	1980	1981	1982
%	40.5	40.6	41.2	41.2	46.6	49.3	46.8	43.4	44.1	44.0	47.6	48.0	47.4

Source: *National Accounts*, OECD, various years.

However, by 1973 the pressures to increase expenditure (partly to compensate for the effects of incomes policy) were mounting and when they left office, the Conservatives were actually presiding over a larger public sector than in 1970 (in terms of the government share of gross national product, and number of enterprises owned by government – see Table 1.2). This is crucial because it demonstrates how much the Heath Government was relying on incomes policy to harness inflation; talk of controlling the money supply, which dominated the policy agenda in the late seventies, was almost completely absent.

1974–75: a return to planning? While in opposition, the Left wing of the Labour Party converted its disenchantment with the 1964–70 period into a set of alternative policies. Eventually published as the *Labour Programme 1973*, these called for a dominant role for the state in the British economy. Britain's industrial recovery, so the programme asserted, could be facilitated only by further nationalisation, the creation of a National Enterprise Board (NEB), the introduction of planning agreements between government and individual industries, a new deal for workers in industrial relations and the management of firms, and the protection of vulnerable industries from foreign competition.

Many of these ideas formed the basis of the 1974 Manifesto and on coming to power, the Labour Government set about implementing at least some of them. The Industrial Relations Act was repealed, a National Enterprise Board whose job would be to act as a state holding company to encourage investment and improve productivity was created, and a system of planning agreements between industries and the state established. In incomes policy, a new social contract would bind both government and unions to moderation on incomes matters. In fact, the social contract resulted in anything but moderation, weekly wage increases jumping from 12.2 per cent in 1973 to 29.4 per cent in 1974. Inflation too bounded ahead, reaching 16.1 per cent in 1974 and a staggering 24.2 per cent in 1975 (Table 1.1). Finally, the Conservatives' quite generous public expenditure targets for 1974 and 1975 were met in full.

Nineteen seventy-four was a bad year for all the developed countries; the quadrupling of oil prices by the organisation of petroleum exporting countries (OPEC) in late 1973 had precipitated a sharp downturn in world trade and an acceleration of inflation everywhere. A good part of the 1974–75 inflation must be attributed to these international forces. But Britain suffered from additional problems peculiar to her. British industrial competitiveness continued to decline and British unions were more successful than those in many other countries in keeping wage rates up to or beyond the rate of inflation. In fact up to the end of the 1970s, in spite of general economic difficulties, the majority of the British population enjoyed growing prosperity and a rising standard of living – a striking phenomenon whose effects are explored in Chapter 4. From a general economic and business point of view, however, the combination of a falling national income, accelerating rates of inflation and wages, and a high level of public expenditure could not go on. Moreover, unemployment was rising fast. The assumptions of Keynesian demand management seemed no longer to apply. According to Keynesian orthodoxy, unemployment or under-capacity occurred only when prices and interest rates were low.

Inflation was a product of rapid growth and labour shortages. Now, however, most countries experienced both inflation and high rates of unemployment at the same time. This fact, above all others, was responsible for the revival both of incomes policies and, crucially, of traditional monetary policies.

1975–79: monetarism and incomes policy The Labour Left's policies for radical surgery on the British economy came to very little. Surgery there was, but it was of the conservative rather than socialist variety. The first change came in July 1975 when a Government now dominated by the Labour Right announced a new incomes policy granting £6 a week for all workers earning up to £8,500 and nothing for those earning over this figure. This was not a statutory policy but an agreement worked out between the Government and the Trades Union Congress (TUC). It was remarkably successful (strikes fell to a twenty-two-year low during the £6 a week period) and demonstrated the growing strength of the TUC. This informal agreement was renewed in July 1976 when a 5 per cent limit was agreed, and again in 1977 when a 10 per cent limit was accepted. Five per cent was proposed in 1978 but effectively rejected by the unions. Their resentment at government imposition of this 'ceiling' was shown by widespread transport and public service strikes in the 'winter of discontent' (1978–79) which almost certainly lost Labour the May 1979 election.

As important was the conversion of the Government to a limited form of monetarism. During 1976 investors' selling of sterling reached panic proportions. Fixed exchange rates (the Bank of England commitment to buying sterling for fixed sums in other currencies) had been abandoned in 1971 and the pound left free to fall – and fall the pound did, to a low of $1.57 at one point. Britain was approaching the point where the Government could not meet immediate payments on outstanding debts. In exchange for massive loans from the International Monetary Fund (IMF), Denis Healey, the Chancellor, agreed to new controls on the money supply. Interest rates rose to a record 15.5 per cent and public expenditure was cut. After complex negotiations, the IMF and the Treasury agreed that the Public Sector Borrowing Requirement (the amount needed by the Government to cover the gap between projected resources and expenditure) should be trimmed by £3 billion over two years. In fact, public spending did not fall quite as rapidly as planned (see Table 1.2) but the very idea of using public sector spending as *the* major instrument of economic policy was new (notwithstanding Roy Jenkins's more limited efforts in this direction between 1968 and 1970).

The combination of income policy and public expenditure cuts reduced inflation quite quickly to a low of around 8 per cent between 1978 and 1979 (Table 1.1). However, unemployment remained stubbornly high and Labour's plans both for industrial reorganisation and for social reform were seriously circumscribed by the spending cuts. Like most other recent governments, managing decline rather than implementing programmes of social reform became the Government's overriding preoccupation.

1979–85: the new monetarism The new Conservative Government of 1979 was determined to avoid the expediency and pragmatism of the 1970–74 Heath

Government. With a change of personnel (the leadership plus all the key economic posts), the Conservatives were pledged to solve Britain's economic problems not by planning or incomes policies, but through rigid adherence to monetarist orthodoxy. Once given a stable operating climate (low inflation and taxes), the market would be given full rein to bring about recovery. Government's role in industrial revival would be minimal.

To achieve a low rate of inflation the money supply would have to be carefully controlled. So on coming to office the Conservatives attempted to cut projected public expenditure quite dramatically and raised interest rates to record levels. In order to finance lower income taxes, the indirect tax on sales (VAT: Value Added Tax) was also raised – a fact which partly accounted for a quickly *rising* rate of inflation during 1979–80. Unleashed from incomes policy, wage rates also increased rapidly, although little higher than the rate of inflation.

Reducing the money supply in combination with the world downturn in economic activity which occurred between 1978 and 1981 quickly lowered the level of activity in the British economy, and unemployment increased from an already high 5.3 per cent in 1979 to over 12 per cent in 1982. While it would be over simple to claim that the Government's main strategy was to use unemployment to reduce wage rates and therefore inflation, there is no doubt that this was partly its intention.

On the industrial front the NEB, while not disbanded, was quickly reduced in resources and status, and the nationalised industries were required to operate strictly according to commercial criteria. Any idea of social planning or reform involving increased expenditure was put into cold storage to await economic recovery. Unfortunately this was not even faintly visible until 1982.

As a strategy for rapid and extensive revitalisation of British industry, the new policy was as unsuccessful as its predecessors. It is important to stress, however, that at least one component (a policy of high interest rates and expenditure cuts) had been pioneered by the Labour Government between 1976 and 1979. The major change was a new devotion to market principles which naturally meant rejection of a prices and incomes policy. But from 1981 this came creeping back in various forms, notably cash limits on what government departments, public authorities and nationalised industries were allowed to offer to their employees. The need for some kind of incomes policy was in line with developments under previous governments. Similarly, in the field of industrial policy, even during its first year of office, the Thatcher Government was prepared to continue support for lame duck industries (British Leyland, British Steel) and it actually increased and strengthened the industrial retraining and manpower programmes inherited from Labour. This, together with increasing state payments to the unemployed, prevented the Government from reducing public expenditure as a percentage of GNP (Table 1.2).

An overview of post-war events

Table 1.3 summarises the post-war developments described above within a chronological framework, and with some reference to international as well as

Table 1.3 Governments, policies and events, 1945–83

Labour governments 1945–51 (Attlee)

National Health Service Act 1946	German surrender 1945
National Insurance Act 1946	Japanese surrender 1945
State ownership of coal industry, gas, electricity, transport and steel	
Town and Country Planning Act 1947	Dislocation of international trade after Second World War
Full employment policy; wage and dividends freeze; control of production in many areas; rationing	
Independence of India, Pakistan, Burma and Ceylon 1948	Berlin crisis 1948–49 marks start of cold war with Soviet Union and intensification of Western alliance

---

Conservative governments 1951–59 (Churchill, Eden, Macmillan)

Deregulation of trade and financial controls	Korean War 1950–53
Limited denationalisation of iron and steel industry, and road transport	World economic growth
Invasion of Suez 1956	Formation of European Community 1956

Conservative governments 1959–64 (Macmillan, Home)

Independence of most African colonies 1959–64	
Wage and price freeze 1962–63	Détente with Soviet Union 1960–79
Unsuccessful application to join EC 1962	

Labour governments 1964–70 (Wilson)

Balance of payments crisis 1964–65	
National economic plan effectively abandoned 1966–67	
Increasing credit, wage and dividend restrictions 1966–69	
Devaluation of £ sterling 1967	Vietnam War 1964–73
Unsuccessful application to join EC 1968	
Plan to regulate trade union and industrial relations 1969–70 (revealed in Green Paper *In Place of Strife* 1969)	
Intervention of British troops in Northern Ireland 1969	

Conservative government 1970–74 (Heath)

Floating exchange rate for £ sterling 1971	
Industrial Relations Act 1971 (legal regulation of trade unions)	
'U-turn' from not interfering in industry or wage negotiations to restrictions on wage and salary increases from 1972–74	Discovery of oil in British North Sea
Suspension of Northern Ireland Parliament and Direct Rule 1972	Rise in world oil prices 1973–74
Reorganisation into larger local government units 1972–75	
Entry to EC 1973	
Easy credit and high inflation 1973–74	
Successful strikes by National Union of Mine-workers 1972 and 1974, which disrupt entire country	

Table 1.3 (Cont.)

Labour governments 1974–79 (Mostly in minority) (Wilson, Callaghan)

Major election gains by Scottish and Welsh Nationalists 1974–77	Continued rise in world oil prices
High inflation 1974 onwards	
Social Contract with trade unions, whereby limits on prices and incomes and legal concessions 1975–78	
Referendum on membership of EC 1975	
Balance of payments crisis 1976	
Severe credit restrictions and increasing cuts in projected Government expenditure 1976 onwards	
High and increasing unemployment 1975 onwards 'Winter of discontent' 1979 (strikes by numerous groups of workers including transport strike)	British oil revenues from North Sea equal payments for foreign oil
Defeat of Government proposals for Scottish and Welsh devolution 1979	

Conservative governments 1979– (Thatcher)

Policy of restricting stock of money to bring down inflation involves further cuts in Government expenditure 1979–82 and central restrictions on local government expenditure	Increasing friction between Soviet Union and West from 1979
Legal restrictions on Unions' rights to picket during strikes and to extend scope of stoppage	
Stable inflation and greatly increasing unemployment 1980–82	
Savage and extensive urban riots 1981	
Foundation of Social Democratic Party and leadership defections from Labour 1981	
Electoral alliance of Social Democrats with Liberals produces sweeping by-election and local election successes 1981–82	Falklands War 1982
Re-election of Conservatives with large majority, Alliance comes close to Labour in terms of votes but not seats	
Miners' strike 1984–5 most bitter industrial dispute since war	
Unemployment reaches 13 per cent	

to non-economic domestic events. During some periods attention was deflected from the imperfections of economic policy to alarming foreign developments and the danger of nuclear war. In the 1950s, when the economy enjoyed a modest post-war boom and trade unions could be placated with a share of increasing profits, both the Korean War and a successful disengagement from most remaining territories of the pre-war colonial empire preoccupied successive Conservative Governments. With diminishing commitments elsewhere, entry to the European Community seemed increasingly attractive as a cure for the ills of British industry, by opening wider markets and intensifying domestic competition. After ignoring the actual formation of the Community in 1956, abortive negotiations for entry occurred in 1962 and 1968, before they succeeded under Heath in 1972, only to be revised by Labour in 1974–75.

The eruption of communal strife in Northern Ireland and intensified demands for some form of autonomy in Wales and Scotland also took up considerable political energy in the 1970s. By the end of that decade, however, even these movements were being seen as tensions generated by economic malaise. As membership of the Community failed to exert any visible economic effects and governments took increasingly far-ranging action to reverse economic decline, they stimulated more extensive reactions against their policies. Thus the moderate Labour Government of Callaghan, with its muted interventionist policy, fired radical left-wing demands for control over the parliamentary leadership to ensure the enactment of social reforms and supporting measures of government economic control. Their success in getting such demands accepted in the Labour Party after 1979 prompted a secession by some established leaders and MPs to form a Social Democratic Party, which in alliance with the Liberals achieved considerable success in by-elections and local elections in the second half of the 1979–84 Parliament.

On the other side, Labour support for more extensive intervention prompted an extreme reaction by Conservatives and support for getting government out of business and industrial relations altogether. This proved impossible as covert controls were placed on incomes in an attempt to slow down inflation, and ailing firms such as Leyland Cars had to be financed to avoid disastrous social consequences. Even so, the unions felt the Government was responsible for the three million unemployed and must be forced to help them through subsidies and programmes for job creation. 'Non-intervention' was almost as much a recipe for political confrontation in the industrial field as earlier governments' positive intervention had been.

The overall consequence of the worsening economic situation and unsuccessful government remedies was a widening of disagreement and intensification of political conflict at all levels of society. At the bottom, violent rioting in many urban centres in the spring and early summer of 1981 warned that socially deprived groups could not be left to bear the consequences of unemployment on their own. The re-election of the Thatcher government and its continuation of restrictive policies was followed by a year long attempt by the National Union of Mineworkers to prevent the closure of 'uneconomic' pits. The resulting strike was bitter but NUM attempts to win the support of other unions generally failed.

Since the major political problems follow directly from governments' diagnosis of economic crisis and their reactions to it, the most relevant question with which to start an overall assessment of British politics is why governments have intervened in the ways they have? What forces explain the particular forms of British government intervention in comparison with those adopted by other national governments? And why have they not been successful? Much of the book will be indirectly concerned with these points, but we consider them explicitly in the rest of this chapter.

The British experience in perspective

The usual explanation of the variations in economic policy is in terms of competing political traditions. Differences in the stance of successive Conservative Governments, for example, can be related to the contrasting traditions of Liberalism (minimal state intervention) and Toryism (paternalistic intervention to solve particular problems), both of which are combined in the modern Conservative Party (see Ch. 4). Certainly such an analysis has validity. The contrast in Conservative approaches between, on the one hand 1951–59, 1970–71 and 1979–80, and on the other 1960–64 and 1972–74, conforms nicely to the two traditions. Similarly, contrasting traditions on the left of the political spectrum could be invoked to explain the Labour experience. Although in recent years social democratic policies have prevailed in government over more interventionist socialist policies, the latter have now been adopted as the programme for the mid-eighties.

While accepting that an explanation in terms of differing traditions is plausible – and also acknowledging that these traditions are in no way static but are constantly changing – it is only of limited analytic value. It does not, for example, enable us to compare the British experience with that of other countries. One way in which this can be achieved is to identify common characteristics over time and thus judge whether state intervention in Britain, whatever the government responsible for it, has certain peculiar characteristics which can be contrasted with those displayed, for example, in West Germany, France and Japan. From our historical summary we can trace the continuities described below.

Structural economic decline

Indisputably this has dominated the policy agenda over the last fifty years. While some of the issues may have changed (from protectionism to payments deficits, to sterling balances, to regional policy, to the reorganisation of industry), competitiveness has been declining. Scholars and politicians have laboured long and hard to explain the decline, but even today the true causes are uncertain. They relate to such basic factors as the provision for technical education, investment habits, and the institutionalised relationships between industry, finance and trade unions. Whatever they are, the preoccupation with managing decline has been a consistent theme in recent British politics. The fact of secular decline does not in itself tell us very much. But politics in such a context are likely to be different from politics in countries where the economy has experienced high rates of growth. A declining economy results in a shortage of resources and consequent cutbacks in government provision which create the social and political tensions already noted. Specifically political and social arrangements may also have contributed to economic decline. Indeed, there are some who see Britain's economic malaise primarily in such terms, particularly in the difficulties faced by governments resisting pressures from strong groups such as trade unions or the financial interests of the City of London.

Fragmented policy-making

Every political system is characterised by conflicts, anomalies and inefficiencies in its policy-making processes. In some, these problems are sufficiently serious to cause revolutions or frequent outbreaks of political violence. While Britain's system is generally secure from such threats (apart from Northern Ireland where separate causes operate), there is increasing evidence that policy-making arrangements are under serious stress. Later chapters will show in detail how this appears in particular institutions and processes. But from the preceding summary it clearly applies to the key areas of economic policy-making and planning. The most popular and also the crudest way to explain these stresses is to point to the increasing 'overloading' of governments, and in particular to the growing power of trade unions and other groups external to representative institutions. There is no doubt something to this thesis, but again it is analytically limited. Union power may have seriously circumscribed policy-makers over the last ten years, but it can hardly account for the failure of the National Plan or of Macmillan's attempts at indicative planning.

There are more fundamental reasons for policy failure, many of which relate to the strangely fragmented nature of the British policy-making system; this is strange because in a highly centralised state with a skilled and loyal civil service, one would expect fragmentation to be the least of the problems. Fragmentation occurs at two levels: within government, and between government and key economic interests. Both have related causes. The history of economic policy graphically illustrates how institutionally fragmented the British system is. In spite of acquiring vast new government responsibilities during and after the war, the central administrative machine changed very little. New departments were created and others merged, but, the Treasury apart, remarkably little co-ordinating or planning machinery was established. This remains true even today, although institutional controls over public expenditure have been strengthened. The British system has never acquired guiding bureaucracies like the French Commissariat Général du Plan (CGP) or Délégation à l'Amenagement du Territoire (DATAR), which have been crucial in co-ordinating the programmes of disparate government departments towards specific ends. So a major characteristic of British politics today is the functional fragmentation of government departments. Virtually the only co-ordinating function is performed by the Treasury, whose role is essentially the negative one of controlling expenditure. Given the sensitivity of the Treasury and the associated Bank of England to financial interests, Treasury control also operates to subordinate general economic concerns to financial ones. As a result, almost all the administrative experiments with planning and co-ordination, from Labour's post-war economic surveys to Neddy, to the DEA, to Policy Analysis and Review, to the 1975 Planning Agreements, have either failed or had limited success.

Fragmentation also characterises the relationship between government and the country's major industrial interests. Both the unions and employers' organisations play an important and increasing role in economic and industrial policy. However, neither are integrated into the policy-making process as in some countries. Instead the unions have come to perform the largely negative if powerful role of resisting incomes policies. Rarely have they been brought directly into the overall decision-making process, although as we shall see in the next chapter, they may be closely integrated with particular departments. The same is true for employers' organisations (the Confederation of British Industry, and trade associations). Of course, these are frequently consulted and when their interests have been threatened they have exerted powerful pressures on government (as with protectionism during the 1930s and nationalisation during the 1940s). But in the absence of an established corporatist tradition emphasising the values and interests shared between government, industry and unions, attempts to integrate the three have often looked contrived. Very often, new corporatist arrangements such as Neddy, or Labour's planning agreements, have been condemned in the press even before they have started; and have in any case never got to the level of detail necessary to put general agreements into practice.

Organisational inertia

A high level of public expenditure is not always synonymous with a co-ordinated economic policy, and in Britain the failure of planning has hardly reduced the size of the public sector. What explains the apparent antipathy to planning? Insitutional fragmentation is part of the problem and this phenomenon itself requires explanation. Of course it occurs everywhere and organisational theorists would be quick to provide general explanations. But given Britain's economic problems and the myriad attempts to plan and co-ordinate policy, the failure to achieve anything more than *ad hoc* measures requires a more specific diagnosis. One factor stands out: a continuing failure to extend collectivist ideas about politics to institutional and organisational arrangements. The collectivist ideas (socialism, corporatism) of the twentieth century transformed British politics, but the impact of these ideas on organisations was minimal. More often than not, parties and politicians have attempted to superimpose organisational innovations on existing structures, with little thought of how the new arrangements will impact on the powers and values of existing bureaucracies. British civil servants are more resistant to planning and state intervention than are their European counterparts, owing to their preference for an aloof style of government which intervenes indirectly through tax and monetary policy rather than by engaging itself in detailed social engineering. As a result, the reception given by Whitehall to Neddy, the DEA and other innovations has been cool. In France, planning and co-ordinating initiatives have actually been led by civil servants. Further, within the political parties there has been remarkably little theorising on how and to what extent the state should intervene in economic and social life. Since 1950, the parties have tended to perceive a serious economic problem, to adopt a simple solution and then rather unthinkingly apply it. In a book on physical planning, Donald Foley interprets this tendency in British politics as an overriding sympathy with unitary solutions. His characterisation of the way in which post-war land use planning was formulated could equally be applied to economic policy:

It characteristically builds around seemingly self-evident truths and values and, in turn, bestows a self-justifying tone to its main propositions and chains of reasoning ... while it may contain highly rational arguments, it is characteristically superrational in its overall spirit (Foley 1963).

The failure to appreciate the importance of organisational values and interests has not affected those collectivist forces accounting for the growth of the public sector over the last fifty years. As a result, Britain has, perhaps in a more acute form than many other countries, acquired a large and cumbersome public sector but little in the way of controlling or central co-ordinating structures. It is not unreasonable to assume that this has reduced the efficiency both of public services and of economic policy-making generally.

A final characteristic of the economic policy and planning experience in British politics has been the very limited role played by Parliament. Chapter 3 will cover more specifically the problems of representation and accountability raised by the relegation of Parliament to the role of legitimiser. In some countries (notably the United States) there is often a trade-off between the 'efficiency' function of the central administration and the representative functions of the national legislature. Hence, in theory at least, what society may lose in the way of efficient government it gains in the way of increased accountability. In Britain, where Parliament plays a much less prominent role than does the US Congress, there is the possibility that the public have been denied both efficiency and accountability.

But this would be far too simple a diagnosis. No discussion of political processes in Britain can be undertaken without reference to the secular economic decline which has affected the country over the last fifty years. As previously noted, dealing with decline is much more difficult than dealing with growth, and many of Britain's political and administrative problems have been aggravated by the country's continuing economic sclerosis. Neither would it be fair to imply that economic policy or economic planning could ever conform to some ideal mode. Planning is relative, and whatever its variety and in whatever country it has been tried, problems, anomalies and inefficiencies have occurred. Planning of the positive or even indicative type – the government making all major economic decisions or at least setting the main economic goals and specifying the ways to attain them – may, indeed, be incompatible both with the pluralism of modern democratic states, and with the unpredictability of an economically interdependent world. This accepted, the speed of economic decline in Britain and the urgency of our economic problems has called for a coherent and radical response on the part of governments and major economic interests. As we have seen, policies have rarely been coherent and when radical have floundered badly. In the next chapter we examine the fragmented relationships between governments and central ministries which account in part for the failure of a cohesive and effective economic policy to emerge.

Chapter 2
Central decision-making

The theory of the British constitution is simple. The leader of the party with a majority in the House of Commons forms a Government which, subject only to the attenuated power of the House of Lords to delay legislation, is free to enact its programme; there is no counterpart to the checks and balances built into most government structures, notably those of the USA. The extreme simplicity of the constitution has been criticised in recent years. Governments elected with a share of the popular vote far short of a majority have been able to initiate policies which enjoy little popular support. Labour was able to enact controversial legislation between 1974 and 1976 despite the fact that it was elected with a share of the popular vote lower than it had received since the 1930s.

The constitutional ease with which British governments can act has become more of a problem recently because of the degree to which policy differences between the major parties have increased. Immediately after gaining power, governments in the 1970s tried to reverse the policies of their predecessors to a degree rarely paralleled in British politics or in the governance of other Western democracies. Frequent sharp switches of policy are self-defeating and at best spread confusion. This tendency is strengthened by the constitutional freedom of governments in Britain to change policy, particularly economic policy, in an attempt to buy popularity in the run-up to an election. Policy is changed not because it is right but because the change may produce votes though (as with the Conservatives in 1964 and 1972–74) the cost to the country can be high. The frequent claim that Parliament in general, and even the back-bench supporters of a government, have lost influence, strengthens fears about the power and essential irresponsibility of the executive.

Many political systems are criticised because of their inability to take authoritative decisions. In the British system, on the other hand, major government decisions can be taken too easily. Cabinet government, as we shall see, facilitates the quick decisive adoption of policies. But divisions and conflicts between and within the departments responsible for putting policy into practice (documented below) prevents top-level decisions being fully effective.

The secrecy with which government and administration operate also means that the opinions of key groups whose co-operation is necessary are often ignored. Not unnaturally this results in diminished support or even opposition to policy on the part of crucial interests such as trade unions. Thus once they are implemented, serious disagreements on the nature and extent of government programmes often emerge. A growing body of critics have in fact argued for a slower pace of top-level decision-making which will gain greater acquiescence in the end through frequent consultations, more open government, adoption of a Bill of Rights, proportional representation with coalition governments, and similar measures.

How does the central machinery of government work, and why is it that such a constitutionally tidy system fails to encourage efficient policy formulation and implementation?

The Civil Service

The first political relationship within the executive which confronts British politicians is that between individual ministers and their civil servants. British administrators have been traditionally organised into broad clerical, executive

Table 2.1 Major departments and ministries of the central government

Ministry or Department of	Ministry or Department of (cont)
Agriculture, Fisheries and Food	Home Office
Agriculture and Fisheries for Scotland	Industry
Agriculture for Northern Ireland	Inland Revenue
Attorney-General	
	Lord Advocate
Cabinet Office	Lord Chancellor
Civil Service Department	
Civil Service for Northern Ireland	Northern Ireland Civil Service
Commerce for Northern Ireland	Northern Ireland Office
Crown Office (Scotland)	
Customs and Excise	Prime Minister's Office
	Scottish Development
Defence	Scottish Economic Planning
Director of Public Prosecutions	Scottish Education
	Scottish Home and Health
Education and Science	Scottish Office
Education for Northern Ireland	
Employment	Trade
Energy	Transport
Environment	Treasury
Environment for Northern Ireland	
	Welsh Office
Finance, Northern Ireland	
Foreign and Commonwealth Office	
Health and Social Security	
Health and Social Services for Northern Ireland	

Source: *Civil Service Year Book 1980*, HMSO. Index to Departments and Sub-Departments. In addition to the 38 selected above, another 218 full Departments are listed.

and administrative classes. Recent attempts at reform (notably the Fulton Commission in the late sixties) tried to break down these divisions and to nurture specialist skills, such as those possessed by the statisticians, economists and scientists – each a separate career grade within the Civil Service. In spite of these attempts, British civil servants continue in the main to conceive of themselves as general administrators rather than specialists, to promote circulation between departments and ministries rather than dedication to a particular speciality, and to maintain broad distinctions between the hierarchy of classes. The typical higher civil servant enters directly as an administrative trainee, and rises rapidly to principal with a fairly autonomous area of operation, whether it be supervision of mortuaries in the Home Office or collation of information on Southern Africa in the Foreign Office. If very successful, the principal will rise through assistant and deputy secretaryships to become permanent head of a ministry, whether as under-secretary or permanent secretary.

Civil servants are grouped into administrative sections with a startling range of functions. Outside the twenty to twenty-five large ministries, most headed by Cabinet ministers, there is no agreed list. Taking departments as those agencies voted on separately in the Parliamentary Supply Estimates, there are about seventy at the present time. Table 2.1 gives a summary listing of the most important.

In his early years, an administrative class civil servant may shift between two or three departments. For most of his career, however, he will be located in one of these in spite of the 'generalist' ideology of the Service.

Minister and civil servants

In theory the relationship between civil servants and ministers is uncomplicated because it is part of constitutional dogma that the elected government is supreme. In terms of this theory civil servants exist to do the bidding of ministers and help them carry out their policies. Civil servants may warn politicians of the difficulties which their proposed policy will cause. If the minister persists in the policy, however, the task of civil servants is to obey. Indeed, the good civil servant should be familiar with the views of the minister and the governing party as set out in election manifestoes and policy statements.

To some extent, the relationship described in constitutional theory also exists in fact. Cases of outright defiance of ministers by civil servants are rare, and civil servants do read with care relevant sections of the election manifestoes of both major parties. Yet few politicians, either Labour or Conservative, would say that constitutional theory captures the reality of the relationship.

Civil servants certainly do much about which their minister in practice knows nothing. Richard Crossman, on taking over the Ministry of Housing in 1964, was told that any documents or letters put in his in-tray and returned by him unmarked would be sent out by the Ministry as though Crossman had personally approved the text. The practice was not reprehensible. It reflected merely the pressure of work on ministers. In spite of working very long hours, they are lucky to be able to read the papers sent to them by their own and other departments or ministries on major issues, let alone minor decisions.

Compared with their counterparts in other countries, British ministers are at a particular disadvantage in attempting to change the routine decision-making – that is, the standard operating procedures – of their ministry. Unlike French politicians, the British are not supported by a *cabinet* of their own staff when they take office. Unlike American cabinet secretaries, British ministers do not have the right to make political appointments to ensure that key posts in the ministry are filled by acceptable people. Ministers are by and large expected to deal with the civil servants in 'their' ministries only through the permanent secretary and a relatively few high-ranking officials. Even the minister's personal office is staffed by young, promising civil servants who are aware not only of the need to be loyal to the minister but also of the cost to their careers of antagonising the permanent secretary. Though traditions vary from department to department, in most cases advice from the lower ranks of their ministry reaches ministers only after it has been filtered and commented upon by the higher officials; the Home Office is a notorious example. It is a determined minister who can discover the pattern of decisions made in his name on routine issues, and changing that pattern will be even harder.

Most politicians who criticise civil servants are extremely sensitive to their power to limit the options from which policy choices are to be made. The comment 'I don't care who makes the decision as long as I define the options' though applied originally to American politics, has a more general validity, and certainly applies to Britain. Modern British politicians of both major parties – perhaps because both have aimed at making radical departures from past policies – have been intensely suspicious of the Civil Service, believing that it presents politicians with an artificially restricted range of options and offers selective criticisms of proposals. This suggests to them that the Civil Service, far from being neutral, has strong policy preferences of its own.

It might seem natural that British civil servants should have strong policy preferences; many people do. Yet British civil servants are trained to believe that they should not embarrass their minister. British representative democracy is based in part on the assumption that ministers are accountable to Parliament and so to the electorate. Only if ministers are prepared to be responsible for the work of their ministries is the British executive responsible to the public. Until recently the constitutional fiction that ministers were accountable for and by implication at least potentially aware of decisions Civil servants make in their name was very widely accepted. Why is it, then, that civil servants have views on policy?

The reasons are familiar to students of bureaucracy in many countries, not only in Britain. Civil servants may well have strong attachments to existing policies, particularly if they have been in the ministry for some time and have helped shape them. When Crossman took over the Ministry of Housing in 1964, the Permanent Secretary, Evelyn Sharpe, had been in that position for over a decade and had seen many ministers come and go. Not surprisingly, she had pronounced views on many aspects of the Ministry's work. Such continuity in a civil servant's career is perhaps rare. One of the criticisms the Fulton Commission made of the Civil Service was that transfers of civil servants between totally different policy areas were too frequent. Nevertheless, politicians are moved between ministries even more often (not so much due to elections as to the extreme frequency of 'reshuffles' and transfers of responsibility in British government). Thus the ministers' expertise with an average of about eighteen months in their ministry, is nearly always less in any policy area than that of their civil servants. Indeed, there is no particular reason to suppose that a British Cabinet Minister will have any experience of a policy area before he or she is appointed to the ministry which supposedly governs it. Thus Crossman, who had specialised in the social services in opposition, was appointed to the Ministry of Housing and spent several months fearing that his ignorance would be exposed before it could be corrected. This is quite typical.

Behind the attachment of individual civil servants to their policies is the tradition of the ministry. Every department in Whitehall has what is known as the 'departmental view' – a set of assumptions about what is good or bad policy in its area which is slow to change. The Ministry of Agriculture, Fisheries and Food tends to assume that farmers should be given more help, and has clear ideas on the best way of doing this. The Foreign Office has been said to have a number of fixed ideas including a strong desire to out-manoeuvre the French. The Department of Trade has a continuing attachment to free trade by reducing tariff and non-tariff barriers.

Civil servants would claim that departmental views are merely expressions of collective wisdom, the lessons from trying to make policy in the past. In fact, departmental views also reflect other factors. The first of these is what might be called bureaucratic politics, or even bureaucratic self-defence. Ministries are not eager to see their powers curbed and their functions taken over by others. Crossman offended his permanent secretary by far too easily conceding control of planning for land use to another ministry. The Permanent Secretary devoted the early weeks of the first Wilson Government to retrieving the situation. Later in the first Wilson Government, Crossman was locked in battle with the Home Secretary, James Callaghan, over allocation of responsibility for certain social services which Crossman was unwilling to concede to the Home Office. Such jurisdictional disputes may seem petty but certainly affect the way in which departments react to proposals.

Departments also feel that they have a responsibility to ensure that certain views and interests are represented or considered when policy is being made. Civil servants believe they should ensure that the policy issues with which they are concerned are considered adequately by the government as a whole. The best way to do this is for each department to act like barristers, putting forward the case for programmes they administer for their beneficiaries or clients. Thus, to take a well-known example within Whitehall of the advocacy department, the Department of Education and Science fights (though with diminishing success) to ensure that education is adequately funded and escapes the worst of public expenditure cuts. Civil servants also argue that the best way to make good policy is for each department to argue for its own corner. As in a trial, truth (or at least good policy) is supposed to emerge from the clash of interests and opinions. Departments are supposed to show a certain degree of restraint and propriety in defending their programmes. Thus it is not considered right for departments to suppress information which might be used by other departments to challenge their arguments. But it is not expected that a department alert another to the weakest part of its case – it is up to that department to spot the weak points itself.

Ministries and interest groups

The 'departmental view' is strengthened by the regular contacts which many departments have with 'pressure' or 'interest' groups in their policy field. Any body, ranging from a local trust to the largest trade union, which tries to influence government policy without directly fighting elections, can be regarded as a 'pressure' or 'interest' group. Usually they will have elected spokesmen and some form of permanent secretariat who will take an active part in making their views known. Some groups, such as Friends of the Earth, will be organised specifically to promote a particular cause; others will group individuals or other organisations which have a wider range of interests in common, and will perform many other functions for their members (e.g. providing insurance and sickness benefits), besides representing them politically. This type of group tends to be longer-lived and more in the confidence of the Civil Service. All such groups perform a very important representative function, supplementing or even replacing Parliament and political parties as channels through which individuals can make their views known to the executive and thus affect policy.

British interest groups can thus under a favourable combination of circumstances be very influential in government policy-making. On the other hand, they also have weaknesses deriving from their federal character and from restrictions on their access to a closed and secretive administrative structure. For a balanced view of their influence on departments, we need to consider both strengths and weaknesses.

Compared with fifty or seventy years ago, most major interest groups operate in a climate of opinion which respects the right of citizens to be represented not simply as voters but as workers, businessmen, consumers, farmers, churchmen, etc. The comments of interest groups on policies affecting their members receive wide publicity and demand some kind of response from official spokesmen (even if it is only to contradict them). British interest groups thus enjoy considerable freedom to make 'news' for the media. A further strength is that most are grouped into a single overall or 'peak' association, which acts as national spokesman. Instead of three trade union 'peak' organisations, for example, as in France or Italy, there is only one; the Trades Union Congress (TUC).

British interest groups have also enrolled a high proportion of members from the sectors they cover, so they can genuinely claim to act as representative spokesmen. Because of this they can be a valuable source of information and support for ministers or civil servants seeking to administer that sector; the latter can find out fairly cheaply and easily from the interest group what effects a policy change would have. In one anomalous case (the financial markets and institutions known collectively as the 'City' because they are physically located in the City of London) the interests involved refrained from organising themselves until the late 1960s, thus preventing government from having easy access to financial information. By presenting decisions on interest and exchange rates as immensely technical and complicated, and providing no information about them, they ensured that they were effectively adminstered at one remove through the (City-based) Bank of England. Thus politicians and civil servants were effectively excluded from a range of central economic decisions.

The opposite extreme is also atypical but instructive, as it reveals what civil servants and interest group leaders can get out of a very close and intimate relationship. This is the case of the National Farmers' Union (NFU) and the Ministry of Agriculture and Fisheries. Relationships here are confidential, cordial, based on technical not party arguments, and above all frequent. When the Chairman of a Commons Select Committee on Agriculture suggested that preparations for negotiating British entry to the European Community were inadequate because there had not been a formal conference between the Ministry of Agriculture and the National Farmers' Union on the issue, he received little support from the President of the NFU, Sir Gwilym Williams. Williams explained that such conferences were unnecessary because officials of the NFU and the Ministry were constantly in touch: there was no aspect of agricultural policy on which their views were not known to each other. Such contacts are almost hourly, in fact, and are reinforced by social contacts (at least at the highest levels) through membership of the same London clubs. Naturally, this frequent exchange reinforces the tendency for the department to have views which serve the interests of their clients.

The position achieved by the NFU is made possible by the technical nature of the questions involved and the marginality of the area to government concerns – governments do more or less carry on the agricultural policies of their predecessors. The NFU has also relatively fewer divergences to reconcile among its membership and only a few constituent unions.

It is on economic and social policy that parties disagree, adopt sweeping courses of action which do not always depend on technical information (although perhaps they should) and increasingly seek to impose programmes rather than have them shaped by discussion with interested groups. When a broad policy consensus existed in the 1950s and to a lesser extent in the 1960s, relationships between interest groups and ministries approximated more to the agricultural model, and information and support were traded for concessions on policy and implementation. As governments resorted to more radical policies in order to get the economy going again, they sought to impose these on recalcitrant unions and local authorities, on the assumption that government knew better than any sectional group where the national interest lay.

Such a lead reinforced the natural secretiveness of the Civil Service and its highly selective choice of interests to consult. Debarred from an influence over the making of policy, groups like the unions and environmentalists have taken to direct action as a more or less normal tactic; (for example stirring up opposition to legislation in Parliament; legal public protest through marches and demonstrations, and even defiance of the law in an attempt to make it unworkable). Trade union opposition to industrial relations legislation, which slightly reduced their power from the late sixties to the eighties, passed through all these stages.

Of course the unions are one branch of the overall Labour movement, whose political wing is the Labour Party. When Labour is in power there is consequently much more consultation between the TUC and the government than under the Conservatives. The Labour Government of 1974–79 made numerous concessions to trade unions on their legal rights and industrial power, partly to buy their approval of incomes restraint. Yet as we saw in Chapter 1, the last pay norm was imposed by the Labour Government of 1978–79 against union opposition. Even when the 'Social Contract' (1974–78) was in full bloom the unions were not in close touch with civil servants (as opposed to ministers) outside the Department of Employment.

Business influence is more pervasive under all governments. Economic growth cannot be achieved if business confidence is low. 'City' and financial interests–since 1970 extensively organised into 'peak' defence associations like the British Bankers' Association and Committee of London Clearing Banks – must be left reasonably happy, otherwise capital will flee overseas rather than into home investment.

The need to consider these interests has prompted suggestions that Britain has become a 'corporatist' state in which policy is made by government negotiating as an equal with all relevant organised groups. Yet this does not fit the reality sketched above, of unequal access to decision-making for different groups, and a situation in which governments have unilaterally imposed their policies even on the City (as in the enforcement of greater competition within financial markets during the late 1960s).

Besides free and equal access to government on the part of all powerful groups, the corporatist thesis also assumes that the participants can bind their members to observe agreements reached in top-level negotiations. A second major weakness of peak associations like the CBI and the TUC is, however, that they incorporate representatives from many diverse industrial and commercial sectors. Their concerns often conflict, and in any case they may have independent and often stronger links with ministries, and governments generally, than their nominal representative, the peak association. Moreover the CBI does not represent financial and banking interests, reflecting a wider divorce between the two in economy and society.

Where concern for stability of the currency conflicts with industrial expansion, the former usually wins, not so much because of the hidden power of financial interest groups, which are themselves divided, but because a currency crisis constitutes a more immediate danger to economic wellbeing than gradual erosion of business confidence.

Thus although the CBI is represented on many government committees it generally has to fight much harder, and on a broader front, than the farmers to get its views accepted. This is what makes both corporatism and tripartism (the idea that economic policy could be underpinned by agreements between business, unions and government) rather suspect. The rival financial interests at least would also have to be consulted and reconciled.

The relative weakness of business representation helps account for the 'stop-go' policies of the 1960s and the cuts in public expenditure even under Labour Governments of 1966–70 and 1976 onwards. These also stem from the weakness of union influence within the administrative machine. Like the CBI, the TUC has to contend with the difficulty that major constituent unions, representing millions of workers, themselves have conflicting interests and direct links with the Civil Service. Moreover, union views affect the core of the government programme and are often unwelcome. Even at the institutional level, however, unions have much more limited access than business or financial interests. Effectively their links are solely with one ministry, the Department of Employment. Thus their representatives are unable to propagate their views widely within the executive and they are correspondingly less likely than other interests to shape final policy.

This is one reason for the unions' greater willingness to take direct action and put external pressure on government through demonstrations, strikes, picketing and organised protest of various kinds. Even the Labour Party has been more susceptible to union arguments when in opposition than when in government, so the unions' inability to penetrate further into the Civil Service constitutes a fundamental weakness.

Administrative secrecy

The example of the unions demonstrates that involvement in government policy-making is not automatic, even for organisations with a membership of one-fifth, approximately, of the British population. Civil servants decide whom they will consult on what. They can be even more selective in regard to smaller, less well organised groups such as consumers' associations or environmentalists, which lack the resources of unions.

Consultation between interest groups and civil servants is not, therefore, an open debate. On the contrary, it is usually shrouded in secrecy like all other administrative processes. This gives civil servants an important advantage in dealings with outsiders as detailed information, instead of being provided free, is traded like a commodity with the interest groups (which include local governments in this context), in order to involve selected ones in shaping and supporting government programmes. Once the trade is made, the agreed line of policy enters into the fixed 'departmental view'.

The Civil Service monopoly of information (which is further hoarded inside individual ministries) is based on the Official Secrets Act of 1911, Section 2 of which makes it illegal to communicate to any 'unauthorised person' *any* information obtained as a servant of the Crown, or *entrusted by* a servant of the Crown. Although both Conservatives and Labour committed themselves in manifestoes during the 1970s to eliminate unnecessary secrecy in the administration, both failed as governments to do anything about it. The justification for this has been the need for government to take strong and decisive action without further consultation where it (or its civil servants) deem this necessary. The implied assumption here, that wide consultation inhibits rather than facilitates strong action, is quite revealing of attitudes within the executive and indicates why government initiatives so often break down under opposition. The hoarding of information also strengthens civil servants in relationships with their nominal political masters, who come to office without the detailed information they need to muster effective arguments for their policies. However, the unsuccessful attempt to convict Clive Ponting for passing on papers on the sinking of the Argentinian cruiser *General Belgrano*, put Section 2 into further disrepute.

Ministers' effectiveness within departments

The responses of ministers to their complex administrative environment varies widely. A power struggle is unavoidable if they wish to assert their own views. Of course, not all ministers do wish to impose themselves. Many are happy to accept their department's advice and represent it within the government. Some find fulfilment in a role acceptable to their civil servants. Those who do not share departmental views and assumptions obviously have a more difficult time and must think about the strategies which civil servants will use against them, and which they can use to overcome their nominal subordinates.

The easiest strategy to prevent a policy being implemented is not to comply with a decision. Civil servants are unlikely to defy their minister openly. However, they often overlook formal decisions to change policy, or interpret the decision very narrowly, failing to apply it to similar cases.

A more legitimate tactic is to persist in offering advice or options which have been rejected. Thus the Foreign Office continually rejected the use of the word 'détente' to characterise relations with the USSR, in spite of clear rulings from the then Prime Minister, Harold Wilson, that the word was to be used. Every major foreign policy speech or statement would witness a repeat of the battle as the Foreign Office hoped to wear down the Prime Minister on this point. Crossman found his pension reform plan attacked by Treasury officials just before the plan went to Cabinet on grounds which had been considered and rejected months before. Again, a decision had not stopped the criticisms of the civil servants opposed to the plan. Such steadfast opposition may either convert or wear down a minister; indeed, unless he is vigilant the Civil Service may slip past a section in a memorandum or a policy statement which the minister dislikes, but which because he has had an opportunity to reject it, will be treated as though it was his own policy. Ministers are very busy, and the risk of letting something slip through is ever-present.

One Civil Service tactic which greatly upsets politicians is for civil servants overruled by their minister to use contacts with other ministries to mobilise support. Civil servants have many meetings with colleagues on interdepartmental committees; there are also many unofficial and entirely natural meetings between civil servants in the London clubs or over lunch. These meetings, or even telephone conversations, give civil servants the chance to explain the weaknesses in their minister's case to other civil servants – and through them, their respective ministers – in departments predisposed to be critical. Thus, if civil servants at the Department of Industry were opposed to Benn's plans in 1975–78 to make grants to workers' co-operatives, a tactic open to his officials was to alert officials in the Treasury, which always tends to be critical of increased expenditure. The tactic smacks of disloyalty, but is difficult to expose.

The most common concern of those who fear that civil servants manipulate politicians is that ministers are presented with options which either do not cover all possible forms of action or are accompanied by lists of advantages or disadvantages in a form likely to prejudice the decision. Clearly politicians who are not experts must to some extent be dependent on the expertise of their advisers, the civil servants. Predictions of the likely effect of a change in interest rates, the best way to reduce inflation, or the likelihood of persuading the European Community to treat Britain more equitably, must come from civil servants. This is particularly so given their monopoly of technical information. Yet civil servants have not only opinions but unconscious biases.

These do not favour any of the major parties to the detriment of the others. It is perhaps a testimony to the degree to which civil servants avoid overt party bias, that both Conservative and Labour have been convinced that the Civil Service is unconsciously biased against them. Labour politicians are alarmed by the class and educational background of civil servants. In particular, civil servants are recruited disproportionately from amongst the graduates of Oxford and Cambridge and seem to Labour supporters to be part of that establishment which it should be their party's task to challenge. Marcia Williams, Harold Wilson's personal secretary and an influential figure among his private advisers, was sure that there existed an instinctive *rapport* between civil servants and Conservative politicians and an instinctive suspicion of Labour politicians among civil servants. Conservative politicians suspect that there is an inherent conflict between the assumptions made by civil servants and Conservative policy. Civil servants, whose job it is after all to make government work efficiently, are presumed to share a belief in the efficacy of government action which Conservatives, at least in the area of economic policy, do not endorse. Conservatives suspect that the Civil Service will criticise plans for deregulation and disengagement of government from intervention in the economy (although in fact they are probably not averse to shedding responsibility for individual firms or sectors, as opposed to general macro-level direction).

It is extremely difficult to assess the validity of these complaints. It is argued by the Civil Service Department that the heavy recruitment of Oxbridge graduates is accidental, reflecting the distribution of the ablest applicants to the Civil Service among British universities rather than bias on their part. Some of the difficulties between Marcia Williams and the civil servants with whom she worked may have reflected the prickliness of her own personality. The most common and reasonable assumption is that the Civil Service is resistant to change. As noted, civil servants are likely to have some investment in existing policies; they have created and administered programmes which politicians, regrettably, are always proposing to alter. Moreover, the intellectual style implanted in civil servants by British university education makes them more inclined to criticise than to innovate. All this is of course speculation, and will remain so while the Civil Service Department opposes academic research on the Civil Service. What is certain in an era in which both major political parties have been pursuing more radical, and more radically different policies, is that both Conservative and Labour politicians have been experimenting with strategies for imposing their ideas on civil servants.

Before considering these we should note that the relationship between administrators and ministers is not necessarily adversarial. In fact, civil servants need strong not weak ministers for their departments to flourish. Perhaps the crucial determinant of the success of a minister with a department is how successful the minister is *outside* the department. In the last analysis only the minister can, in the political give and take between departments, ensure that the department receives its fair share of government expenditure and parliamentary time for legislation. The minister who unexpectedly or against the odds wins for the department a higher priority in the queue for legislation or saves programmes from expenditure cuts will find his or her authority within the ministry considerably enhanced. Success in Cabinet is a sure way to gain Civil Service approval. A competent minister can win the loyalty of a department through force of personality. Civil servants are always evaluating their ministers, and a minister who is receiving a good press, is performing well in the House of Commons and is successful in Cabinet debates, will usually be popular within the department. Obviously, some ministers are better than others at establishing a working relationship with their civil servants, and occasionally dramatic attempts have been made to inspire them. Tony Benn held mass meetings of his Department of Industry in an attempt to get his message across to officials.

Nonetheless, politicians of both parties have been increasingly unwilling to rely solely on the Civil Service for advice. Ministers have recruited both part- and full-time advisers from outside the Civil Service. One of the main reasons for the friction between Richard Crossman and the Permanent Secretary in his early days at the Ministry of Housing was that Crossman was determined to take advice from outside advisers, including Lord Goodman, on the Rent Act. In time the civil servants came to accept the participation of Crossman's unofficial advisers in policy-making because that at least provided a chance to refute – or attempt to refute – their arguments. Moreover, a large number of ministers of very varied ideological character have actually taken advisers into government with them. The purpose of appointing such advisers is not so much to check on the routine workings of the ministry but to ensure that a wider range of options is considered and that the political implications of proposals are considered. All advisers have had to struggle to be genuinely involved in policy-making. Key issues have been access to papers within the department, so that they are aware of imminent decisions, the options under consideration, and physical proximity to their minister so that discussions with him are easy and frequent.

Fear of the Civil Service has also prompted party leaders to make more detailed policy in opposition. Attention in recent years has focused on man-oeuvres within the Labour Party to bind future Labour Governments to the contents of a manifesto itself the product of the Party's National Executive. The Conservatives have also attempted to avoid contamination by the Civil Service. Between 1965 and 1970 under Heath, the Conservatives made the greatest effort in recent times to draw up in opposition – away from the pres-sures of government, the Civil Service, and interest groups – detailed policies on a wide range of issues, for implementation after gaining office. To the extent that politicians can enter office with a clear idea not only of what they want to do but also how they want to do it, the power of the Civil Service is reduced. It is striking how vague even long-standing political commitments are. In spite of the prominence of housing in British politics during the 1950s and 1960s, the Labour Party had no idea how to implement its manifesto commitments on rents when it came to power in 1964. Yet if this represents one extreme, the attempt to evolve a detailed industrial relations policy in opposition by the Conservatives in the period 1964–70 also suggests that there are considerable limits to this strategy: the policy suffered by being imposed in its entirety on the unions in the face of their absolute refusal to co-operate.

Collective decision-making

It remains a powerful convention in British government that ministers are collectively responsible for major government decisions. A minister who cannot support or defend the important decisions of the Cabinet, particularly if the minister is of Cabinet rank, should resign. How strongly this convention sur-vives is debatable. On the one hand, the lowest ranking of those holding a position in the government, such as parliamentary private secretaries, have been forced to resign if they made an overt show of defiance against a Cabinet decision, that is, abstaining rather than supporting the government in parlia-mentary votes. On the other hand, there have been several instances of Cabi-net ministers disagreeing with collective policy. Thus James Callaghan was known to oppose the industrial relations policy of the 1964–70 Labour Government and indeed used his position as Treasurer of the Labour Party to encourage opposition to legislation based on the White Paper, *In Place of Strife*. In spite of a strong feeling within the Cabinet that Callaghan should resign, he did not. Tony Benn returned the compliment during Callaghan's prime ministership, refusing to resign in spite of sharp differences with the economic policies of the Government. Benn used his position on the Labour Party's National Executive Committee openly to oppose the Cabinet's policy. Again, perhaps because he had learnt an important lesson from Harold Wilson, Cal-laghan decided that it would be best not to ask for Benn's resignation. Cer-tainly the latter might have been a greater political problem if set free to oppose government policy rather than remaining under some constraint as one of its members. However, these instances remain interesting qualifications on the general principle of collective responsibility rather than proof of its demise.

Because ministers ultimately have to support them, it is essential, therefore, that government decision-making should provide for collective consideration of key policies.

It is also the case that few important decisions can be seen as exclusively the concern of only one department. Most obviously, nearly all government programmes cost money and therefore have both financial and economic implications. The Treasury, the main financial department, is naturally involved. Parliamentary time for debating legislation is also a scarce resource, so that collective decisions about the relative priority of government Bills must also be made. Decisions about defence policy must be taken with foreign policy in mind. Decisions about aid to industry have implications for Britain's trade policy and position within the European Community. It is a practical necessity, therefore, that there be interdepartmental consideration of all key legislation, and other policy initiatives. On the other hand, ministers are extremely busy people scarcely able to keep track of their own ministries, let alone other departments as well.

In fact, key policy decisions are the product of inter-departmental consultations. These constitute one of the key political processes in Britain, and proceed on two levels. The first involves the civil servants. There are a large number of permanent inter-departmental committees which on a continuing basis consider the recurring issues in British government; for example, annual forecasts of public expenditure. A standing committee of civil servants considers the state of British agriculture, and what changes in farm subsidies are required each year. New legislation on, say, social security, is discussed by civil servants representing all the relevant departments, including Health and Social Security and the Treasury. In addition, new proposals are considered by specially formed inter-departmental committees of civil servants. In all cases the civil servants will be trying to identify crucial points at issue between departments. Arguing on the basis of some combination of long-standing departmental preferences and the attitudes of their ministers, the civil servants will then refer points which they are unable to resolve to committees of ministers. During the discussions between civil servants, representatives of each department will be alerting their ministers to points for which they will have to fight on ministerial committees. In view of the limited time ministers can devote to considering proposals from other ministries, this sifting by civil servants is essential.

For every committee of civil servants there exists an inter-departmental committee of ministers. These committees, committees of the Cabinet and reporting to the Cabinet, are amongst the most important institutions in British government. Yet their existence is supposedly secret, and their membership is never publicised. Their general composition is well known, however. The ministers from the departments most involved belong, and there are usually a small number of ministers, one of whom acts as chairman, who have no departmental interest in the issues at stake. Thus on farm subsidies, the committee will have representation from Agriculture, Fisheries and Food, the Home Office (responsible for agriculture in Ulster), the Scottish and Welsh Offices (responsible for Scottish and Welsh agriculture), the Treasury (concerned about costs to the Exchequer), the Department of Trade (concerned with trading links with overseas suppliers of food) and the Foreign Office (also concerned with trading links with overseas suppliers and with the European Community).

The need to have a chairman with no departmental interest indicates that these committees frequently witness fights between departments, which are understood best as conflicts between their enduring attitudes and interests. To continue our example, in any government, Conservative or Labour, the Ministry of Agriculture presses for more help for farmers; the Treasury resists increases in expenditure; and the Department of Trade opposes any proposal which increases protection and conflicts with trade liberalisation. Many of the major departments – Agriculture, Employment, Education, Trade and Industry – have links with approved interest groups, and the clashes between departments in Cabinet committees constitute one of the most important ways in which outside demands are voiced and combined into an overall policy. Of course this process takes place within the rather strict and selective limits noted above, so that outside interests constitute only one element in the 'departmental views' being advanced.

Ministers may of course differ in the way in which they conceive their role and act it out on committees. Some ministers are primarily ambassadors for their departments, while others give this function a low priority. Again, not all issues are equally important to all the ministries concerned, and lower ranking ministers may deputise at some committee meetings for a senior colleague. Neither is it the case that all crucial issues are settled in cabinet committees. Although Harold Wilson during his first term as Prime Minister attempted to restrict the flow of issues from Cabinet committees to the full Cabinet by saying that committee decisions could be appealed to the full Cabinet only with the consent of the committee chairmen, many crucial issues cannot be settled without discussion in Cabinet. And here more is at stake than simply the rival interests and attitudes of departments.

Collective decision-making and the Cabinet

British political parties have long been plausibly regarded as coalitions. It has been common to emphasise divisions in the Labour Party between the more socialist or 'left-wing' elements and the 'moderates', or right-wingers. How consistently these categorise divisions on specific issues may be doubted. Thus Barbara Castle, clearly identified with the left wing, emerged as a proponent of legislation which would restrict the powers of trade unions, usually regarded as a right-wing position. Anthony Crosland, a revisionist socialist writer and intellectual hero of the Labour moderates, was in fact one of the ministers least prepared to accept the deflationary economic policy dictated by the International Monetary Fund in 1976. Richard Crossman, hard to categorise ideologically but not on the far left of the party, was one of the most sceptical about the Wilson Government's futile attempt to maintain the value of the pound and avoid devaluation in 1967. Yet it is possible to identify a set of issues which by and large divide the left from the right in the Labour Party. On any one of these issues it is possible to point to individuals who do not fit the categories, but it is still possible to make broad generalisations. The Labour left is more likely to reject orthodox economic deflationary measures, more critical of British participation in the European Community and NATO, and more opposed to restrictions on trade union power (including incomes policies) than the Labour right. The striking of a balance between the left and right in a Labour Cabinet is part of the intra-executive political process.

Over the 1970s divisions within the Conservative Party became almost as deep and predictable as those within the Labour Party. Mrs Thatcher's Cabinet divided between 'wets' and hardliners. The 'wets' were more sceptical about monetarist economic policies, programmes which seem likely to produce confrontation with the trade unions, and more anxious to preserve the remnants of consensus between the two major parties. Though the derogatory term 'wet' was coined by Mrs Thatcher to describe the wing of the party which disagreed with her, her first Cabinet contained a majority of 'wets'. Both Conservative and Labour Cabinets, therefore, are forums within which important differences within the political system are resolved.

What, then, will be going through ministers' minds at Cabinet or Cabinet committee meetings? Of course both Crossman's and Barbara Castle's diaries show that ministers do not always find the debate compelling and some turn to doodling or making out shopping lists. More frequently, when ministers are paying attention, their reactions to proposals reflect a combination of the factors we have encountered. Ministers will be thinking *departmentally*, and thinking about how the proposals affect the interests, attitudes and policies of their own ministry. If any of these are affected adversely, the minister will tend to oppose the proposal. Ministers will also evaluate proposals politically. Does the proposal conflict with ideals (such as greater equality or lower public expenditure) which the minister espouses? Is the proposal one which will cost the Government popularity and, above all, seats in Parliament? The Crossman diaries are replete with calls to ministers to evaluate a wide range of proposals – including local government reform and the redrawing of constituency boundaries – in terms of how they would affect the Labour Party electorally. Ministers also react on the basis of regional loyalty; the Wilson Government of 1964–70 blocked the modernisation of Bristol's docks because the Welsh MPs in the Cabinet thought that blocking Bristol would help the South Wales ports across the Bristol Channel. Finally, to some extent ministers function as an intelligent but critical audience pointing out ambiguities, contradictions and flaws in other departments' reasoning. Which of these influences ministers' approach to proposals depends partly on their personality. It depends also on the character of the issue before them. It would be a rare minister indeed who acquiesced in the cutting of his or her department's budget.

Not every major government decision has been the product of genuine collective discussion. Attlee's decision to build a British atomic bomb; the decision of the Wilson government to modernise Polaris submarines; Eden's invasion of Egypt after it had taken over the Suez Canal; Wilson's application to join the European Community and his further attempt to maintain the value of sterling in 1966–67, are all cited as examples which were not the product of the collective decision-making process supposed to characterise British government. In these cases it is suggested that the Prime Minister was able to restrict discussion, or to rig discussion in such a way as to determine the result. This raises a difficult point about the power of the Prime Minister in the British political process, relative to his Cabinet colleagues, a question to which we shall soon return. It is noticeable, however, that examples of the Prime Minister acting on his own are usually of decisions which were afterwards regretted. There was little advantage to a Labour politician after 1967 in claiming to have been fully involved in the decision not to devalue the pound and several wished to exaggerate their unhappiness with decisions to apply for membership of the European Community. Crossman, who before he served in a Cabinet had been a vociferous proponent of the view that British government is more prime ministerial than collective, in fact provides very mixed evidence on this point in his diaries. It is certainly the case that discussion of devaluation was discouraged by the Prime Minister and the Chancellor of the Excheque, using the plausible argument that if it were known that devaluation was being discussed the foreign currency reserves would suffer considerably. Yet Crossman also records that by 1966 devaluation had been much discussed by members of the Cabinet and one gains the impression that what was lacking was not so much the opportunity to mention devaluation as the political determination of members of the Cabinet to impose it. Again, it is quite clear that the decision to apply for membership of the European Community was much debated by members of the Wilson Government. Opinion within the Government was certainly divided, and it is even possible that half the Cabinet opposed membership. Yet its opponents were not prepared to veto the application. Crossman's justification for this is interesting, particularly from one so committed to the view that we have prime ministerial government. He was forced into arguing that it was not institutionally impossible for members of the Cabinet to provoke a debate on a major government policy of which they disapproved, but politically and almost psychologically impossible. Using an analogy which showed his unfamiliarity with contemporary universities, Crossman argued that for him to challenge a major policy with which the Prime Minister is associated would be like a member of a university Senate dissenting when the Vice-Chancellor had decided to take disciplinary action against students involved in a well-publicised riot.

Crossman might well have been able to argue, however, that collective decision-making on major issues often came too late and after damaging commitments had been made. It is probable that Harold Wilson could have presented his Government with a *fait accompli* on Rhodesia had he been able to reach an agreement with the Rhodesian rebel Prime Minister, Ian Smith, which Smith was prepared to honour. Certainly the Cabinet discussion of legislation arising from the White Paper *In Place of Strife* was in one sense a textbook example of collective debate, with Cabinet argument exposing many instances of muddled thinking in the proposals. However, the doubts expressed by members of the Cabinet did not prevent the Government being identified with a difficult course of action, one which would damage its position in the country, with the Labour Party and the trade unions who fund the Labour Party. Doubts expressed in Cabinet, relayed to the unions by Callaghan, weakened the Government's position, but collective debate had not taken place early enough to ensure that the Government was genuinely prepared for the political risks it was running. Crossman in power, obstinate man that he was, nonetheless was forced to admit that collective debate and responsibility made more difference to government than he had imagined. Yet Crossman could justifiably complain that collective debate tended to come late in the day, and to have largely negative results. Collective debate and responsibility sometimes served to *stop* proposals; it rarely served to start them. There was little opportunity for even the senior members of the Cabinet to discuss what positive initiatives should be undertaken.

Direction from the centre and the setting of priorities

The central decision-making process used to be one of the most widely praised aspects of the British political system. Aided by an impartial and experienced Civil Service, the most senior government ministers would discover by debate amongst themselves policies which embodied their priorities and, precisely because of the preceding debate, decisions would be of an unusually high calibre. Members of the Wilson Government staged a mock Cabinet debate for the benefit of President Nixon, then on a state visit, and were vastly pleased with themselves. Where else, they wondered – encouraged by Nixon's flattery – would one find government conducted in such an intelligent and civilised manner?

The reality is, as we saw from the discussion of economic policy, very different and reflects on the adequacy of the input into policy-making not only from individual departments but from the government collectively. Certainly, the British system ensures adequate discussion of proposals from an individual ministry. If, for example, Environment wishes to launch a new road-building programme, then contributions from numerous departments such as the Treasury, the Ministry of Agriculture and the Department of Industry will ensure that ministers making a decision have been alerted to all the crucial facts. A poor decision might still be made, but that will not be the fault of the system. Costs, benefits and alternative options will have been fairly thoroughly explored. Yet criticisms are still made, even if they are often contradictory. Perhaps the most damaging have been that power within the British executive has been centralised into the hands of the Prime Minister, and that British government, in contrast to the received view, provides inadequately for central consideration of strategy and priorities.

Prime ministerial power

The question of the relative power of the Prime Minister and Cabinet is the most debated issue in the study of executive politics in Britain. This is in spite, or perhaps because, of the imprecision of the terms used, the difficulty of establishing criteria which would settle the debate, and the attempts by British politicians, including supposedly reforming Labour Governments, to keep intact the veil of secrecy which cloaks executive processes. This is one reason why debates over prime ministerial power seem oddly abstracted from the complex political processes in British executive politics which we have attempted to outline. They also involve other issues discussed later, such as the degree to which Parliament, or at least the House of Commons, continues to have a significant influence over government policies.

The main reasons why some believe the Prime Minister dominates Cabinet are easily summarised. In an era in which television is the dominant news medium, attention focuses on the Prime Minister and the Leader of the Opposition. It is assumed that for most voters, the parties have become synonymous with their leaders. Once the election is won, the Prime Minister enjoys considerable freedom in deciding whom to include in the Cabinet and what positions they should hold. The Prime Minister is relatively free to move or dismiss ministers and through the power of appointment and dismissal can determine the broad direction in which the Government is moving. If the Prime Minister joins with the appropriate minister in advocating a course of action, the Cabinet in practice has little choice but to support them. Thanks to jet air travel and telephone links, heads of government have come to dominate the conduct of diplomacy leaving little freedom of action for mere Foreign Ministers. In the course of such prime ministerial diplomacy, commitments are made which the Cabinet and parliamentary party can do little to alter. Finally, the Prime Minister has a more or less unfettered right to decide the date of the general election and thus to decide the point at which the entire government will put its future and plans to risk at the polls.

There is a reply to all these points. Modern electoral research shows that party images and loyalties are shaped by many other forces than the image of the party leader (see Ch. 4). Far from being free to include or exclude whomever they choose, recent Prime Ministers have been forced to accept in their Cabinets people whose views they disliked. Thus Wilson retained Callaghan, Callaghan retained Benn in spite of policy differences; and Mrs Thatcher was forced to change her attitude to Cabinet-making. Before the 1979 election she said in a famous interview, that there was no point including in a Cabinet people with whom one disagreed; too much time would be spent arguing with them. Yet when the Thatcher Cabinet was announced in 1979 it contained a majority of Conservatives from the non-monetarist wing of the party, the future 'wets'. The need to appoint a Cabinet which would have the confidence of the full parliamentary party was overriding. Foreign Secretaries have not disappeared from view; Lord Carrington played a major role in the settlement of Rhodesia in 1979 and in later negotiations involving the European Community on Afghanistan, Poland and the Middle East. Moreover, British Prime Ministers have not so much strutted the globe unrestrained, as been buffeted by domestic and international forces such as the unions, industry, International Monetary Fund and Organisation of Oil Exporting Countries, which they have been powerless to restrain.

It is apparent from even this brief account of the debate that it is highly anecdotal. There is no way of telling whether the instances quoted are typical or not. The possibility that single-party governments commanding a Commons majority may give way to coalition or minority governments dependent on outside support (see Chs 3 and 4) does argue, however, that if government has not been unambiguously prime ministerial when it is single-party, it is even less likely to be so when the Prime Minister has to negotiate with equal partners whose support is crucial.

One weakness of the debates over prime ministerial power is their failure to analyse the relative impact of personality and the institutional nature of the office. On the one hand it is unreasonable to view the prime ministership as such a structured institution that its character varies little according to who fills it. At least superficially it would seem that British Prime Ministers in recent years have varied quite considerably in their style and almost certainly in their ways of doing business. The detached air of Douglas-Home, the compulsion of Wilson to be at the centre of events, the directing zeals of Heath and Thatcher and the avuncular calm of Callaghan, have presumably had significant consequences for the character of the office. How far the Prime Minister allows individual ministers to pursue their work without interference from 10 Downing Street, and how energetically the Prime Minister leads the Cabinet in a particular direction is at least as much a reflection of personality as of the continuing nature of the prime ministership itself. Unfortunately, few attempts have been made to examine the impact of personality on the prime ministership; what discussion there is has focused more on supposed common personality features which explain the ambition required to take politicians to the prime ministership, than on the effect of personality differences between Prime Ministers on their conduct ot the office.

The debate about the power of the Prime Minister ought to have stimulated more discussion of the central institutions of British executive politics and the criticisms made against them. One of the best objections to the argument that Britain has prime ministerial government, is that the Prime Minister has no department. Where can the Prime Minister obtain the staff help, policy analysis and advice which would enable him or her to play a dominating role in policy making? Equally, critics of the British system of government may ask, where are the people who think about policy from the viewpoint of the whole government, and not just in terms of how their own operating department will be affected? These are points related closely to the discussion of economic policy in the preceding chapter, and to the absence highlighted there of any sound administrative base for central co-ordination.

Treasury control

The major source of co-ordination in British government was traditionally Treasury control. Operating departments might be so close to their own concerns and to associated pressure groups as to be incapable of taking a sufficiently detached view of the true value of their plans or of how the plans fitted into the Government's priorities. The Treasury, with the right to comment on any proposal from an operating department, would in contrast have the opportunity to see the wood from the trees. Its critical evaluation of proposals would enable ministers to think over their true priorities.

In recent years, however, scepticism has grown about the adequacy of Treasury control as an instrument of policy review. In the first place, orthodox Treasury review is directed to changing, not continuing, policy. The Treasury comments on the implications of changing policy but not on the implications of continuing policies which may well have outlived their usefulness.

Moreover, Treasury review is based on the assumption that the struggle for resources between the spending departments is a winner-take-all situation: when one department gains the others must lose. Faced with such a situation, ministers will reveal their real preferences on the relative importance of policies. Yet in practice ministers in charge of the spending ministries may well band together to defend their programmes, forcing the Treasury ministers to increase taxation or the budget deficit. Different spending departments may be allies, not enemies, in a common fight with the Treasury.

Treasury review also suffers from limitations inherent in the budgetary process. Budgeting is typically an incremental process in which most expenditure goes unquestioned. This is partly because much government expenditure this year will be the consequence of decisions made in the past which cannot be changed without severe consequences. It would be perverse to leave a school half built, and difficult to end an entitlement such as retirement pensions to which people had long contributed. Most current government expenditure is, therefore, relatively untouched by Treasury review.

During the 1960s and 1970s a number of innovations were designed specifically to give the Treasury more direct control over expenditure. The first of these, the Public Expenditure Survey Committee (PESC), resulted from an official inquiry into spending control (the Plowden Committee) and the new system dominated policy between 1961 and 1973. In essence PESC attempted to impose on the budgetary process a longer-term view with expenditure projected five years in advance. However, the new system continued to decide on expenditure *before* revenues were calculated and neither departments nor the Cabinet had much incentive to economise during these years. Indeed, public expenditure as a percentage of Gross Domestic Product (GDP) increased from 33 per cent in 1961 and rose steadily (pausing briefly under the Chancellorship of Roy Jenkins) to reach a peak of 46.5 per cent in 1976. Since the mid-1970s governments have resorted increasingly to cash limits as a means of expenditure control. So, instead of fitting cash totals to projected needs, needs have had to be tailored to the amount of cash available in any one year. This change helped Denis Healey impose his draconian public expenditure cuts to great effect in the 1976–78 period.

Since then cash limits have had limited success in holding down expenditure. There are a number of reasons for this. First, the nationalised industries are subject to a separate form of control and not even the avowedly free market government of Margaret Thatcher could resist the pleas of British Leyland, British Steel and British Rail in the 1979–82 period. Second, cash limits or not, many ministers have continued to fight hard in Cabinet to prevent spending cuts from biting too deeply into their departmental budgets – and sometimes successfully. Finally, and most important, many expenditures are almost beyond government control because they are automatically increased by broad societal change. When unemployment increases so must unemployment benefits. When the number of over-sixty-fives increases so must old age pensions. Governments could control these benefits by reducing their value or altering eligibility rules, but such changes would be highly unpopular electorally.

From 1982 another initiative in the continuing saga of expenditure control was launched. *Volume* planning was introduced and in combination with cash limits should enable ministers to project ahead how much in cash terms will be available given inflation – and, crucially, what *revenues* are expected to be in any one year.

Other innovations to improve co-ordination

Partly in recognition of weaknesses in planning and co-ordination, two experiments were launched by the Heath government of 1970–74: the creation of the so-called super-ministries and the Central policy Review Staff (CPRS). The super-Minister - Trade and Industry linking two former ministries, and Environment formed out of the old Ministry of Housing and Local Government and the Ministry of Transport) were to help consistent policy-making, in two ways. First, the Cabinet could be made a smaller and more coherent body better able to think about the broad direction of government policy. The belief that a large Cabinet and strategic thinking are incompatible is a recurring theme in the writings of politicians in all parties. Second, by grouping ministries along supposedly functional lines, certain recurring policy conflicts could be resolved by senior members of the Cabinet in super-ministries covering both aspects of policy, an obvious example being the placing of the road programme (along with the other responsibilities of the Ministry of Transport) within the new Department of the Environment, which was also charged with conservation.

Perhaps the boldest innovation of the Heath Government was the creation of the Central Policy Review Staff (CPRS), known as the Think Tank in popular parlance. The CPRS grew out of the recognition that both ministers and civil servants approach questions with pre-established views or interests, and that normal processes of policy review are inadequate to establish priorities. The CPRS, bearing in mind the broader philosophy of the Government as reflected in, for example, the manifesto on which it had fought the election, was to examine broad areas of policy, including those in which no major changes were planned; or major issues such as population changes, which in spite of their long-term importance did not command the attention of the Government. Areas for study would be selected by either the Prime Minister and Cabinet or the Director of the CPRS.

Neither super-ministries nor the CPRS have had the impact which was hoped. Super-ministries have proved unwieldy and too large for effective control by a top Cabinet member. The attempt to confine recurring differences in policy within them tended to impede the consideration by Cabinet of inevitable choices. If the minister responsible for a section of a super-ministry's work was in Cabinet, then relations between that minister and the Secretary of State for the super-ministry were difficult. If the lower-ranking minister was not in the Cabinet, an important source of advice was neglected.

The CPRS was handicapped because the analysis of the nature of British executive politics on which its proponents had rested their case proved all too accurate. Though Treasury control of expenditure was not an adequate form of policy control, the Treasury had no wish to share its power with the CPRS. The other departments and ministries had no more wish to see their programmes challenged effectively by the CPRS than by any other institution. In battles with the CPRS they had one immense advantage: when CPRS reports were discussed in Cabinet the CPRS might be represented by its Director, but the departments concerned with its report would be represented by a Cabinet Minister. The CPRS had no one with political rank to act as advocate for its views. It has therefore been vulnerable to counter-attacks by the established departments which can use links with other civil servants through the Whitehall machine, and contacts with the press and pressure groups, as well as spokesmen in the Cabinet, to defend their views. When the CPRS produced a critical analysis of Britain's overseas representation which argued that the British diplomatic corps and other aspects of overseas representation were insufficiently geared to commercial work, the Foreign Office organised a massive campaign of denigration of the report. Though the example is more dramatic and public than most aspects of CPRS work, it illustrates how vulnerable the office can be. Not surprisingly, it has learnt to pull its punches and not challenge the interests of government departments so directly. Thus a CPRS enquiry into agricultural subsidies narrowed its focus considerably for fear of offending the Ministry of Agriculture, Fisheries and Food. In brief, the CPRS has not had a dramatic impact on the policy process.

One of the fears expressed by its critics was that it would increase the powers of the Prime Minister. However, as we have already seen, one of the standard arguments against the theory that Britain has prime ministerial not Cabinet government is that the Prime Minister lacks sufficient staff support to make detailed decisions on government policy. The distinctive character of Lloyd George's prime ministership between 1916 and 1922 was precisely that he developed through the 'garden suburb' (his private executive section located in the garden of 10 Downing Street) the capacity to make and implement policy without reference to the relevant ministers or even departments. Some feared that the CPRS would form the nucleus of a Prime Minister's Department increasing the Prime Minister's ability to take control of particular areas. In fact, Mrs Thatcher abolished the unit in 1983, deeming it unnecessary. Yet staff support for the Prime Minister has grown. In addition to a personal press officer appointed from outside the Civil Service, Prime Ministers now have a retinue of personal advisers, not regular civil servants, inside Number 10. While in charge of his personal office, Mrs Marcia Williams enjoyed greater access to the Prime Minister than most Cabinet ministers. Both Wilson and Callaghan used a policy unit headed by Bernard Donoghue, an historian from the London School of Economics, again recruited from outside the Civil Service.

In addition, Prime Ministers have come to employ top civil servants as advisers or chiefs of staff. Thus for most of his first Government, Sir Harold Wilson used Sir Burke Trend, the Secretary to the Cabinet, in much the same way that an American President might use the head of his White House staff. Trend was the close confidant and companion of Wilson, playing a major role whenever the Prime Minister stepped outside the conventional way of doing business. Thus when Wilson aimed at personally negotiating an end to Rhodesia's unilateral declaration of independence, it was Trend who advised and accompanied him on a mission which was unknown to important Cabinet ministers until the last minute. Crossman records how Trend's influence was reduced only after the Prime Minister, acting on Trend's advice, had been much embarrassed by his handling of 'D' notices, through which the government regulates press coverage of issues with a security aspect. The late Lord Armstrong during his period as Head of the Civil Service became an extremely influential figure in the Heath Government. Armstrong was one of Heath's closest advisers during the Government's unsuccessful attempts to impose pay policy on Britain's coalminers and was so closely associated with the Prime Minister that after the Conservatives lost the 1974 general election, Armstrong left the Civil Service to become Managing Director of Midland Bank. The example of Armstrong shows how the concept of the civil servant as an impartial, bipartisan executor of government policy can become a myth. Armstrong was a fully committed member of the Heath Government's team and, like the politicians, was in effect forced to leave office by defeat at the polls. Mrs Thatcher has also made use of a number of personal advisers including, until 1982 Sir John Hoskyns as Head of the CPRS. Although the CPRS was abolished in 1983, the Prime Minister now has a 'policy unit' and has been just as eager to make use of personal advisers, especially on economic matters, as her predecessors.

The impact of government processes on policy

The co-ordinating institutions of British government have grown in importance. New units of government have been formed. Formal controls over public expenditure have been strengthened. Established posts, such as the Secretaryship to the Cabinet, have been used in new ways. The capacity for centralised, collective policy-making and evaluation has increased. Yet few would suggest that recent British governments have greater consistency or sense of purpose than their predecessors; the reverse is probably true. Since the Heath and Wilson/Callaghan governments, the question usually asked by commentators is not whether but when there will be a 'U' turn in important government policies. Even under Mrs Thatcher a gradual return to old policies was discernible. The explanation for policy reversals lies of course partly outside Whitehall. The intractability of Britain's problems, the vulnerability of the economy to external pressure particularly on the pound, sharp differences within the major parties on central issues, and increased voter volatility all combine to blow policy off course.

But some of the reasons why British politicians change course so frequently are to be found in the processes of government itself. Opposition politicians happily embrace proposals with little thought of important underlying assumptions or the crucial details of their schemes. Monetarism is adopted on the Right without consideration of what the money supply actually is or how it might be controlled. Import controls are the magic solution of the Left, even though little thought is given to their impact on Britain's trade links. There are many policy issues about which politicians in opposition have not thought at all, such as what the correct exchange rate for the pound was in 1964. Even when politicians know what they would like to do, they have little idea how to do it. The short British election campaign gives little opportunity for them to be pressed hard on their proposals. The politician in power not only finds himself in an unfamiliar institutional environment, but discovers that this environment is highly charged politically. There are enduring pressures to adopt certain policies from civil servants, departments and interest groups with privileged access. On certain issues such as funding for education, constant battles will be fought between the department concerned and the Treasury. The name of the party in power may change but the process and the result will be much the same.

It is true that parties arrive in office determined to make a sharp break with the policies of the past. For example, both the Labour and Conservative parties have repudiated incomes policies in opposition and criticised their opponents for implementing one. In power, however, the two major parties have come to accept – slowly and belatedly – the value of incomes policies. Whether this is seen as corruption of party doctrine in office, or the education of politicians in reality, is immaterial; the impact of the political processes of Whitehall may be readily admitted. Politicians who have no clear and practicable policies are easy prey for civil servants who have. But such tacit re-emphasis of policy continuities comes too late, and only after a damaging period of confusion and change. It is no wonder that many top civil servants now see their role as one of damage limitation and devote their energy to minimising the disruption caused by politicians.

On the other hand, the obsessive concern of the Civil Service with secrecy and its concomitant restriction of informed debate to limited Government circles, itself contributes to the naiveté of Opposition policy. Politicians out of office have no more access to detailed technical information than anyone else. Privileged interest groups are given information on a confidential basis, and would forfeit access if they shared it with opposing politicians. The press is debarred so far as possible from reporting debates within the executive or from divulging the contents of unpublished reports under the Official Secrets Act, through which offending journalists can be, and often are, prosecuted in the courts. There are besides a variety of unofficial sanctions which can be brought against proprietors, editors and journalists to discourage investigation of Whitehall. Internal executive processes are also closed to academic research.

Given their lack of supporting information, there is little that Opposition politicians can do but formulate broad policies in the abstract (though they also share the general British predilection for this approach, noted in the last chapter). In government, politicians are hardly better placed. Relying almost totally on the Civil Service for technical advice, which is initially selective, their consideration of options is blinkered. Like the Opposition they cannot benefit from informed discussion of alternative policies by experts and interested parties outside the Civil Service, as they are simply not given enough detail to evolve costed and planned programmes. Like the political Opposition, outsiders are restricted by the information monopoly to general and probably unrealistic proposals.

Of course the Government in office and the Civil Service do release a large amount of information – from trade statistics to scientific and cultural publications – in the shape of official Blue Books, White Papers and reports of Royal Commissions. (The latter are bodies of experts, usually from outside Government but selected by the Civil Service, and charged to investigate a certain area. They complement and sometimes overlap the Parliamentary Select Committees which we shall discuss in the next chapter.) Nevertheless this is still information which the administration has decided to disclose. Usually it appears too late to affect the policy decisions to which it might be relevant.

Commission Reports and also government Green Papers lay out arguments for and against selected lines of policy and invite general discussion of them. Again, however, these cover the minority of areas on which a deliberate decision has been made to encourage debate. It is the more sensitive and policy-relevant areas which need detailed debate most but fail to get it.

By the early 1980s a wide range of bodies, including committees of the Labour, Social Democratic and Liberal parties, were working on proposals for reform of the Civil Service, spurred by economic failure to the conclusion that structural change was needed to render it more efficient. The ideas being floated included greater use of political advisers and recruitment of top Civil Servants on short-term contracts from industry and finance, thus breaking down its constitution as a separate class with a lifetime vocation in government. All schemes, however, agreed on the need for free information, thus undermining many of the administrative practices discussed above.

For two reasons this seems likely to have limited effects in the immediate future. First, general legislative and government regulations are hard to impose on an established bureaucracy. There are many ways of ensuring that information is restricted even if the definition of official secrets is narrowed. This is particularly true as media reporters would take time to accustom themselves to the new situation. Secondly, parties in power are reluctant to suffer the potential embarrassment which freer circulation of details might entail. For the 1980s we can safely assume that administrative secrecy will continue.

An effect of this on Parliament, the subject of our next chapter, should be noted; it results in Commons debates being very general and unrelated to policy as it is being made. This is particularly true of foreign affairs and economics, where most government actions do not require preliminary legislation, even though decisions in these areas are possibly the most important for the general population. We consider in Chapter 3 what becomes of Parliament's representative role in such circumstances and how far recent attempts to improve its scrutiny of the executive have succeeded.

Chapter 3
The place of Parliament

Although we generally equate 'Parliament' with the elected House of Commons, it also comprises the nominated and hereditary House of Lords. Because this is removed from the centre of affairs it is, paradoxically, better able to achieve the collective and detailed assessment of government policy which reformers would like to see in the Commons.

The effective membership of the House of Lords is increasingly weighted in favour of notables nominated by governments to a 'life peerage', and judges and bishops who have achieved their position by merit. While hereditary peers still attend (some, of course, being distinguished in their own right), they do not dominate proceedings.

This House has only delaying powers over legislation – which can, however, effectively kill it when a government is approaching the end of its term or would find difficulty reintroducing a Bill in the Commons. Being largely composed of old, well-established personages, its sympathies incline towards the Conservatives, and it grew increasingly out of sympathy with Labour during the 1970s. Delays and obstructive tactics are more likely to be directed at Labour than Conservative legislation, although on technical Bills close to its members' interests the House is liable to take an independent stand against any government: an example was the controversial Countryside Bill promoted by the Thatcher administration in 1981, which was amended on many points before it passed.

Nevertheless the major influence of the House of Lords is through persuasion and correction of details rather than direct defiance of the Government. It is still worthwhile to get the support of its members because of their personal influence and weight, and the publicity this attracts for views promulgated in the House.

In the last analysis, however, the role of the Lords is peripheral and it is in the House of Commons that governments are formed and major debates take place.

The House of Commons meets for about 200–250 days of the year, on a reasonably continuous basis from late October to July or August. General debates, questions to and statements from ministers, and certain stages of legislation are debated in full meetings of the House from mid-afternoon to around midnight. Much work is done in specialised committees which meet in the mornings and often in tandem with meetings of the House.

Such committees are of two general kinds. Standing committees consider the technical details of legislation. Each government Bill put before Parliament receives a perfunctory first reading and then a second reading on its general principles. This involves the whole House of Commons. By definition since a Government can last only so long as it gets majority support in the Commons, government Bills are almost always approved. After the second reading the Bill goes to a standing committee for a clause-by-clause review of its details. Occasionally the whole House of Commons may constitute itself a committee for this purpose. Generally, however, standing committees consist of forty to ninety members. A few of these are specialised (for example, the Scottish and Welsh Standing Committees, to which Scottish and Welsh legislation is referred) and have a relatively permanent membership. Generally, however, the question of which standing committee a Bill goes to is arbitrary, and membership shifts. Each is selected so that the government party or parties have a majority. After the technical parts are approved the Bill goes back to the full House of Commons for its third reading, and subsequent approval by the House of Lords if it has not already passed there. Bills introduced by MPs without government backing, and Private Bills sponsored by an outside body (normally some local government) also go through these general stages. Without government backing, however, it is unlikely that Bills will survive all these stages to become law.

Since the Government in office so strongly dominates legislative proceedings, it is arguable whether the main function of Parliament is to pass legislation at all. Certainly an equally important task is to scrutinise all activities of government whether these require legislation or not, and to publicise criticisms and grievances. For this a major instrument is the other main type of committee, the select committees. These are bodies with a permanent membership, often chaired by an opposition MP, which are expected to produce non-partisan reports on detailed aspects of government policy. They may concentrate on the financial side of government business (as with the Public Accounts and the Estimates and Expenditures committees), or the work of a particular ministry (Agriculture, Social Services) or on a particular region (Scottish or Welsh Affairs). The committees examine documents and witnesses and issue reports on aspects of policy, which can attract widespread newspaper and television comment.

The work of committees is supplemented by the time allotted to questions which individual MPs can put to ministers, including the Prime Minister. Ministers are bound to reply, although their answers may be evasive. Verbal questions put in the House are supplemented by written questions and answers which are reported in *Hansard* (the transcript of parliamentary proceedings published each week). On certain days backbench MPs can also raise questions for a short debate at the end of the day's proceedings.

The opposition parties also debate broad aspects of government policy on the days allotted to them on the parliamentary timetable. These publicise selected aspects of government policy, although at the very broad level already noted. Given the secretiveness of both government and Civil Service and the influence of party rivalries, it is difficult for set debates to be really informed.

The House of Lords follows the same general procedures as the Commons. As we noted, it has only the power to delay legislation for a year, after which the Commons can ratify a Bill on its own. However, since the Commons will also automatically support Bills backed by the majority party leadership, it is doubtful whether the Lords' general debates are more of a formality than those of the Commons. What lends more excitement to the latter's proceedings is the presence there on major occasions of almost all members of the existing government and their rivals in opposition. The tensions which build up in this atmosphere are absent from Lords' debates, which as a result are duller but more considered and sometimes more informative. The main strength of the Lords is their ability to focus attention on areas neglected by the Commons and to improve the detail of Bills. An example of their technical work is the Select Committee on the European Community, which has functioned more successfully than its Commons equivalent (see Ch. 6).

Government and Parliament

The presence of both the actual Government and of the alternative Government (the Official Opposition) in the House of Commons has both advantages and disadvantages. It means that the chief policy-makers directly face elected representatives for most of the year, which makes for close and intimate communication. On the other hand, it means that proceedings are dominated by ritual quarrels between Government and Opposition to an extent which makes it difficult for the House of Commons to organise itself as a distinct entity, or to express an independent point of view.

All one hundred or so ministers in a British government have to be Members of Parliament or peers. In practice most are MPs. This means that most of the people who would replace them were they to be defeated in an election are also MPs. The Government continues so long as it is supported by a majority of MPs, usually all members of the majority party. Its survival, therefore, depends on the cohesion of the parliamentary party. The support of the majority party for the Government is central to the functioning of parliamentary democracy as it exists at the present time in Britain. It is secured by various devices, such as the existence of a special office and officials (Whips) to maintain agreement and discipline, weekly party meetings to discuss policy, distribution of party and government patronage, etc. We consider these along with evidence of some weakening in cohesion below.

Party unity implies that even if a minority of MPs disagree with the majority in their party, they will still normally vote with them against the other party or parties. The presence of most ministers in the Commons means that out of the 350-odd members in a majority party, a proportion approaching a third actually form the Government. Only an equal number of backbench MPs need to be won over to gain a majority in the parliamentary party and thus in the House of Commons.

While in theory a mere 200 MPs could dominate business in the House of Commons, in practice any party which was split down the middle so sharply would be in serious trouble. Much more reliance is placed in persuasion and widespread agreement. Here again, the presence of so many ministers actually in the House of Commons is of great importance. It does, however, act against the House developing views independent of the Government in office. Although the leaders of the other major party (recognised as the Official Opposition) are much more in the position of ordinary MPs, their constant desire to criticise their rivals along party lines with a view to winning the next election also inhibits the House from developing a 'Commons' view of most matters.

Within the government there is of course a whole hierarchy of ministers, from parliamentary private secretaries who act as factotums for the more important ministers, through deputy ministers of various kinds and non-Cabinet ministers heading their own departments, to Cabinet ministers who normally take responsibility for an important department or ministry and also participate in discussions of overall government policy. Usually this takes place in the weekly Cabinet meeting (chaired by the Prime Minister) and in its committees, which may include non-Cabinet ministers as well (their functioning has been described in Ch. 2).

Whatever their status or role in the Government, all its members are formally bound by the doctrine of collective responsibility. That is, they are supposed to support agreed government policy in speech and action, whatever private doubts they may feel, or no matter how fiercely they opposed it in private. If they disagree publicly they are expected to resign or may be dismissed. The support this practice gives the Government in the Commons and in its parliamentary party is considerable.

Again, however, practices may be changing to some extent. We have already noted important breaches of the doctrine in recent years. Unattributed leaks to the press allow ministers to challenge Government policy without exposing themselves. The Wilson and Callaghan Governments had to tolerate public dissent from important ministers in the referenda campaigns on the European Community (1975) and on Scottish and Welsh devolution (1978–79). During 1980–81 the clearly identified Conservative 'wets' in the Cabinet consistently opposed monetarist policies in private and deplored their implications in public.

Internal party disputes of this kind are generally fought in Committees and spill over into the press, rather than provoking debates in Parliament. The last thing major parties want is to have internal clashes aired in general debate. Collective responsibility and party cohesion still operate to maintain the semblance, at least, of the united effective government so important to British political traditions.

Parliamentary scrutiny of government

In one sense it is paradoxical to talk about Parliament supervising government as though the latter were quite a distinct entity. The Government in office after all occupies its position only by virtue of majority support in the House of Commons, and all its members are normally MPs or peers.

As we have seen, however, departmental processes are too complicated to be controlled by one minister (or even a team of ministers in the more important departments). The Government as a whole hardly exists as a decision-making entity. Only the twenty or so most senior ministers meet in Cabinet, and neither Cabinet nor Prime Minister has the administrative staff necessary for close supervision of what is done in their names.

Thus while members of the majority party or parties in the Commons may generally approve of their Government's intentions, and hence vote on their side on crucial divisions, much that the executive does is unintended. Moreover, ministers, exposed to new information and Departmental views, may rapidly develop different ideas from those originally shared with their parliamentary supporters. In this sense Governments do form a distinct body over and against other MPs; this distinction is even more evident when we consider that the Government assumes responsibility for all that the Civil Service does.

Parliamentary scrutiny of government actions, in the sense of critically reviewing what ministers and civil servants do or intend to do, is important for two reasons. First the wider discussion, sometimes by experts, may improve the quality of the policies being pursued. And secondly, Parliament is in constitutional theory at least the main national institution representing the views of the population. In part the latter are expressed in support for parties in elections, which we shall discuss in the next chapter. The leader of the party with the largest number of elected members in the House of Commons is assumed to have had his policies approved and will therefore be asked by the monarch to form a Government.

However, many problems unforeseen at the time of the election campaign emerge in the three to five years separating most elections. These will particularly affect certain individuals or groups. If sufficiently large and powerful, they will negotiate directly with civil servants and ministers. But they will probably also try, particularly if the Government is not responsive, to get support in Parliament. For individuals or smaller groups ignored by the Civil Service, Parliament must often be a first recourse.

This is particularly true of groups organised to promote a particular object (such as changes in the law regulating abortion of unborn babies, or divorce) rather than acting as representatives of a particular sector of society. These 'causes' are often too controversial for civil servants to wish to decide a policy. Since they are peripheral to the main issues dividing parties, governments too have usually no wish to act, at least until they have tested the degree of popular and parliamentary support which a change might attract. Promotional groups therefore concentrate on finding sympathetic individual MPs who will seek opportunities to publicise the proposed change or bring it forward as a Private Bill. The permissive legislation extending opportunities for divorce and abortion at the end of the 1960s was carried in this way. Promotional groups thus form an exception to the general tendency for interest groups to concentrate their prime lobbying on the Civil Service. To the extent that trade unions are excluded (particularly under non-Labour governments) from normal executive consultations, Parliament also becomes a focus for their lobbying attempts. The enquiries and hearings of the new select committees (discussed below) have also given a better opportunity for aggrieved groups to make known their views about current policy.

Group representations often involve cases of individual hardship. We shall discuss the very active response of most MPs to constituents' needs at the end of Chapter 4, along with the role played by local governments and courts, and even the European Community institutions, all of which offer alternative means of redress to individuals affected by government actions. Parliament's representative role requires not only action in individual instances, however, but a collective response to aspects of general policy which may cause individual hardship. In other words, a concern with effective representation also implies attentiveness to the success and quality of government programmes, so the function of representation and the need for informed discussion of policy converge.

It is the contribution of Parliament to the general discussion of policy which we examine below. How effectively is Parliament organised for this task?

Strong government versus open government

We should start by noting two major obstacles to informed debate on policy alternatives. The first is the way in which parliamentary processes and procedures are designed to facilitate the party battle. The domination of business first by the Government, and secondarily by the official leadership of the next largest party, constitutes perhaps the major obstacle to independent collective initiatives by the House of Commons as such.

This institutional monopoly is, however, buttressed by constitutional doctrine and the entrenched attitudes of many MPs. They consider that the government's ultimate responsibility to serve popular interests is guaranteed by exposure to a general election at the end of its term. In the interim, decision-making will only be disrupted by undue parliamentary interference. The task of the parties in Parliament is, therefore, to support their Government, or if out of office to keep up morale by attacking the office-holders. As Parliament is simply an arena for partisan encounters it can have no collective and independent role *vis-à-vis* the Government.

This belief is in turn linked to a broader, traditional emphasis, also embedded in constitutional theory, that government knows best what to do in the public interest, and should be left (at least between elections) to get on with it unhindered. This colours opinion on a wide range of practical questions besides the nature of parliamentary debate. It covers government secrecy (desirable, because it prevents too much outside intrusion into business); reform of the relationship between party votes and seats in the House of Commons (undesirable, because the present system, though grossly unfair to third parties; generally allows one major party to take clear responsibility for forming the Government); accountability of the leadership to members inside parties (undesirable because it renders leaders, who may become ministers, less able to act decisively on their own initiative).

We shall take up the last two points in Chapter 4. It is clear, however, that support of strong, unfettered government militates against effective outside scrutiny, inside Parliament or anywhere else. The justification is that 'the public interest' (a term often used to justify government action) can only be served this way. Governments must not be put under pressure to meet immediate demands, for to do so might result in an inability to plan for the future. There is obvious justification for this argument in the area of economic policy, when trade unions press for immediate wage increases which would render British products dearer than competing goods, thus producing factory closures and massive unemployment in a year or two's time. As a result governments have increasingly resorted to control of incomes (or attempts at control) as we saw in Chapter 1.

One theory (termed the theory of 'government overload') in fact attributes many of Britain's problems to weak governments capitulating to popular demands. As a result the government has taken on too many responsibilities which it is not able to discharge properly and which get in the way of its primary functions. As against this, there is no evidence that popular demands are excessive (Ch. 4). Nor is it obvious that we do have a detached and impartial Civil Service unerringly determining what the nation will need in four or five years. Errors and biases too often creep in.

The case would be different if policy debates were simply about agreed goals. In a very broad sense there is of course agreement on the need to promote greater prosperity. Disagreements arise on intermediate objectives: will nuclear development safeguard energy supplies or is it better to rely on self-renewing sources (sun, wind, tide) or on more efficient use of traditional fuels? There is no guaranteed answer to these often technical problems, and it is at least as likely that wider and more informed discussion would help government find better answers, as hamper it unduly. The growing belief that this is the case has spurred many MPs to develop new procedures for discussing government policy – and in the first place finding out what it is.

The obstacles to establishing even the simple facts can hardly be exaggerated, given the administrative secrecy already discussed. The selective management of information by government is best illustrated in the parliamentary context by the 'lobby system' of specialist journalists attached to Parliament. Incidentally it is significant that British political reporters, almost without exception, are concentrated within Parliament rather than in the executive offices, where they have of course no official place assigned to them. This means that news about government comes secondhand rather than directly from within the system itself.

The parliamentary lobby itself is a name given to specially privileged parliamentary correspondents of the main newspapers who spend most of their time in the 'lobbies' of Parliament. They are given confidential information and have ready access to ministers (rarely to civil servants). It is understood that in return they will reveal only what they are expressly authorised to publish, and use the rest solely as background material in preparing their reports. Failure to observe the understanding leads to exclusion from their privileges. A further consequence is that the information which gets published is that divulged at the initiative of the administration and therefore consisting of what it wants to reveal rather than what it wants to keep hidden. Two developments have undermined this way of managing news. One is the increasing practice of ministers and administrators briefing selected journalists, usually in order to have the story published as part of an attempt to resist or push policy proposals within the administration. This is an especially common tactic when resisting budget cuts, even on the part of such figures as the Joint Chiefs of Staff, the supreme military commanders (see Ch. 8). The briefing shades into the 'leak' of unauthorised news in the case of nominally subordinate administrators opposed to policies backed by their superiors.

Briefings still represent selective management of information in someone's own interest. The other process undermining the lobby system is the development of a more independent stance on the part of political journalists towards so-called 'investigative journalism' where stories are pursued at the initiative of the newspaper and followed through without buying information for silence. In line with this trend, journalists and newspapers have also been prepared to risk prosecution under the Official Secrets Act, the D notices circulated by governments to editors to prevent discussion of topics relating to national security, or the severe British libel laws, while refusing to reveal the sources of their information.

In spite of these breaches, however, the ethos of the lobby system still predominates in British government. Information is for insiders rather than outsiders and government (or at least its constituent ministers and administrators) determines who shall be insiders. As peers and MPs depend heavily on published material for their own information, to supplement erratic personal contacts and the selective confidences of party leaders, government management of news deprives them of a major source of information just as much as it does the general public.

It is unlikely that live radio or television coverage of parliamentary proceedings will change this situation much, as what is broadcast tends to be set debates, covered by newspapers anyway. Only if Parliament itself develops procedures for uncovering and evaluating important information will broadcasts be more illuminating.

Scrutiny through select committees

One way to make information more widely available is to utilise parliamentary privileges to force investigation of important policy areas and publish the findings. Attempts to do this in the last twenty years have concentrated on extending the remit, and strengthening the organisation, of an old parliamentary institution – the select committees. As mentioned earlier, these are bodies with a relatively permanent all-party membership often chaired by an opposition

MP and traditionally nonpartisan, which are designed to investigate detailed policy areas and to produce agreed reports. In these, if anywhere, a parliamentary view can be expressed, and technical detail accumulated.

Moreover the experience of other legislative bodies operating in Britain seems to indicate that they are workable. In district and regional councils there is not the strict division between Government and Opposition which is made in Parliament. Instead all elected councillors are appointed to executive committees covering the main areas of policy and corresponding to ministries in the central administration. Party groups are represented on each committee according to their numbers, so the minority party in the single-chamber council is also in the minority on all committees, which are chaired by a majority member. Nevertheless the minority leader on each committee has special status. While practices vary according to the bitterness of party conflict within the locality, minority members participate in all confidential business. Since the chief officer of each affected department sits with the committee and its conclusions are usually accepted by the full council, the minority has a good opportunity to influence policy. Often indeed the committee view overrides party lines. Where parties are strongly opposed, the majority party members will meet separately to decide on a line they will push through the committee. Nevertheless the system favours compromise and gives all elected representatives some say in administration. What becomes a great difficulty is co-ordination between committees.

Similarly the single-chamber European Parliament (see Ch. 6) handles much of its business in specialised subject committees, with debates generally being initiated by a statement of the committee's view through a *rapporteur*. It cannot be said that the European Parliament's views have carried much weight with the chief executive body of the Community, the Council of Ministers, nor with the European Commission of technocrats. But that is less the fault of its structure than of Parliament's late arrival on the scene and the effective national veto exercised by member countries over Community policy. Certainly the Committees are successful in getting an agreed view and providing informative reports.

We can therefore set the development of the Commons select committees against the practices of corresponding bodies. In the period after 1966 the select committee system was modified as part of the general reform of business procedures carried out by the then Leader of the House, Richard Crossman. The House during this period created six specialist committees. Three of these were concerned with the work of a single department. The Committee on Agriculture 'to consider the activities in England and Wales of the Ministry of Agriculture, Fisheries and Food' was created in 1966 and ceased to exist in February 1970. The Overseas Aid Committee 'to consider the activities of the Ministry of Overseas Development' was created in 1968, disbanded in 1971, reformed as the Overseas Development Committee in 1973, and finally ceased to exist as a result of reforms in 1979. The Committee on Education and Science 'to consider the activities of the Department of Education and Science and the Scottish Education Department' was created in 1968 and disbanded in 1970. The other three committees were concerned with policy areas:

the Committee on Science and Technology 'to consider Science and Technology' was created in 1966 and disbanded in 1979. The Committee on Race Relations and Immigration had more complicated terms of reference 'to review policies, but not individual cases, in relation to (a) the operation of the Race Relations Act 1968 with particular reference to the work of the Race Relations Board and the Community Relations Commission and (b) the admission into the United Kingdom of Commonwealth citizens and foreign nationals for settlement'. It was created in 1968 and ceased to exist in 1979. The Scottish Affairs Committee 'to consider Scottish Affairs' existed between 1969 and 1972.

The next major attempt to reform select committees occurred in 1971 with the creation of a new Expenditure Committee which replaced the older Estimates Committee and took over some of the functions of previous specialist committees. This reform followed from the report of the Procedure Committee of 1968/9 which was sitting at a time when dissent within the Labour Party caused the Government to withdraw a major Bill on industrial relations and thus lose prestige. Partly it was developed as an agency for modernising procedures in the field of public expenditure planning and management. It was also seen as a way of upgrading specialist committees in face of the Labour Government's hostility to them in the late 1960s. The Government responded cautiously to the proposals and appeared far from keen about the suggestion that an Expenditure Committee be created. In contrast the new Conservative Government of 1970 produced a Green Paper on select committees of the House of Commons based upon the Procedure Committee's report. The new Committee was established and started work early in 1971.

The terms of reference of the Expenditure Committee required it 'to consider how, if at all, the policies implied in the figures of expenditure and in the estimates may be carried out more economically and to examine the form of the paper [i.e. the new *Departmental Expenditure White Papers*], and of the estimates presented to this House'. Though its mandate was determinedly technical there was obvious potential for expanding its scope. The work of the Committee was in fact carried out through six subcommittees: General (which was concerned with the work of the Treasury); Defence and External Affairs; Employment and Social Services; Trade and Industry; Environment, Education, Arts; and Home Affairs. Each sub-committee developed its own style and method of working and they were almost totally autonomous.

The third major reform of select committees in thirteen years occurred in 1979. On 25 June 1979 the House of Commons voted by 248 votes to 12 for a drastic revision of the system. Once again the reform resulted from the report of a parliamentary Committee on Procedure which was set up in 1974 for the life of the Parliament and reported in August 1978. This report was radical by most standards. It asserted that: 'the balance of advantage between Parliament and Government in the day-to-day working of the Constitution is now weighted in favour of the Government to a degree which arouses widespread anxiety . . . the Committee believes that a new balance should be struck.' The main proposal of the Procedure Committee was that the existing Expenditure Committee with its sub-committees, and the four specialist committees – the

Nationalised Industries Committee, the Race Relations Committee, the Overseas Development Committee and the Science and Technology Committee – be wound up and replaced by twelve select committees divided on departmental lines. In addition the committee recommended that: Committees should be empowered to order the attendance of ministers and the production by them of papers and records from whatever source; time should be set aside in the business of Parliament for debate of the committees' reports; committees should have more resources at their disposal; and perhaps most controversially, a new legislative committee be established to hold evidence-sessions to precede discussions in standing committee. The debate on 19 and 20 February 1979 on the Committee's Report was notable for its unanimity. All speakers, with the exception of Michael Foot, Leader of the House, and one other Labour MP, supported the main thrust of the Committee's Report. The Government, however, revealed little interest in the proposal and it was left to the new Conservative Government and Norman St John Stevas as Leader of the House to introduce the proposals based on the Procedure Committee's report; these were approved by Parliament in June 1979.

All the existing select committees were ended except for those dealing with Privilege, Election, House of Commons Services, Sound Broadcasting, Public Accounts, Statutory Instruments, European Legislation, and the Parliamentary Commissioner for Administration. The twelve new committees broadly paralleled the major spending departments: Agriculture; Defence; Education, Science, and Arts; Employment; Energy; Environment; Foreign Affairs; Home Affairs; Industry and Trade; Social Services; Transport; Treasury and Civil Services. In addition a Welsh Affairs Committee and a Scottish Affairs Committee were to be established.

In spite of the Procedure Committee's recommendations, these committees were not given powers to compel evidence from ministers, the chairmen were not to be paid, and they were not provided with any allotment of parliamentary time for the discussion of their reports. In addition, no changes were made to the existing legislative process.

The extent of the changes which have occurred in just over a decade indicates that there is pressure in Parliament for closer scrutiny of the executive, but also offers strong prima facie evidence that previous changes have proved ineffective. This indeed is borne out by a review of the committees' record, which indicates that this attempt to redress the balance with the executive has so far been unsuccessful. The committees did much work and prepared many reports. Departments, however, reacted slowly to most of them. As an extreme example, the sub-committee on education prepared a report on post-graduate education which was published in December 1973 and to which the Department published a reply in August 1976, thirty-two months later. More generally delays of between six and nine months before the department concerned replied were the norm, but delays of over a year were common. In addition very few of the committees' reports were debated in Parliament. In fact over a five-year period there were only nine debates on expenditure sub-committee reports and seven of those occurred on days made available by the Opposition from their own parliamentary time (Robinson 1978: 133–54). If the success of the committees is measured by government reactions, it does not seem great.

The limitations on committee powers derive from their position as secondary institutions which cannot command attention in their own right. Major debates are unlikely to be prompted by a report, still less a major piece of legislation, because the management of parliamentary time is in the hands of the Government. Its parliamentary representatives will not devote time to reports which are at best irrelevant to its immediate aims, and possibly critical and embarrassing. This is eloquently illustrated by the fate of the Commons Committee on European secondary legislation, discussed in Chapter 6. For this reason Opposition parties sometimes take committee reports up in the limited time made available for their initiatives, but erratically and in a negative rather than a constructive spirit. Besides being hampered by party dominance in publicising their reports or forcing policy changes on their basis, committees also experience internal difficulties as a result of partisan loyalties. They are not free to choose topics for investigation, as the choice must afford prospects for agreement among the two or three parties represented on the committee. This often results in technical and administrative investigations being initiated which are important, but less likely to have a major effect on policy than many other areas open to investigation. It may also result in the final report omitting information and proposals that came up in discussion, as these might prove awkward for one side or another.

Of course the reformed committees introduced in 1979 may prove more successful than their predecessors. As the preceding discussion makes clear, the problem lies not in organisation but in the inhibitions imposed by party loyalties and the dominance of parliamentary proceedings by the Government. Changes in committee structure will not affect this. What may radically transform the situation is a weakening in party loyalty or shifts in the balance of parties within the House of Commons which produce a Government based on minority support or a coalition, and thus less able to assert an unquestioned domination of proceedings.

With the possibility of substantial third party representation in the House of Commons based on the electoral Alliance of Liberals and Social Democrats, some transformation in the party balance is already under way. Both Conservatives and Labour also experienced major internal splits during the last decade; in the case of Labour these proved so disruptive that they gave rise to the Social Democratic withdrawal in 1981. These developments have the potential to free the select committees, and indeed general debates in Parliament, from some of the constraints they have experienced in the past, and to permit development of a 'Commons view', independent to some extent of party orthodoxies (a situation which already exists in the Lords).

The party changes have not yet had time to influence parliamentary proceedings very much, nor will they necessarily extend committee autonomy. That will depend greatly on the committees' ability to assert themselves within this new situation. They did not, after all, emerge as markedly more effective during the period 1977–79 when the Labour Government lacked an absolute majority over all other parties in the House and relied on a formal pact with the Liberals and informal support from Nationalists and Ulster Unionists. Nevertheless, individual MPs felt freer to assert themselves during this period even against their own party leadership, as we shall see.

Fluctuations in party discipline and loyalty certainly carry major consequences for the contribution Parliament can render policy-making as well as for the overall organisation of its proceedings. In the next section we consider the factors making for party cohesion and dissension, with particular attention to developments since 1970.

Party cohesion in Parliament

The British parliamentary parties, particularly in the House of Commons, display a striking degree of internal cohesion – one without parallel in most countries of the world. Party discipline stems in part from the government's close association with the Commons. Instead of legislature and executive being separated constitutionally to the extent that a legislator become minister has to resign his parliamentary seat, in Britain the situation is reversed to the extent that a minister almost invariably has to have a parliamentary base. Government dependence on a Commons majority means that a critical and independent legislative stand is a costly luxury for MPs in the majority party, who may thereby jeopardise 'their' government in a way which cannot occur where there is legislative–executive separation.

Nevertheless this association also existed in the mid-nineteenth century, when MPs were notably more independent of and critical of government than they are today.

Intensified party discipline and stronger internal agreement have been associated with two developments over the last hundred years. The first was the increase in sheer numbers of electors associated with successive extensions of the franchise. This put pressure on MPs to keep a united front as they increasingly owed their election to party support in the constituency and depended on it for re-election. A second factor was the growth in government business, associated with policy-orientated parties and the administrative complexities of a developed society. This in turn made it necessary for government to increase its control over Commons procedures in order to get its legislation through, and decreased the independence of the ordinary member.

These developments continue to exert their influence today through a number of related channels. For the sake of convenience we can divide these into constitutional, party, constituency and ideological. The situation in all of them is changing, and we shall examine both the influences which continue to make for cohesion and those which encourage dissent.

Constitutional influences

Perhaps the most important factor here (which we will be considering in the next chapter) is the single constituency simple plurality system, which makes it difficult for third parties and independent MPs to get elected. Its workings produce majority governments and encourage legislators and electors to think of Parliament in terms of two adversaries, alternating power between them. This makes MPs reluctant to defy the whip or to dissent because of the difficulty of being elected as an independent and because the defeat of one's own party may lead to its replacement by the opposing party.

However, this is an influence which is likely to change radically during the 1980s. Because of the growth of the Alliance of Liberals and Social Democrats (also described in Ch. 4), the simple plurality system is under criticism. A situation can readily be envisaged where Conservatives, Labour and Alliance all get around one-third of the votes but one or two get disproportionate shares of the seats. In a representative democracy such as Britain, such a grossly unfair possibility is hard to justify, even in the name of strong government. Besides, the Alliance have a vested interest in relating vote-shares to seats, and are highly likely to change to some kind of proportional representation system if they take a hand in government.

As such a system is likely to produce more parties, individual MPs will have a better chance to threaten resignation from their existing party. Even under the existing electoral system, twenty-five Labour MPs and one Conservative defied their existing parties to join the Social Democrats in 1981 and aroused considerable popular support. So a strong precedent has emerged for greater dissent, not necessarily attended by electoral penalties.

A second constitutional factor often cited under the traditional two-party system is the size of the government majority, the presumption being that a government with a very small majority of seats in the House of Commons will be overthrown if many supporters vote against it. Recognition of this influences Members to vote consistently with their party. Since many postwar governments have operated on small majorities, this factor would go a long way to explaining internal cohesion. In fact, however, the evidence is mixed. With large majorities before 1970 (Labour 1945–50 and 1966–70 and Conservative 1959–64), members were more likely to vote against their Government than in the case of small majorities in other years. But in the 1970–74 Parliament, when the Conservatives had a small to medium majority, one or more Conservative back-benchers voted against the whip in 18.5 per cent of the divisions. More spectacularly, in the 1974–79 Parliaments when the Labour Party was often in a minority, one or more Labour back-benchers rebelled in 28 per cent of all divisions – more than a quarter.

A third constitutional factor tending to cohesion could be provided by the Prime Minister's (and to a lesser extent the Leader of the Opposition's) power to appoint members of the Government (or party spokesmen in opposition), and to a lesser extent to grant honours. Although this may not be employed as a direct inducement, it could contribute to cohesion by increasing goodwill among ordinary Members. Certainly Edward Heath's technocratic approach as Prime Minister, and his lack of personal warmth, combined with a failure to distribute appointments and awards more widely, produced much dissent between 1971 and 1974.

The last constitutional factor to have an effect on party unity is the Prime Minister's power of dissolution. If defeated on a crucial Commons vote, the

Prime Minister has the power to dissolve Parliament and call a general election, through a formal request to the Queen. The uncertainty of the result inhibits the Prime Minister from threatening dissidents very often, but it can successfully promote cohesion on a particular issue. Heath was able to secure a majority of 309 to 301 on the second reading of the European Community Bill in February 1972, by making the vote an issue of confidence, and thus indicating his willingness to go to the country if defeated. It is likely that the Government would have been defeated on this issue given the other voting on the Bill if this dramatic tactic had not been employed.

Party influences

The second set of influences promoting internal cohesion are the activities of the party officials known as Whips, selected from MPs not in the Government (or alternative Government, in the case of the Opposition Party). The picturesque name comes from the analogy with the whipper-in of foxhounds, hardly a flattering analogy for backbench MPs! One of the Whips' powers is withdrawal of the whip from a dissident, with resulting loss of access to parliamentary order papers and backbench party committees. The ultimate sanction is expulsion from the parliamentary party, with an almost inevitable loss of party endorsement at the next election and, until recently, near-certain electoral defeat. On the side of positive inducements, while the Whips do not control access to office they do in effect allocate members to standing committees on government Bills, recommend members for standing committees on Private Members' Bills, and choose members for parliamentary and party delegations abroad. Once again, such incentives can be used to improve the atmosphere on the backbenches and thus encourage cohesion. If fact, as opposed to theory, Whips have three separate if related functions. They act as a channel of communication between the front and back benches; they organise and manage the business of the House; and they attempt to encourage cohesion. There seems little doubt that it is the first two functions which are more important. Various Whips have publicly admitted their limited disciplinary powers and dissenters have boasted that they ignore them at will. Whips can and do encourage cohesion but cannot enforce it; similarly the Whips' patronage is limited and is employed to promote general good feeling rather than to influence Members directly.

Constituency influences

Where MPs were elected by small majorities they may feel particularly dependent on party support and fear constituency reprisals if they thwart the Government. Their party workers may not unreasonably feel that they campaigned for overall government policy, not the Member's personal views. In addition, if the MP belongs to a government party, his action may contribute to parliamentary defeat and thus bring the day of electoral reckoning closer.

This is a plausible argument but again encounters mixed evidence. In the 1959–64 Parliament it was found that the Conservative backbenchers 'most likely to join [the major rebellions] were those who had lower career aspirations, weaker socialisation into Conservative identities and group orientations, and lower vulnerability to renomination challenges' (Schwartz and Lambert, 1972, 1981). However, from 1970 to 1974 these influences worked weakly if at all (Norton, 1978, 220). Indeed, a number of Conservative MPs who during the 1970–74 Parliament voted against European Community membership resisted strong constituency pressure in doing so, and successfully fought off attempts to deny them renomination. The European Community (EC) is often referred to in the UK as the European Economic Community or EEC). What is more, constituency pressure does not always push MPs in the direction of support for their front-bench. In the Labour Party there is certainly evidence that the pressure can work in the other direction, with constituency parties encouraging dissent. In 1981–82 great publicity was given to the number of staunch supporters of the previous Labour Government who were denied renomination in favour of a left-winger. Although the actual numbers involved are small this helped to promote the Social Democratic secession.

Ideological influences

The last and probably the most important factors encouraging cohesion can be labelled as 'ideological'. MPs after all join a party because they agree, broadly, with its views. Entirely of their own volition and without external constraints they may be expected to support it most of the time. Even in cases of slight disagreement they will give it the benefit of the doubt.

Ideology (adherence to a particular doctrine or a programme) is often associated with the Labour Party. In considering the Conservative Party, 'prior socialisation' is usually given as a reason for cohesion. The idea here is that the shared social and educational background of Conservative members predisposes them to unity. In fact this explanation is really ideological as it implies that this common background leads to a shared set of political values, which then predisposes most members to support the frontbench position. Not just support of party views but also dislike for those of the other side may play a powerful part. Although there may be ideological splits particularly in the Labour Party, it can be argued that parties remain cohesive because no matter how much they dislike the other wing of their own party, they dislike the Opposition more. This is an explanation often given of the reluctance of the Left Wing to split away from the Labour Party, and is frequently linked to the argument that the British electoral system would prevent a party formed from the left of the Labour Party having any access to power.

While the argument may still work for the Labour Left, it obviously no longer applies to the Right, where the internal campaign for Social Democracy led to a secession of some of its leading members and the formation of a Social Democratic Party with good political prospects. Yet in a negative sense ideology still seems to have exerted some effect on the Labour rebels, as they did not join the Conservatives but preferred to create a separate party which retained some aspects of Labour ideology. Again in seeking alliances they chose the Liberals rather than the Conservatives.

Certainly ideology did not prevent the Labour split. This may be seen as the end result of a long history of factionalism in the Labour Party, which produced long-standing bodies, such as the Tribune Group, with their own organisation and even newspaper.

Factionalism of this kind has been much more evident in the Labour Party than among the Conservatives – one reason possibly why they have not experienced a secession similar to Labour's. There is, however, at least one area in which Labour, including its former members in the Social Democratic Party, is noticeably more cohesive than the Conservatives. That is the type of permissive legislation mentioned above. On major unwhipped issues (i.e. those where party leaderships do not take an official stand) such as abortion, capital punishment, divorce and homosexuality, there is still a very strong relationship between party and vote. Labour MPs tend to support the extension of abortion and divorce, and freedom for homosexuals, and to oppose the death penalty. Conservative MPs tend to take the opposite line. Labour is almost totally united on its point of view (with the exception of abortion on some occasions), but the Conservative party is split, with roughly one-third agreeing with Labour and two-thirds opposing. One must not make too much of such evidence but it does indicate that there are some shared values among Labour MPs which must aid rather than hinder cohesion.

A last element of ideology which has united members inside both major parties in the past, is belief in the necessity and desirability of strong, effective government. The general prevalence of this view has already been noted but it is particularly influential among Conservatives, because they see themselves as the 'natural party of government'. This implies that a Conservative government has a particular claim on the party in performing the task incumbent on it: to govern.

Dissent within parliamentary parties

Nevertheless governments cannot rely for ever on unquestioning support if things go too badly wrong. The British belief in strong government relies on it being successful, at least in the long run. The lacklustre economic record of the last twenty years has, therefore, weakened this influence on party solidarity. Along with a decline of deference towards government has gone a decay of the other forces making for party cohesion: for example, constituency parties will be less inclined to blame rebels when they themselves feel critical of the leadership. And if his own leaders are not achieving what an MP wants, the prospect of voting to weaken the Government and allowing another party to gain power is less alarming than it used to be. Moreover, the successful rebellion of the Social Democrats sets a precedent for secession, makes the party leadership more sensitive and more responsive to individual views, and renders the party alternatives less stark than when governments were a straight choice between Labour and Conservative.

The secession of the Social Democrats was the culmination of increasing factional tensions among Labour MPs in the 1970s. This extended even to the traditional consensual and hierarchic Conservatives, though internal tensions there are unlikely to show themselves in quite so dramatic a form. Conservative factionalism is obviously on the increase, however. Under the aloof prime ministership of Edward Heath (1970–74) an identifiable body of Conservative MPs emerged with a hard line on monetary policy and social issues. When they took over the leadership with the victory and premiership of Mrs Thatcher, semi-public dissent from the prevailing monetarist orthodoxy became common, and increased in extent after 1980.

The point at which dissent in both the major parties reached significant proportions was the 1970s – hardly surprising in view of the major economic difficulties which successive government policies simply seemed to worsen. Under Heath there were sixty-nine divisions in which more than ten MPs dissented during the period 1970–74. At the same time, there were more persistent dissenters, with forty-one MPs (12 per cent) casting six or more dissenting votes and seventeen MPs dissenting on twenty or more occasions. In fact one Conservative MP (perhaps not surprisingly it was Enoch Powell) dissented 115 times.

Dissent has always been more widespread in the Labour Party, but it became almost epidemic in the 1974–79 Parliament. No less than 45 per cent of all whipped divisions in the 1978/9 session saw some Labour MPs voting against the Government. What is more, only sixty-two Labour MPs (19 per cent of the total) cast no dissenting votes, while forty cast more than fifty and nine more than a hundred dissenting votes (Norton, 1980 provides the definitive treatment of these episodes and the background to them on which this discussion is based).

There can be no doubt, therefore, that dissent within both major parliamentary parties showed a major increase up to the secession of the Social Democrats, and that the 1970s were the crucial turning point in the process (which still continues). Can any reasons for dissent be identified beyond the pervasive threat of economic failure?

Certainly Heath's aloof style did nothing to avert tensions, but it is unlikely in the absence of other factors that it would have produced enduring effects – no more so at any rate than the sweeping Cabinet purges of Macmillan's last administration (1962–3).

A plausible explanation is found in the changing nature of MPs and the critical attitude of younger entrants towards the Government. From 1967 younger MPs have revealed stronger feelings of dissatisfaction about both their own role and the domination of the executive. In all the thirty-five Labour backbench rebellions, both in the full House of Commons and in standing committee, which defeated the Government over the three sessions from 1974–1976, both the background and date of entry of MPs into Parliament were related to rebellion. On the Labour side the newer middle-class MPs, less imbued with traditional notions of party solidarity and discipline, were more likely to dissent and subsequently influenced many older Members to follow their example. The crux of the matter is that new MPs, probably on both the Labour and Conservative sides, have a different perception of their role to that of their predecessors. There is a swing back to interest in the constituency and an increasing tendency to see their role less as a parliamentary party voting machine and more as a representative of local party and constituency interests.

As we have noted, this change of mood is related to the conspicuous failure of governments to solve the economic and other problems of the last decade. It is difficult to believe in the infallibility of government when governments constantly prove fallible. While dissent has also had an ideological base in the internal disputes within parties, these themselves ultimately rest on opposing prescriptions for solving national problems. As the problems pile up owing to successive governmental failures, internal disputes between adherents of a controlled or mixed economy, of social concern versus economic freedom, become increasingly widespread and bitter. What is held in common by the various protagonists is an increasingly critical attitude to the government of the day.

Dissent has not been confined to minor issues. In the 1968/9 sessions Labour backbenchers contributed to two major and humiliating Government defeats, on their industrial relations policy and on House of Lords reform. During the Conservative Government dissent almost cost Heath a second reading of the European Communities Bill and he was forced to accept amendments to the 1972 Industry Act as a result of Conservative back-benchers' cross-voting. Once again it is the Labour Government of 1974–79 that provides most examples of backbench dissent on major issues. Cross-voting led to defeats on the floor of the House on the 1975 Industry Bill, the 1975 Housing Finance (Special Provisions) Bill, the 1976 Dock Work Regulation Bill, the 1977 Scotland and Wales Bill, the 1977 Criminal Law Bill, the 1977/8 Scotland Bill and the 1978 Wales Bill (Norton, 1980).

It is true that governments in office can still expect to win the vast majority of votes if they have a clear majority, and can still rely on backbench support on votes of confidence. But MPs are no longer lobby fodder. Dissent, moreover, is a politicising experience; once MPs rebel they are more likely to do so again and their example will encourage others. In reaction ideological opponents then assert a similar right to oppose on questions on which they feel strongly. This means that governments with small majorities will have to be careful to consult their backbenchers or more ready to accept defeat on a variety of votes. In addition, while dissent has most dramatically manifested itself in the Labour Party, it is not confined to it. All this will make the future role of party leaders and Whips more difficult than in the past, even discounting the possibility of minority or coalition governments under a three-party or two-and-a-half party system.

The House of Commons in the 1980s

With the emergence of the Social Democrats and continuing ideological divisions among Conservatives and the remaining Labour MPs, there is no likelihood that dissent and cross-party alliances will abate. As MPs express their own views rather than those of their party's leaders, this reinforces their own propensity to take a more critical and independent stance, and encourages others to do so. Secondly, governments have increasingly come to accept dissent. At one time a defeat on the floor – certainly a defeat on a major Bill – would have been a resigning matter. Now a government is unlikely to resign except on an issue of confidence, and it will choose such issues carefully. For MPs this must in many cases legitimate dissent. Thirdly, there is evidence of an increase rather than a decrease in ideological differences within the parties. In particular it is now possible for the first time to identify such differences in the Conservative Party. As we have seen, ideological divergence is associated with rebellion.

The increase in dissent is likely to mean more defeats for the Government on the floor of the House and even more in standing committees, particularly when governments have a small majority, or are in a minority. Experience with the minority Labour Governments of the mid-1970s indicates, however, that the Government will still win the majority of votes. Nevertheless the increased opportunities open to individuals to sway the balance means that party leaders and Whips will be forced to pay more attention to backbenchers (the ordinary MPs).

Does this mean that Parliament's role in policy-making will become greater, or only slightly less marginal? Two factors will be crucial here. One is the attitude of the new Alliance of Liberals and Social Democrats to the role of Parliament. It is not so far strongly identified with demands for greater autonomy or more searching scrutiny. None of the former Labour Cabinet Ministers who constitute the SDP leadership took Parliament markedly into their confidence when they held office before, so there is no reason to think they will in the future. The Liberals, during their post-war exclusion from office, have been associated with demands for more open government, but these cannot be described as major commitments.

Simply having three sizeable parties in Parliament could mean a greater making and unmaking of governments in the House of Commons. This might lead to greater interest in its proceedings, but whether it produces more informed debate and a greater influence on detailed policy-making depends very much on whether the scrutinising select committees are capable of shaking off their partisan constraints and formulating a 'Commons view' which overrides party loyalties. This is by no means certain, but they have a greater opportunity to do so now than ever before.

Chapter 4
Parties and electors

Our discussion has amply demonstrated the importance of political parties to the functioning of government and Parliament, and indeed to the making of policy as a whole. The contrasting economic policies adopted by parties in opposition may be disruptive when applied in office, and pushed by circumstances towards an underlying norm of incomes restraint and industrial intervention. But party changes do make a difference in terms of economic policy and even more on distributive questions: on what services and their clients will bear the burden of public expenditure cuts, and how far cuts ought to be made as opposed to raising taxation.

Parties also have a crucial role in formulating political demands on behalf of the public, voicing them in Parliament and other representative bodies, and attempting to translate them into government policy. The responsiveness of government institutions to popular wishes, and thus the whole functioning of representative democracy in Britain, depends crucially on the parties.

This has been recognised in constitutional doctrine with a move away from individually based ideas about representation, to the mandate theory. Originally representation was conceived as a relationship between individual MPs and their constituents: either the MP voted on policy according to his best judgement, and his conduct was assessed by constituents at the election through their support or rejection (the representative theory), or the MP consulted with constituents on each important vote, and acted according to their wishes (the delegate theory). These contrasting viewpoints are still very relevant to the question of internal party representation, as we shall see. But nationally, ideas about representation have had to be revised to fit the functioning of cohesive, strongly disciplined parliamentary parties with whom MPs – at any rate in the recent past – have almost always voted.

The theory of party representation is associated with the idea of the mandate. That is, that parties should at elections present a definite set of proposals which, if elected, they have a 'mandate' from electors to carry out. How well the theory fits actual practice we shall consider below, but it is obvious from what has been said that governments increasingly face emergencies not envisaged at the time of the election where they have to act in the absence of any specific indication of popular feelings.

There are of course many ways in which individuals can try to affect government policy through interest groups and contacts with bureaucrats and ministers. In subsequent chapters we shall explore others: through local authorities, European Community institutions, and the courts and legal processes. Many of these relationships are themselves influenced or mediated by the political parties. And certainly the single most important way in which most individuals can affect the overall direction of policy is by voting for a particular party at a general election. Parties are crucial, therefore, as an institutional link between the preferences and needs of individuals and the government policies which are meant to cater for them. They are the only organisation which directly associates sets of leaders with sets of political activists and electors under a common name and with shared political loyalties. The inclusion of such disparate elements often imposes severe strains on the party organisation. To understand these we shall need to consider the structure of existing parties and of their relationships with each other. We begin, therefore, with a discussion of the parties themselves, before moving on to their basis in social divisions and the relationship between electors' policy preferences and party support.

The changing party system

Until 1974 the parties themselves, and the type of party competition which existed in Britain, were regarded as stable and fixed. This is reflected in the voting percentages reported in Table 4.1. Two large parties, Labour and Conservative, had alternated in office over the post-war period, providing strong single-party governments based on sizeable majorities in the House of Commons. Apart from important but rare occasions (the invasion of the Suez area of Egypt in 1956, the abortive industrial relations legislation of the Wilson Government in 1969), these majorities remained firm in their support throughout each government's term of office. The Liberals had picked up in 1959 and

Table 4.1 British general election results, 1945–83

| Year | Total percentages of votes received by: | | | | % Turnout |
	Conservative	Liberal*	Labour	Other	
1945	39.8	9.0	47.8	2.8	72.7
1950	43.5	9.1	46.1	1.3	84.0
1951	48.0	2.5	48.8	0.7	82.5
1955	49.7	2.7	46.4	1.2	76.7
1959	49.4	5.9	43.8	0.9	78.8
1964	43.4	11.2	44.1	1.3	77.1
1966	41.9	8.5	47.9	1.7	75.9
1970	46.4	7.5	43.1	3.0	72.0
1974 (Feb.)	37.8	19.4	37.1	5.7	78.7
1974 (Oct.)	35.8	18.3	39.2	6.7	72.8
1979	43.9	13.8	36.9	5.4	76.0
1983	42.4	25.4	27.6	4.6	72.7

*Liberal/SDP alliance, 1983

during the 1960s oscillated around 10 per cent, but never appeared very serious challengers of the Conservative–Labour hegemony. Despite one or two by-election and local successes, the Welsh and Scottish Nationalists had remained fringe parties. The Ulster Unionists, who had split from the Conservatives over their Northern Irish policy, could only hope to win some ten seats in that province out of the 635 in the House of Commons as a whole.

By 1974 the failure of both major parties to resolve the country's economic difficulties caught up with them. The Conservatives had presided over massive inflation and boxed themselves into a direct confrontation with the unions, while the memory of stagnation under Labour from 1966 to 1970 was too recent to render them a credible alternative. Economic decline had hit the peripheries harder than the still prosperous Midlands and South East of England. In Scotland the combination of a relatively worsening industrial situation with the prospects opened up by the discovery of oil in territorial waters, seemed to confirm Nationalist assertions about the benefits of greater political autonomy. The same (without the oil) could be said to a lesser degree for Wales. As a result, the Scottish National Party (SNP) took 22 per cent of the Scottish vote in February 1974, and won seven Commons seats: Plaid Cymru, the Welsh (Nationalist) Party, took 11 per cent of the Welsh vote and two seats.

Reactions against the major parties were not confined to the peripheries. In England the Liberals advanced their vote share to an unprecedented 19.4 per cent, though owing to the biased electoral system they obtained only twelve Commons seats. Conservatives and Labour received almost equal vote shares below 38 per cent. Labour, having received a slightly greater number of seats, formed a Government without an absolute Commons majority till October 1974, when it called another election which more or less confirmed the results of the first; the Liberals received slightly less percentage votes but the Nationalists more, and the SNP beat the Conservatives into third place in Scotland with 30.4 per cent of the Scottish vote. For most of the succeeding period, Labour was able to govern only with support from minority parties for which they made concessions (e.g. by introducing Devolution Bills for Scotland and Wales).

In the general election of 1979 the Conservatives restored their vote to almost 44 per cent but Labour returned a post-war low of just under 37 per cent. The Nationalists slipped to their core support of around 18 per cent of the Scottish vote for the SNP and 10 per cent approximately for Plaid Cymru (the Welsh Nationalist Party). The Liberals, retained almost 14 per cent of the voters.

The consistently bad returns for Labour indicated that it was failing to appeal to electors. Disputes about whether this stemmed from the fiscal and economic orthodoxy of the 1976–79 Callaghan Government, or from the activities and extreme policies of the left, racked the party from 1979 onwards .The strengthening of Conference control over the parliamentary leadership, which we describe below, together with the adoption of Left-wing policies on withdrawal from the European Community, abolition of American bases in Britain, import controls and regulation of investment, provoked a secession of many leaders and MPs in 1981 to form the Social Democratic Party (SDP). In alliance with the Liberals, this won important by-election and local successes against a still divided Labour Party and a Conservative Government discredited by the failure of cuts in public expenditure to regenerate the economy. The 1983 election confirmed electoral trends: while the Conservatives lost slightly (but won the election handsomely in terms of seats) the Labour vote slumped to near equality with the Alliance: 27.6 per cent compared to 25.6 per cent. The bias of the electoral system, however, ensured that Labour had 209 Commons seats to the Alliance's 23.

Party factions and ideologies

The ability of party infighting to give birth to a new party demonstrates the importance of internal relationships within the parties. To understand why factions have emerged increasingly during the 1970s we need to review the contrasting traditions incorporated within both Conservatives and Labour. Then we need to look at the structure and organisational changes which have been used by competing factions to increase their strength, and which in the case of Labour produced the secession of the SDP.

The origins of party factions run back to the creation of the modern parties. The present Conservative Party emerged from a long series of amalgamations with groups splitting from its main nineteenth-century rival, the Liberal Party. These took place from the 1880s right up to the 1930s. Their consequence was to combine the paternalistic outlook of the old, landed ruling class, with its stress on an ordered hierarchical society where the poor were helped if they kept to their place, with the free market philosophy of the nineteenth-century business classes. This supported opportunities for the aggressive individualist which often involved the removal of societal restraints and severe economic penalties for failure. The emergence of monetarist economic ideas which involved severe checks on government expenditure and controls has revitalised this line of thinking. In turn, this has led to strong reassertions of the 'one nation' strain in traditional Conservative philosophy. Thus the two traditions of Conservative thought and their supporting factions often combine uneasily. Edward Heath and Margaret Thatcher, the most recent leaders of the Conservative Party, both represented the individualistic free enterprise side of Conservative ideology, in contrast to the previous leaders Hume and Macmillan – scions of the hierarchical and paternalistic tradition. But since both sides wish to preserve the established structures of British society, they never diverge too far: the factional disputes of traditionalist 'wets' and monetarist 'drys' in the first Thatcher Cabinet were about tactics rather than fundamental goals.

Shorn of its business elements, the Liberal Party's preoccupation with individual freedom has led it in the post-war period to oppose censorship and espouse such policies as abortion, while supporting welfare legislation on the ground that it enlarges freedom of action for the masses. It has been less cohesive in support of all these causes than Labour, however, as its few MPs come mainly from peripheral rural constituencies with a traditional social outlook. The Liberals have always been firm on regional devolution, on extending ownership of industry to the workforce, with workers' councils sharing control with management (which they see as a distinct third course between state control and capitalism), and most consistent of all the parties, before the emergence of the Social Democrats, on European Community membership.

The ideological sources of Labour factionalism derive from the two groups who in 1900, founded a parliamentary committee and later, in 1906, founded the Labour Party. On the one hand, there were avowedly socialist groups who believed in class struggle, capture of the state by the workers and enforcement of their control. On the other hand, there were moderate reformers aiming at amelioration of social and industrial conditions in collaboration with the trade union leadership. This 'social democratic' tendency is identified in policy terms with comprehensive as opposed to selective state education and with the foundation and extension of the welfare state – the provision of free government health care and support for unemployment and old age. While this has involved heavier taxation of wealthy groups to pay for services to the poor, it has not led to the eradication of wealth or income differentials. Government takeover of industry has been supported on pragmatic grounds, either as providing needed investment for a particular sector or averting widespread unemployment. This is the ideology, along with support for the EC, which the Social Democratic Party have taken over.

In contrast, the socialists have advocated greater social equalisation through penal taxation of higher incomes, and confiscation of wealth; abolition of private schools; and complete government direction of the economy (including 'social ownership' of the greater part of industry). The difference between the two sides is deeper than exists between the Conservative factions and has given rise to much more bitter and prolonged struggles, culminating in the foundation of the separate SDP.

The Labour Party itself is only part of the wider Labour movement, embracing consumer co-operatives on the one hand and trade unions on the other. Since the latter control the block vote of their membership at the Annual Conference (amounting to some 6¼ million compared to some 276,700 for constituency delegates), they can effectively decide which ideological tradition will win Conference support. Until the late 1960s when their suspicion of government regulation drove a wedge between trade unions and the Labour moderates, trade unions regularly backed reformist MPs, helping to confine the choice of leader to the parliamentary party and to keep in his hands or those of his associates the writing of the manifesto, the authoritative statement of Party policy in an election. Since 1970 their support has been much less consistent. Socialists within the Labour Party have been disproportionately active in constituency associations. They have therefore sought to increase the control and influence of constituency committees and representatives. The organisational changes of recent years have been more connected with battles for control and influence within the party than with technical efficiency.

Party structure and organisation

Superficially, all British parties are organised the same way. The primary purpose of local parties is to fight elections, so their areas correspond to political boundaries. The lowest political and geographical unit is the ward – the local government constituency. Ward parties are grouped in a (parliamentary) constituency party. Both ward and constituency parties hold general meetings throughout the year, with social activities designed to raise funds and recruit members, and a flurry of campaigning activities at election times. Each has an executive committee, with chairman and secretary, who meet throughout the year to plan and organise activities. Unpaid officers of the constituency party may be supplemented by an agent, paid from central funds, who can provide more of an impetus than unpaid part-timers.

The selection of local and parliamentary candidates is usually in the hands of the management committee of ward or constituency parties. Candidates have also to be accepted as eligible by the central party. Affiliated organisations may send their representative to a selection committee meeting (this gives affiliated trade unions through their local branches an important role even in local Labour parties).

Where several constituencies fall under one urban government, they may join together to form a city party. All constituency parties are grouped into regional organisations which do not have much importance except in Scotland and Wales. (Northern Ireland has its own Unionist, Nationalist and Labour Parties which are organised broadly on the lines described here but have no organisational link with all-British parties.)

At the British level, constituencies are represented at the Annual Conference and through its executive or organising committee. Generally constituency associations send one or more delegates to the Annual Conference in proportion to their numbers. Along with representatives of affiliated organisations (womens' and youth groups, trade unionists, etc.), these propose and debate resolutions on policy matters, which are designed to influence party policy.

Two other party organisations exist at national level. These are the central bureaucracy of the party (the central organiser who directs the local party agents, research departments, office staff) and the parliamentary party, consisting of the MPs and members of the House of Lords belonging to it. The Leader of the Party comes from the Parliamentary Party, invariably from the House of Commons, and will become Prime Minister if his party forms the government.

While the formal structure of all parties (even of the Nationalists in Scotland and Wales) conforms to this general description, their internal relationships differ considerably. This is most clearly seen in the relative position of the central institutions: the Conference, representing the mass party, the Leader and parliamentary party, and the central bureaucracy. In the Conservative Party, both Conference and bureaucracy are firmly subordinated to the Leader. The Leader, for example, appoints the Chairman who manages both the Conference and the Central Office. Resolutions sent by constituency parties to the Conference for debate are selected so that only those favourable to the official line are actually raised. Until very recently the Leader turned up to speak only after Conference had officially terminated its business. Needless to say, Conference has no say in selecting the Leader, who is elected by vote of the parliamentary party, and then accepted by the mass Party organisation. Nor does Conference control the Party bureaucracy, who are accountable solely to the Leader or the Leader's deputies.

The parliamentary leadership dominates the rest of the Conservative Party because, historically, the mass organisation was founded only after the parliamentary party had consolidated itself. It was, therefore, designed to function in a purely subordinate role, focusing mainly upon the generation of support for candidates and policies rather than upon discussion of them. There has always been a strong Conservative parliamentary party, so its dominance over Conference and the mass party organisation has been maintained.

A crucial change occurred inside the parliamentary party in 1965. Up to that point, the Conservative Leader had 'emerged' by a process of consultation, which gave great scope to the previous Leader and party notables to bias the selection, normally in favour of the hierarchical traditional side of Conservatism. From 1965, however, Leaders have been elected by the Conservative parliamentary party, giving the more thrusting free enterprise group the advantage. An open election also gave opponents of the incumbent Leader an opportunity which they never had before to canvass support as a group, and in 1975 Mrs Thatcher defeated Edward Heath as an outside candidate for the hard-line monetarists, following Heath's loss of the two 1974 elections. In this way the new, more democratic, Conservative procedure contributed to a sharp break in Conservative Party policy, away from the more consensual Keynesian intervention of the earlier period. By transforming the monetarists into a dominant minority, but still a minority, within the party, it also contributed to the factional quarrels of the early 1980s.

The Liberal Party shows how a similar structure to the Conservatives evolved when its parliamentary representation declined. Reduced to half a dozen MPs in the 1950s, and a mere dozen even when its fortunes recovered, the parliamentary party could not claim to be more representative than the base organisations. This was particularly the case as Liberal policy put much stress on local autonomy and self-reliance. As a result the Conference has become a lively debating body shaping its own resolutions, the Leader is elected by a wide postal ballot of most active Liberals, and constituency parties are self-regulating – they have to be since they generate most of their own finance. The national party has more need of the constituency parties than they have of the national party, so local enthusiasm and participation are at a premium. The same is even more true of the Welsh and Scottish Nationalist parties.

The Labour Party originated as a mass movement outside Parliament, which gained effective representation there only twenty years after its formation. One would expect, therefore, to find grass-roots participation more widespread than in the Liberal Party. Up to 1980, however, the Labour Party most closely resembled the Conservative Party. The Leader was elected by the parliamentary party and simply accepted by the rest of the Party. Although formally the National Conference was the ruling body of the Party able to instruct the parliamentary party on policy, in practice the latter had asserted its complete autonomy under the pretext of deciding when and how agreed policy was to be put into effect. This meant that Conference proposals could often be effectively shelved. The Party programme (the election manifesto) was written under the direction of the Leader just as it was in the Conservative Party.

The Parliamentary Labour Party and its leadership could effectively dominate the mass organisation in the constituencies because of the structural peculiarity of the Labour Party already noted. The Party is part of a larger body, the Labour movement, also incorporating consumer co-operatives and trade unions. These are represented at the Annual Conference in proportion to their membership, or rather, the proportion of their membership who contribute money to the Labour Party. Contributing members of the trade union are those who pay, with their subscriptions to the Union, a political levy – non-payment of which is entirely the responsibility of the individual who must declare his desire not to pay (contract out). The number of paid-up contributors far outweighs the membership of the constituency parties. So long as the trade union leadership was dominated by fears of Communist and left-wing penetration, and had a fairly unstrained relationship with Labour Governments, they supported the parliamentary leadership. The union 'block vote' at the Conference was thus cast in support of policies the latter favoured and a National Executive Committee (NEC) elected who supported them. This was important because among other things the NEC controlled the central bureaucracy and constituency agents of the Party.

Over the 1960s and 1970s Labour Governments along with Conservative governments tried to exert more control over trade union activities, as part of a general effort to reform industrial relations and render British firms more competitive. This strained relationships with union leaders, who were also less worried about left-wing influence inside the unions as international tension slackened. The unions therefore ceased to exert their block vote automatically in favour of the parliamentary leadership, and hence the NEC and Conference became increasingly assertive and critical of the moderate leaders' policies.

This criticism focused on three demands. The first was for parliamentary and local candidates not only to be initially chosen by constituency selection committees, but to be fairly frequently reviewed and if necessary dismissed by them. The introduction of mandatory reselection in 1981 was obviously a move towards making MPs and councillors delegates who reflect the views of their supporters, rather than representatives exerting their autonomous judgement. The second demand was that the National Executive Committee should control the writing of the party programme and manifesto. The third was that the Leader and Deputy Leader should be elected by a wider electoral college in which active constituency members would have an influence, equal or greater than that of MPs. In the electoral college as it finally emerged, trade unions have 40 per cent of the vote and MPs and constituency parties 30 per cent each.

While to some extent support for, or opposition to, these proposals rested on beliefs in internal party democracy, accountability of elected representatives, and open versus strong government, they became increasingly symbols in a battle for power between socialist sympathisers, who dominated the constituencies, and the Social Democrats entrenched in the parliamentary party. The success of the former in forcing through most of their demands by late 1980 was exacerbated by personality disputes involving their main spokesman and aspirant for the leadership, Tony Benn. Although a member of the 1974–79 Governments, he had consistently criticised their record and was consistently at loggerheads with the Party leaders, James Callaghan and his successor Michael Foot.

To fight the socialist drive for domination of the constituencies, various Social Democratic organisations had been founded within the Labour Party. Despairing of the Labour Party both as a likely election winner and as a vehicle for their policies, several prominent Social Democrats (David Owen, Bill Rodgers and Shirley Williams) left Labour at the end of 1980, joining forces with another former minister, Roy Jenkins, to form in 1981 an independent Social Democratic Party. This appeared an attractive compromise between the public expenditure cuts of the Thatcher administration and the sweeping controls now advocated by Labour. Thus it won, with the Liberals, a string of impressive by-election successes. Concurrently its membership grew to 60,000 during the year, while it attracted double the number of MPs belonging to the Liberals – all but one, defectors from Labour.

The SDP from the outset aimed at building a strong constituency organisation on the general British model. It also encouraged full internal participation of its membership through extensive working parties and circulation of discussion documents. Like the other parties, it established a National Conference to debate resolutions and hear reports. Its arrangements in regard to leadership were its most novel feature. It started off with the 'Gang of Four' who had founded the Party meeting as an executive. Arrangements to supercede this still have a collective character. The Chairman is elected through a postal ballot of all party members, not just constituency representatives; as is the Leader of the parliamentary party. The latter is the more important figure since he has most weight in negotiating coalition arrangements or in determining what section of the party programme to implement. The exact relationships between Chairman and Leader obviously depend on who they are. It is unlikely that the Leader will emerge as quite so dominant as the Labour Leader was in the old days. Given the origins of these arrangements in recent Labour controversies, however, it is possible that similar working relationships will emerge.

All British parties have chairmen but they are normally much less important than the Leader, if not subordinated to him. The only parallel with the SDP is found in the case of the Welsh and Scottish Nationalists, where their limited parliamentary representation has usually made the chairman, selected by the mass party, a more dominant figure than any of the MPs. The Nationalist MPs have usually been forced by the nature of their position into a more gradualist position than that of enthusiastic activists outside Parliament, and this has made for tensions in periods of electoral success.

Election arrangements

Just as internal organisation may favour one faction at the expense of another, so the rules for translating party votes into Commons seats are far from neutral or purely technical. In Britain not only do the biases of the electoral system determine the relative political success of the parties (since it is Commons seats rather than popular votes which decide which is to form the Government), they also affect the composition of party representatives and leaders, so materially affecting the result of internal struggles.

Popular votes are translated into Commons seats through the 'first-past-the-post' or 'single-constituency simple plurality system'. Britain is divided into 635 constituencies, each represented in Parliament by a single MP. The seat goes to the candidate who attracts more votes in the constituency than any rival – a plurality – regardless of whether or not this proportion is over 50 per cent – a majority. Indeed, in a four-candidate contest the proportion voting for the winner could be as little as a third.

The results of such contests throughout the country then determine the overall balance of seats in the House of Commons, and hence the Government. Almost all the candidates elected attract support as the nominee of a party. (Votes given on the individual attractiveness and personal appeal of the candidates in the normal urban or suburban constituency are less than a thousand out of an average party vote of thirty to forty thousand.) Consequently they will all vote in the House of Commons to support the Government chosen by the Party Leader and will continue this support on all issues that do not create acute internal divisions within the party.

Constituency outcomes thus determine the party composition of the government but such results are as much affected by the method of counting and the division of constituencies as by the popular vote for parties. Where the electorate vote strongly in favour of one party or another, the result is reasonably reflected in the distribution of seats. Where there is a relatively even split, the distortions created by the existing system can push the result arbitrarily in favour of one side.

The most spectacular examples of bias on a national level have been where a major party with slightly less of the popular vote than its rival actually gained more Commons seats and formed the Government (the election of February 1974 is the most recent example). This has not had much practical significance since in such cases popular support was clearly moving towards the party which took power and the outcome was accepted even by the ousted party. Such results tend to emerge because Labour, for example, wins a disproportionate number of small, depopulated central city constituencies and of Scottish and Welsh seats, which are more numerous in relation to population than English. The Conservatives win more country seats which in the peripheries have a limited population over a large geographical area. Despite periodic adjustments by Boundary Commissioners, such anomalies are probably inevitable in any constituency-based system which takes other criteria into account than simple equalisation of population within constituencies.

Since these anomalies tend to balance out they are not too serious in terms of the national result. What does introduce systematic bias is winning by pluralities inside a large number of constituencies. This means that parties with a minority of supporters scattered over a lot of constituencies pick up no Commons seats at all. This is true for Labour in the South East of England and for the Conservatives in the North of England, Wales and Scotland. It is not that the other party lacks substantial support in these areas, but simply that the system of apportioning seats does not reflect it. The result is that the parliamentary leadership of both Labour and Conservatives is regionally biased in a way their voters are not. Labour MPs almost exclusively represent the big cities of Wales, Scotland, the North of England and also Inner London. Conservative seats are disproportionately located in the Midlands or South East of England and usually form rural or suburban constituencies. The regional and urban-rural division between the parliamentary leadership of the two parties is very marked, and was even more exaggerated by the 1979 election. Out of a total of 334 parliamentary seats, the Conservatives held only seventy-eight outside the Midlands and South East, of which only twelve were in big cities. A marked difference emerges in Parliament, which is just not apparent in the voting bases. Up to 1979 both Labour and Conservatives polled strongly in all parts of Britain.

Through the mechanics of the system the major parties gain in areas of relative strength what they lose elsewhere. But smaller parties lose out entirely. If they have concentrated support in one region they may gain a block of Commons seats in rough proportion to their strength, as did the Scottish and Welsh Nationalists in 1974. If they attract wide support which is not particularly concentrated they may gain next to no seats although they receive a large percentage of national vote. The prime victim of this bias is the Liberal Party, which with almost 20 per cent of popular votes in 1974 and almost 14 per cent in 1979 received roughly 2 per cent of Commons seats. The Liberal alliance with the Social Democrats also has this bias operating against it as shown by the result of the 1983 election.

There are, of course, many alternative systems of counting votes employed in other countries. These are generally referred to as proportional representation systems, since their aim is to bring the party proportions of legislative seats into line with their overall proportions of the national vote. Most of the proposed systems would require larger constituencies represented by several MPs; this is to allow large minorities to be able to elect at least one MP. Instead of solely determining the choice of MP, the largest proportion of party supporters would then elect say two MPs, and the two minorities perhaps one each. Various technical ways of apportioning constituency votes exist, but all would have roughly similar effects.

Depending on which scheme of proportional representation was adopted and the particular level of their vote, the Liberal–SDP Alliance could place from 50 to 350 MPs in the House of Commons with Labour and Conservatives getting proportionately less. Not unnaturally the Alliance plans to legislate for some kind of proportional representation whenever it gets a share in government. Given the present distribution of political support in Britain, this would make it likely that no party had an absolute majority of seats in the House of Commons, so that any wishing to form a government would require the support or collaboration of some other parties. Instead of the single-party governments we have had up to date (even when they did not have a complete legislative majority, as in 1976–79), we should always have coalition government grouping a number of parties. This would produce great changes in the way governments behave, but the situation would reflect more closely the distribution of preferences among the electorate.

In Britain, though without much justification from the history of other countries, peacetime coalition governments have generally been regarded as weak and indecisive. Proportional representation has been discussed in stark terms of greater representativeness at the cost of weaker government, if the electoral system is changed: or stronger government at the cost of less representativeness, if it is retained. Given the general bias towards strong government discussed in Chapter 3, it is not surprising that the majority of politicians have opposed moves towards proportional representation. Even on the left wing of the Labour Party, it has been felt that if Labour were not in power, it would be better to have a Conservative Government with clearcut policies than an amorphous group in the middle. Proponents of electoral reform argue against adversary politics of this type on the grounds that the simple plurality system and single-party government lead to crushing party discipline, opposition for its own sake and constantly changing policies with changes of government. Greater representativeness should not only be supported for itself but because it improves opportunities for individual representatives to respond flexibly to popular preferences.

Now that a significant political group is pushing for change, some proportional election system is likely to emerge in the foreseeable future. Not only would it alter the shape of the party system and government formation by providing permanent niches for smaller parties, it would also – owing to a more representative selection of MPs – affect the nature of internal party leadership. No longer, if their national support holds up, would Labour MPs be predominantly urban and northern, and Conservative MPs suburban and southern.

For most of the post-war period, however, this contrast has obtained, and has been partly responsible for pushing the parties into opposing lines of policy which can also be seen as regional: the Conservatives favouring a free enterprise economy tailored to the more prosperous regions, whereas Labour endorse subsidies and protection from foreign competition in order to reduce unemployment in the peripheries.

Parties and social cleavages

These divergences also stem from the fact that parties (like the government ministries examined in Chapter 2) tend to defend the interests of associated groups – particularly those they see as voting for them. We have already identified regional divisions between parties. Another obvious division is class, the Conservatives attracting most of the middle-class vote and Labour most of the working-class vote. Region and class are not, of course, independent of each other, nor of other social factors such as race and religion. They all exert complicated and interwoven effects which we consider below.

Region, religion and race

Regional differences used to be considered irrelevant to British politics. The rise of nationalism in Wales and Scotland highlighted differences previously masked by a common language, the facade of unitary government, the economic preponderance of the South East and Midlands of England and the national coverage of the London press and other media. None of these factors works unambiguously to eliminate regional differences. Welsh nationalism has as a major goal the preservation of the Welsh language (now, with about 500,000 speakers, shared by a fifth of the population of Wales). Scottish nationalism also finds symbolic support in indigenous literary and linguistic traditions.

As Chapter 5 demonstrates, unitary government in Britain is largely a myth: under its forms lurk a variety of governmental arrangements with much scope for local resistance to centralising tendencies. Economic disparities between a relatively prosperous core and declining peripheries provoke nationalist feeling as much as they damp it, especially when discoveries such as North Sea oil seem to indicate that the region might be more prosperous on its own (e.g. in Scotland, 1972–76).

The case of the press is even more striking. Britain is unusual for the countrywide circulation of newspapers produced in the capital, as also for their sharp division between 'quality' newspapers with serious analysis and discussion of news, aimed at the wealthier and more educated groups, and 'popular' newspapers with limited news coverage conveyed in screaming headlines and simple, direct presentation of sport, sex and gossip. The papers which carry these techniques to their extremes, with a corresponding reduction of print compared to pictures, may attain a national circulation of up to $5\frac{1}{2}$ million. The best-selling quality newspaper attains just over one million, again on a national basis.

These facts, however, have obscured the equally striking point that some local and regional newspapers have not only survived but have flourished more vigorously in recent years than the London papers. Most of these papers are evening or weekly, but the further one gets from London the more well-established dailies are found in the main cities. These have a different character from the London press: since their basis is regional rather than class, they bridge the gap between quality and popular coverage. For such papers almost anything that happens in their locality is prime news. In Scotland, for example, with a distinctive Press, regional issues are bound to get extensive coverage, so there is inbuilt encouragement for nationalist feeling of some sort.

Television and radio have in the past been centralised, although they have always had a regional structure. Under the impact of political events and the consequent rise in regional consciousness, this has been strengthened. Only 44 per cent of directly produced television programmes on the more popular television channel of the British Broadcasting Corporation (BBC I) now emanate from London, compared to 36 per cent from the regions. Whereas the regional companies' contribution to national independent programmes used to be nominal, more emphasis both in guidelines and in practice is now devoted to directly produced regional programmes. Local radio stations based in each large city are attracting larger audiences. All these developments mean that within a nominally centralised structure, regional voices are increasingly heard. In turn, regular expenditure by the media in each region builds up a core of professionals in journalism and the arts which is available to repertory theatres and other local ventures. Arts Council spending in the regions grew from 50 per cent of its total to 70 per cent in the 1970s, financing a network of local theatres and arts centres which operate fairly independently of London, and undermine its cultural monopoly.

Government recognition of the social distinctiveness of Wales and Scotland, and attempts to stall off nationalism with some political concessions, have resulted in the areas having separate legal and institutional arrangements. The extreme case is Northern Ireland, which not only had a devolved government and parliament for fifty years (1922–72) but also its own savage religious conflict between Catholics and Protestants, a near civil war, and an even more precarious economic base than the rest of Britain.

The English regions are less distinctive, partly because they lack traditions and institutions to focus their grievances against the centre. Urban riots which have occurred disproportionately in the North and West in recent years indicate, however, that grievances are there, though their base is economic and racial rather than nationalist. But even Scottish and Welsh feeling results from a complex interplay of these factors rather than pure cultural nationalism.

One of the historic differences between the North of Britain and the rest of the country is the impact of massive Irish immigration there during the nineteenth and early twentieth century. This was compounded by the settlement after the Second World War, predominantly in the same areas, of a quarter of a million Poles and Ukrainians. The primary legacy of Irish and East European immigration (as well as of lesser foreign influxes such as the Italian) has been to augment the strength of the Catholic Church in the northern areas. One quarter of the population of Glasgow is Catholic and the same balance obtains in Liverpool. Education in religious schools as opposed to the largely non-denominational state system perpetuates social differences, which have been sharpened by the close ties of both religious communities with the opposed factions in Northern Ireland. Labour party support in the West of Scotland and in Lancashire has been centred on a Catholic working-class vote rather than a purely working-class one. This contrasts with the insignificance of religion as a social and political division in southern England.

The increasing settlement of West Indians, Pakistanis and Indians (3.6 per cent of the British population) has also produced disproportionate regional and local effects owing to their concentration in particular areas. Generally a deprived section of the British population, their position is worse when they are settled in poorer inner city areas or in cities and regions whose economic base has declined since they arrived – the West Midlands and the textile towns of the North.

All these developments interpenetrate with pre-existing differences to heighten regional distinctiveness, which in turn is preserved by the low level of geographical mobility among the British. Regional differences do not simply or even mainly contribute to Nationalist Party support of course. Given the Liberals' long-standing support for regional home rule, their new effectiveness in the Alliance with the SDP may well attract former Nationalist supporters. Labour's policies of active help and subsidy for the peripheries also render them natural regional spokesmen except for periods when they are in power in Westminster, or discredited by recent failure as a Government to cope with regional problems.

The fact that Labour has been at one and the same time the representative of the peripheries and the spokesman of the working class testifies to a certain overlap of class and regional loyalties. One major regional difference is precisely the distinctive working-class ambience of the North compared to the middle-class ethos of the South of England. These differences arise in the first place from the different class proportions living in each region: more working-class in the North and middle-class in the South. Each dominant class group tends to shape the outlook and aspirations even of the other class living there to a disproportionate extent, a tendency which is also reflected in voting behaviour. The 'ecological' effect of class (the pervasive social influence of the dominant class in the neighbourhood) rather than straight occupational effects of belonging to a particular class accounts for most of the class effect in English voting (Miller 1978).

Class

At the present time, therefore, class influences are also regional influences and vice versa. The effects of individual membership in a social class, independent of region and area, have been more and more muted by the social developments of the past two decades. Like the political developments reviewed earlier, these are intimately bound up with the functioning of the British economy in the post-war period.

As noted in Chapter 1, Britain has been in the paradoxical position, during these years, of achieving economic growth and greater prosperity in absolute terms (i.e. in comparison with its own past performance) while declining relatively, through experiencing a markedly lower rate of growth than most other countries. Internally, absolute growth, combined with a certain redistribution of income from clerical to skilled manual workers, and the increasing employment of women who contribute a second family wage, has provided the bulk of the population with more money than in the past, has indeed produced an 'affluent' society spending large amounts on both the basics and the comforts of life (see the *Family Expenditure Survey 1979*, H. M. Stationery Office, 1980, for detailed evidence of increasing individual prosperity after a decade of national economic difficulties).

The decline of British exports and manufacturing industry over this period has on the other hand meant that the British population increasingly spent more money than the country as a whole had earned, leading to a recurrent imbalance between what is earned by exports and paid for imports. Increasingly effective foreign competition has destroyed many British enterprises, particularly in sectors such as textiles, steel and shipbuilding, and produced long-term unemployment, particularly in outlying parts of the country (again accentuating regional discrepancies). These trends have been aggravated by the slackening in world trade and economic activity associated with increasing energy costs. Simultaneously, therefore, individuals have experienced greater prosperity, combined with greater insecurity as prices rise and jobs are threatened. What effects has this had on class differences?

The most obvious is the increasing affluence of the population as a whole, including most manual workers. As the latter acquire better housing and consumer durables and patronise the same supermarkets and multiple stores as the middle class, they become less distinctive in terms of overall lifestyle. The elimination of the more glaring class differences is also speeded by attendance at the same type of (comprehensive) school and similar housing in large modern estates on the fringes of cities. However, the working class still live predominantly in rented and council houses while the middle classes generally purchase theirs through a long-term mortgage. Thus the standards of amenity vary. The contrasts are still much less than between the slum and substandard properties near city centres, in which most workers lived sixty years ago, and the substantial villas and semi-detached houses with gardens, where the bulk of the middle class lived at that time. Increasingly many manual workers have also become owner-occupiers.

Writers of the 1960s saw such trends as contributing to the 'embourgeoisement' of the working class – their assimilation to a middle class outlook, leading in politics to a weakening of the Labour Party and strengthening of the Conservatives. With hindsight we can see that tendencies to assimilation have worked both ways. As differences in income decline, members of the middle class have in many respects become more like the manual workers. They too are provided for by supermarkets, comprehensive schools and a National Health Service. With the application of computer technology to clerical and higher level tasks, their traditional job security is undermined and they are threatened with immediate redundancies and structural unemployment. Cuts in public expenditure designed to stimulate private enterprise or to bring imports into line with exports, even threaten the permanency of government employment, a long-standing bastion of middle-class professionals and managers. To some extent this opens up the possibility of a new politico-economic cleavage between those workers supported by public taxes and those who gain no direct benefit from them.

In such circumstances it is perhaps not surprising that the last decade has seen a major increase in the strength of white-collar unions (which in 1974 had a membership of almost 40 per cent of clerical and related workers, with a heavy concentration in government employment). White-collar unionism may undermine the cloth-capped image of earlier periods, but it also subverts the bowler-hatted image as well. For example, the traditional association between trade union membership and Labour voting has been weakened – at least partly as a result of so many more professionals and clericals becoming trade unionists. At the same time a unionised worker has been more prone to vote Labour than a non-unionised worker, whatever his occupational level. Assimilation proceeds from both sides of the earlier divide.

A major indication of the extent to which this is being bridged comes from the decreasing numbers in the population who spontaneously identify with a class, when asked to do so in surveys. This declined from a low 50 per cent in 1964 to an even lower 41 per cent in 1974. Declining class-consciousness is associated with declining electoral support for the major parties whose appeal has been heavily class-based. Surveys reveal that British problems are not primarily associated with class by most of the population.

All this provides opportunities for political parties which have a new, non-class image and seem capable of transcending the old divides. Political history in the decade 1972–82 can indeed be interpreted in these terms and viewed as a watershed between the old class-based politics and a new politics concerned above all with sensible management of the economy and industrial regeneration. Even the Nationalist parties can be viewed in this way within their own regional settings, for their successes were associated with strongly economic themes. More obviously, increased Liberal voting over the 1970s, and the wide immediate response to the Social Democrats and their Alliance with the Liberals, testify to a general feeling that class-based confrontations are not only irrelevant but positively damaging. In this sense the older parties' unpopularity stems not only from their perceived economic failure but from their association with vanishing social divisions. The political revulsion against these, symbolised by the response to the Alliance, itself contributes to lessening their political relevance.

Underlying these developments are massive occupational shifts. Social mobility in Britain has been very great over the past two decades. Many members of each 'occupational' class (in some cases as much as a half) have origins or parents in a different class. While many people have moved down, most have moved up with the expansion of the economy. It is no wonder that people who have improved their social position and experienced many class locations in their lifetime cease to use these as a major political reference point.

Another shift in the occupational structure has occurred with the decline of purely manual occupations; the growth of clerical, professional and managerial categories; and especially the expansion of service occupations – covering an enormous area of work from catering to nursing, retail and wholesale business and transport. Unlike the traditional manual or clerical worker, persons in the service trades tend to be in contact with a wide range of 'customers' of diverse social types. Given the environmental effects noted earlier – the tendency to follow the lead of 'people around us' rather than 'people like us' – this expanding group is likely to be less set in class ways than occupational groups mixing solely with their own members. The tendency of service workers to be less class-conscious than others has been noted over a long period of time. What is important now is their sheer numerical weight compared to any previous period. They are also disproportionately in government or public employment.

Of course these tendencies towards a breakdown of class barriers are less where society and economy have continued on traditional lines. There, ways of life are still distinctive as between the different classes, mobility is lower and the service sector has not expanded to the same extent as elsewhere. Hence class consciousness is higher: in Glasgow over three-quarters of electors spontaneously identify with a class compared to slightly over half in London. Here again we find regional and class differences entwined; Scottish images of the English, for example, assimilate national and class differences, endowing Scots with all the working-class virtues and vices and seeing the English as inherently middle and upper-class.

All this suggests that class consciousness and class feeling are not spread equally throughout the population but inhere particularly in certain 'purer' areas and groups. This is particularly the case as the groups at the extremes of the class structure have experienced less mobility than others. Britain has a lower-working-class which is predominantly descended from generations in the same position; thus traditional attitudes are accentuated in the least mobile, lowest manual group.

A worker in a traditional manual occupation, living in established working-class housing, belonging to an old craft or labouring union, tends to divide up the world in terms of traditional distinctions between 'them', the bosses, and 'us', the working people. Similarly a top manager or professional, living in a middle-class enclave, will blame a unionised workforce for the lamentable state of productivity and industrial discipline, while absolving himself and his fellows from responsibility.

Class conflict

An awkward question remains. If class divisions and class consciousness really are in decline among the majority of the population, how can we explain the poor state of industrial relations evidenced by the frequent strikes which in 1979 were responsible for more working days lost in Britain than in 1926 – the year of the General Strike? How also can we explain the resurgence of socialist feeling in the Labour party which fuelled the disputes examined earlier and resulted in the breakaway of the SDP?

However we diagnose this internal party conflict, we can hardly present it as a class struggle, where a bourgeois right wing confronts working-class socialists on the left. Studies of the social background of party members, local councillors, MPs and Cabinet ministers concur in showing (a) that they predominantly come from a fairly privileged, middle-class background, (b) that those higher on the political ladder come from more solidly middle-class backgrounds than those lower down, and (c), that as time goes on these tendencies intensify. The major exceptions to this general rule are the union-supported and sponsored MPs, who tend to originate in a working-class environment. Members of this group, however, like the unions themselves, are somewhat more likely to appear among the defenders of the *status quo* in the Labour Party than among its critics.

Apart from this exceptional group, all MPs, regardless of party, share a similar, non-working-class background. Conservative MPs are distinguished only in appearing even more exclusive in terms of higher income, private education, political connections, religious affiliation and family wealth. Labour MPs come from the middle and lower middle class and on the whole practise the 'talking professions' of teaching and journalism. Conservatives come from the business classes and traditional professions like medicine and law. (But both Mr Heath and Mrs Thatcher, the last two Leaders of the Party, come from a modest middle-class background like that of most Labour MPs.)

There is, therefore, no clearcut social division between left-wingers and right-wingers within the Labour Party leadership. Their dispute cannot be said in any literal sense to form a confrontation of two opposed classes. The radical side does claim, however, to represent working-class interests, and explains the heightening of party and factional conflicts by a resurgence of class feeling in the 1970s, as demonstrated most dramatically by the major strikes and industrial unrest of that decade.

To understand why these manifestations can occur alongside a general weakening of the class structure, we have to return to the idea of 'pure' working-class and middle-class groups. Society is a complex of many different groups and individuals enmeshed in diverse socio-economic situations. While many of these involve a relaxation of rigid class divisions, working-class groups which continue to perform traditional manual jobs in a relatively isolated social environment will continue to be as class conscious as before. They will react to declining economic circumstances with increasing militancy, as they suspect employers of trying to maintain their profits by reducing the real value of wages.

Although the members of this group constitute a minority (reckoned at around 19 per cent of the electorate in 1970), they are of course just the kind of worker to be found in big, large-scale industrial locations. The very nature of the employment helps to define their outlook. They will tend to be miners, car workers, factory workers of all kinds – exactly the type of industry where a strike has massive effects on the supply of energy or of components, and thus spreads widespread disruption through the rest of industry. It is significant that the major strikes of the last decade involved the miners (1972, 1974, 1984/5), the Ford car workers (1978), the engineering workers (1979) and steel workers (1980). Only the transport strike in the early months of 1979 involved another group, centring on the lorry drivers, who in terms of their 'service' status do not appear as purely working-class as the others.

Such industrial confrontations are exacerbated by the concentration of the other relatively stable class group, the employers and managers, in positions of authority in these enterprises. These are the very people whose political attitudes are diametrically opposed to those of class-conscious workers. The very institutions – employers' federations and manual trade unions – which are responsible for industrial relations are dominated by representatives of these groups and tend as a result to adopt quite inflexible tactics against each other. This confrontation then becomes a recipe for industrial unease and unrest.

In the juxtaposition and conflict of these polarised class groups we find an explanation for the extent of industrial trouble in Britain. This explanation also demonstrates that the class attitudes underlying such strife are confined to a minority of people within the society and are indeed capable of continuing as class barriers break down elsewhere.

It is true that the habit of industrial action spread in the 1970s to sections which had previously avoided it: white-collar workers and professionals in the Civil Service, ancillary workers in the National Health Service, teachers. Here, however, outright withdrawal of labour has been rare, and a variety of forms of non-co-operation practised which have not had the massively disruptive effects of the industrial strikes. If class assimilation involves other groups taking over some of the traditional outlook and behaviour of the working class, increased white-collar militancy paradoxically becomes an indication of the breakdown of class divisions rather than its enhancement.

Generally, one must put the whole question of strikes into perspective. In Britain they are generally of low intensity (involving, for example, minimal violence) but perhaps because of this, of relatively long duration. No side is under intolerable pressures, so both can hold out longer. In assessing the level of class feeling and conflict which strikes reflect, their conduct as well as incidence should be taken into account. The absence of associated violence supports the conclusion to which all our other evidence points, that in contemporary British society as a whole class conflict is muted, and class itself not the only factor shaping individual preferences and attitudes.

Electors' preferences and values

This conclusion still leaves us with the task of explaining why most working-class individuals have generally voted Labour and most of the middle-class Conservative (even if this is now declining and some of it is attributable to area influences). Voting is linked to what individuals feel the parties can do for them. Before looking at voting directly we should explore the nature of the personal preferences which electors take into account and see what influences these.

Individual preferences are often described as though they were naturally public and political, rather than personal and private. Thus assessment normally begins with attitudes towards the regime and leading national institutions, such as Parliament and monarchy, democratic processes, and the rule of law. All these receive widespread endorsement from the British population. It is worthwhile noting, however, that while the British are proud of their political institutions they are also capable of appraising the performance of governments coolly and realistically: 29 per cent of schoolchildren in one sample felt the government can on occasion do more harm than good, and even at the height of wartime success in 1944, 57 per cent of adults felt that politicians were either out for themselves or for their party (Dennis, Lindberg, McCrone 1971).

General reactions of this kind obviously have importance for the climate in which politics is conducted, but they do not relate closely to party support. To relate this to electors' concerns we have to examine demands more closely related to immediate political action.

On this, survey responses detailing choices on current political issues are often taken as the main evidence. Over the years these have shown national samples of electors as generally opposed to greater nationalisation and immigration; desirous of reintroducing the death penalty for murder and of upholding traditional moral standards; supportive of the welfare state and lower taxation; enthusiastically in favour of greater prosperity, and maintaining Britain's general status overseas. Attitudes towards entry to, and membership of, the EC have varied. Where hard choices are put to the public greater divisions occur. For example, as between reducing unemployment at the expense of higher inflation, or vice-versa: generally, most people would like to do both, just as they wish to have lower taxes and extended welfare services. The juxtaposition of these preferences has usually been viewed as evidence of the inconsistency and irrationality of the general population, since expanded social services have to be paid for, and how else but through higher taxes? We should note, however, that there is not a necessary contradiction here, since the enhancement of government revenues through greater prosperity would make it possible to expand services without raising taxes: and of course electors do favour prosperity as well.

Generally one gets the impression that electors think in terms of goals to be achieved rather than specific policies to be adopted. The latter are the concern of governments, and electors evaluate their success in terms of reaching obvious, agreed objectives rather than by how they have sought to attain them. To gain some inkling of what electors think the most important goals of public policy are, we should look at replies to general questions on important problems facing the country and the individual, rather than to questions on specific issues.

Overwhelmingly (to a level of 70 per cent) answers to general queries stress economic concerns – cost of living, prices and employment – as the ones which are central. Housing, rising crime and the problems associated with immigration are also emphasised, but less heavily (an average level of 20 per cent or below). All replies are concrete and immediate, relating to prices for the week's shopping, the adequacy of incomes to meet them, and the comfort and safety of the home environment. They are the factors which most closely affect the day-to-day existence of individuals and families within their local community. General national concerns such as defence, or abstract causes such as aid to the underdeveloped countries of the Third World, scarcely figure at all (rarely attracting endorsements of more than 10 per cent).

We hardly need surveys to tell us that individuals' most important concerns are their own and their family's wellbeing. Nevertheless general, and in particular, political concerns have often been assumed to bulk larger. In fact little difference between the classes does emerge in regard to their basic concerns. And there is certainly no evidence of a great interest in politics, as can be seen by examining the extent of political participation in Britain. Places on public bodies are limited in number so it is not particularly surprising that elective councillors and MPs constitute less than half of one per cent of the adult population. Voluntary participation in party and other political work is also limited. Individual membership in a political party (often nominal to the extent of being in arrears with subscriptions) extends at most to 5 per cent of the population; the proportion engaged in active political work, whether within or outside the established parties, is certainly lower. While three-quarters of registered electors turned out to vote in the general election of 1979, it is an exceptional local election which attracts as much as 40 per cent. The first direct election for the European Parliament in June 1979, an occasion of considerable political significance, attracted only 32 per cent of electors.

If politics do not predominate, what does concern British electors? Evidence on the primacy of personal and family goals comes from surveys on 'the quality of British life' carried out in the mid-1970s. Asked what the quality of life meant to them personally, the largest single number (23 per cent) referred to family and the home, with another 10 per cent mentioning friends and neighbours. Rather surprisingly perhaps, 16 per cent stressed traditional values and priorities, among which bringing up children held pride of place. Half the sample therefore spontaneously mentioned traditional family-centred concerns.

These were not challenged by any of the qualities mentioned by the other half of the sample. Eighteen per cent mentioned money and the cost of living, and 17 per cent their basic standard of living (in the sense of obtaining adequate necessities). While clearly worried about their material circumstances, such electors could be equally concerned for their families as for themselves. Certainly very few wanted to improve their personal standard of living (only 3.5 per cent wanted more consumer durables, luxuries or more extravagant ways of enjoying themselves). Support for these conclusions comes also from a survey of London electors interviewed in the early 1960s, at a high point of post-war prosperity, which tried to establish the complete range of their overall values and aspirations. Out of eight possible concerns into which answers were classified (public-political, social status, moral, family-centred, basic health, monetary, technical and educational), personal goals came overwhelmingly first. Eighty-six per cent put basic health among their leading three concerns, while 80 per cent put family and friends. Public or political interests were mentioned first by only 6 per cent and money was rated as a leading objective by just 19 per cent. Technical expertise was valued highly by a third, and social status by only slightly less, while morality was a leading preoccupation for a quarter. Education similarly concerned one-fifth.

These rankings are perhaps not surprising, but they are of great interest in showing which personal concerns predominate. The wellbeing of family and friends is paramount. While basic health attracted slightly more attention, it was clear from the context of the replies that this was directed more to nature than to the National Health Service. Most people worried about the consequences of a fatal or crippling illness rather than about the quality of the medical care they would get if it occurred. And part of their anxiety was for the effects on family as well as on themselves. This is confirmed by replies on basic aspirations from a national survey carried out in 1980: people's strongest motivation was to provide a better life for their family, while there was almost as strong a desire for the children to do better in life (*The Times*, 26 June 1980). The solidarity of families is also attested by the enormous extent to which children continue to model themselves on their parents. Friends and media influence their leisure and clothes, but basic beliefs and values are derived from parents.

On this evidence, government will most clearly meet the wishes of electors when they serve the needs of the family, and of kinship and friendship networks. How can they best do so? The concern with health gives one pointer: towards adequate medical services. The earlier evidence we have cited also shows electors to be strongly (though not exclusively) concerned with the economic wellbeing of the family unit, with the effects of prices and inflation and unemployment. They say so repeatedly when asked about important problems. It is just possible that in their aspirations for their family, they could be equally greedy and unrealistic if they simply pursued individual advantage. That their economic expectations are inflated is asserted by commentators who see Britain's current problem as aggravated by the 'overloading' of governments with far too many new problems and concerns. According to them, postwar electors in Britain as in other developed countries demand ever-expanding help and financial aid from governments. Since they will not be re-elected if they do not comply, policy-makers have expanded the range of government services far beyond practicable limits, with a consequent decline in administrative efficiency (as most of the problems they face are insoluble anyway).

The rather homely nature of British electors' support for the family does not fit this picture of vaulting aspirations. Nor does their mild scepticism about government competence. The most relevant evidence comes from studies of the relationship between government economic performance and voting intentions (as recorded by the polling agencies). These give the reactions of electors in aggregate to upsurges in prosperity and downturns into recession. Possibly the most striking finding is that electors punish governments for economic downturns by changing their intention to vote for them (or at least many electors do). But greater prosperity does not attract votes to anything like the same extent. Governments are not, in other words, rewarded for giving the population more, but get sharp adverse reactions when they give them much less.

Such behaviour is obviously not a product of rising popular expectations. It is simply aimed at retaining the present standard of living rather than constantly expanding it. Further evidence for this is found in the tendency of electors to downgrade their expectations in the face of bad economic performance, to accept in the face of rising inflation that their standard of living will get slightly worse, and to recognise that governments can do little to affect it. All they ask under these conditions is that the situation does not deteriorate markedly – in which case, understandably, the existing government experiences widespread losses in voting support.

Electors' private preferences therefore relate primarily to the stability and well-being of the family and of its relatives and friends. They are much more anxious to preserve it from disruption (whether through financial troubles, bad housing or neighbourhood changes) than to raise its standards and ambitions to any very marked degree, though they have hopes in the long term for their children. Obviously immediate benefits and improvements will not be spurned – in some cases they may be essential to prevent family disruption, where living conditions are very bad. Nonetheless, a prevailing impression is of electors struggling to preserve what they have, and initially suspicious of change because they expect things to get worse rather than better. They have certainly been encouraged to believe so by all the social and economic forecasts of the last decade.

Social influences on electors' preferences

What shapes these private concerns of electors, and what consequences do they have for political processes? The first is easily answered. In spite of an escalating divorce rate and the publicity given to marital breakdown, the family is still the main agency through which individuals orientate themselves to the world. Not surprisingly, a major value inculcated by this experience is of the importance of the mutual bonds binding its members and of the necessity of preserving them from undue strain. These are lessons which prevail regardless of class, milieu, or region of origin. Even single individuals continue to be oriented to the parental family, and most of those divorced start a new one or at least retain their children within a truncated family unit.

Class, region and other social influences enter at a later stage, that of defining the family's needs in light of its social conditions. Low income families have as their most obvious need some improvement in their material standards. Families in better circumstances may be more concerned with crime and social problems in the neighbourhood, which particularly affect their children's upbringing. Where both financial and environmental problems are less immediate, declining moral standards and a lessening respect for authority may seem to constitute the major threat to family well-being.

There is no evidence of any manipulation or distortion of natural desires by outside bodies. Indeed, all the evidence points to the inability of the press or television to affect individuals' basic outlook and values, which are directly derived from parents within the family. Antisocial attitudes and behaviour stem primarily from broken or deprived families rather than from media influences, though where the break-up has already occurred television may give pointers to antisocial actions.

Different social locations point the common concern with family security in different directions – towards diverse perceived needs and preferences. Translating family needs into policy terms is not straightforward. If the prime need is for greater material support, how does this facilitate a voting choice between incomes policy and free collective bargaining, especially when both are advanced as the quickest way to greater prosperity and economic specialists disagree about their effects? If an elector wants to avert the decline of an inner-city neighbourhood, does he choose more immigration plus money for inner-city renewal, or less of both? This is the choice he was offered in 1979. Are declining moral standards to be redressed by greater censorship, and restrictions on divorce and abortion, or is political action counterproductive within this area?

In assuming that electors can make an easy jump from their private preferences to the public policy options available, most discussions of voting and party competition (not to mention other forms of political action) make a great mistake. It has proved impossible even for highly trained specialists to weigh up the costs and benefits of such relatively simple choices as the site for a third London airport. Lacking their skills and resources, electors cannot even hope to translate their need to increase family income, for example, into the economic alternatives being urged. If British democracy works in the sense of citizens being able to select party policy alternatives on the basis of their own needs, it must be through some kind of simplification which relate the party programme they choose at elections to their personal situation, at least in the long term.

Party competition

The way the parties present their policies is crucial to simplifying public choices in a relevant way. At least in the period since the 1920s, major British parties have avoided direct arguments about the merits of their own policies or demerits of their rivals'. Instead their election manifestoes, detailing the party record in government and future programmes, talk about policies and problems almost as if the other parties did not exist. Reading the manifestoes put out by different sides for a campaign leads to a delusion that several quite different elections are taking place, so radically do their definitions of the situation differ!

The reason for the contrast is the different emphasis placed by rival politicians on different policy areas. Table 4.2 shows these in terms of the average percentage of sentences in the Conservative and Labour manifestoes devoted to each of twenty-six broad topics. Apart from references to social services (where, however, Labour supports their expansion and Conservatives advocate economy and more efficient administration), the parties clearly differ in the attention they pay to various areas. The Conservatives stress the importance of Commonwealth, regional priorities, individual enterprise and efficient administration much more than Labour. Conversely Labour emphasises a controlled economy, social justice (i.e. equality) and support for international co-operation.

These differences closely reflect the divergent ideologies of the parties. Labour focuses on central government planning, basic services and equality. Conservatives stress government economy, decentralisation and individual enterprise. Clearly, therefore, the contrasting emphases of the rival manifestoes are deliberate. British parties compete for votes by highlighting those issues which they think will appeal to electors and on which they are more likely to be associated with a generally approved course of action. Conversely they ignore issues on which they think their competitors might have the advantage. Selective emphasis, rather than direct confrontation, is the essence of party competition in Britain – a tendency exaggerated by the mass media both for simplicity of presentation and more dramatic impact. Selective emphases are also the tactics employed by Liberals and likely to be adopted by the SDP in

Table 4.2 Mean percentage of sentences devoted to each broad area of policy by Conservative and Labour manifestoes, 1924–83

Areas of policy	Labour (%)	Conservative (%)
Empire, special foreign relationships	2.0	5.5
Decolonisation	2.0	1.0
Regionalism	1.1	4.1
Freedom	0.3	2.0
Enterprise	1.4	8.2
Democracy, constitutionalism	3.4	3.1
Controlled economy	11.5	1.0
Economic planning	7.6	1.7
Regulation	2.0	3.2
Labour groups	3.8	1.9
Agriculture, farmers	4.0	5.3
Other minority groups	1.5	2.2
Culture	1.8	1.8
Economic stability	8.5	6.1
Protectionism	1.2	3.8
Productivity	4.0	3.7
National effort	0.4	0.5
Social justice	4.3	0.9
Technology	2.2	3.2
Conservation	1.3	1.3
Military	1.6	3.2
Government performance	1.9	7.1
Incentives	1.0	4.5
Peace	3.3	2.6
Social services	17.5	15.3
Internationalism	9.2	6.0

the future – not that the positions of these parties will have much direct effect so long as they appear moderate. Before they develop a stronger image of their own through actual association with government, the Alliance will gain more from the lack of attractiveness of Labour and Conservatives than from the positive inducements they themselves can offer.

Electors' voting decisions

How do parties' selective emphases ease the translation electors make between their personal and family need for more money or a better environment, and the public alternatives available to them? Or do the parties' selective emphases distort individual preferences and make them appear other than they actually are?

The parties' presentation certainly simplifies electoral choice. For the parties discuss issues as if they fitted neatly into a number of sharply separated areas, in each of which there exists an obvious policy of 'betterment' which one party is more qualified to tackle than the other (taking the choice as lying between the Conservative and Labour parties as it has up till now). Because electors are at the receiving end of the whole simplifying process as relayed through the media, they divide current issues into 'areas' or 'problems' which are even broader and more basic than the ones used in the manifestoes. Table 4.3 lists the fourteen problem areas into which British electors generally classify the specific issues which confront them in national elections. Issues regarded as falling within one area are judged as though they had no implications for others.

These broad policy areas do not interest electors equally. More are affected by welfare and redistribution of wealth than by government regulation of monopolies; crime in the streets has also a more general impact than foreign affairs. Whether an issue, once it comes up in an election, causes large, medium or small numbers of electors to shift their vote is indicated in the third column of Table 4.3.

Table 4.3 Areas into which electors classify issues

Broad policy area	Specific issues corresponding to each area	Extent of impact	Favoured party
1. Civil order	Law and order: measures against crime: death penalty: rioting: strikes and demonstrations: anti-system parties and problems caused by their strength	Large	Conservative
2. Constitutional	Questions involving established institutions (e.g. monarchy, Parliament and relations between them): democracy: civil rights	Medium	Conservative
3. Foreign relationships	Membership of NATO and other foreign alliances: *détente*: attitude to Communist powers: membership of EC: national prestige abroad: colonies and decolonisation: overseas aid: attitudes to war and peace	Small	Conservative or Labour
4. Defence	Military spending increases or reduction; importance *vis-à-vis* other policy areas: nuclear arms	Small	Conservative
5. Candidate	Likes and dislikes about candidates: leading candidates' performance	Variable	Labour or Conservative
6. Government record and situation	Current financial situation and prospects: expectations: economic prosperity, depression: incidence of inflation and unemployment: government corruption, inefficiency: satisfaction with government in general	Variable	Labour or Conservative

7. Traditional morality	Support of traditional/Christian morals and Church: abortion and birth control: temperance: religious schools and education	Large	Conservative
8. Ethnic	Immigration and foreign workers: attitudes to minority groups and their advancement: discrimination: school and housing integration: language questions	Large	Conservative
9. Regional	National unity: devolution and regional autonomy: regional equalisation of resources	Large	Conservative
10. Urban/rural	Farmers and rural interests: agricultural subsidies	Small	Conservative
11. Socio-economic redistribution and welfare	Social service spending: importance of social welfare: housing as a problem: housing subsidies: rent control: health and medical services: social reform: pensions: aid to other services such as education: action in regard to unemployment: full employment, employment guarantee	Large	Labour
12. Government control and planning	Nationalisation: state control of the economy: general government power and control: management and regulation of environment	Small	Conservative
13. Government intervention in favour of small men	Action against monopolies: big business power, trade union power: protectionism and free trade	Small	Conservative
14. Individual initiative and freedom	Closed shop and action in relation to it: incentives: level of taxation: support for free enterprise economics	Small	Conservative

Not all of these areas will be relevant in any one election, of course (see Table 4.4 below). Typically, electors are confronted with four or five important issues, each of which fits into one of the broad policy areas.

How does the emergence of an issue affect party fortunes? This depends on which party is seen as best in the area to which the issue belongs. To decide this we must return to the question of personal needs. The evidence points to electors' overwhelming concern with personal and family security. This renders them cautious on the whole and rather pessimistic in their expectations about social and political change. The large-scale upheavals of the post-war period (urban renewal and resettlement, unemployment and industrial uncertainty, immigration, technological change) have all disrupted settled patterns of behaviour, including traditional family relationships. These have been further undermined by political enactments which have made divorce easier and

Table 4.4 Issues in British general elections, 1950–79
* The numbers attached to each broad policy area are those given in table 4.3.

Election date	Specific issues important in campaign	Broad policy area*	Extent of impact	Party favoured	Estimated net gains from issues Conservative (% vote)	Labour (% vote)
1950	Military threat from USSR	4 Defence	Small	+ Con.		
	Attlee as successful PM	5 Candidate	Medium	+ Lab.		
	Churchill as inspiring alternative leader	5 Candidate	Medium	+ Con.		
	Cost of living, unemployment	6 Govt. record	Medium	– Lab.		
	Achievement of Welfare State	11 Redistribution	Large	+ Lab.		
	Nationalisation of steel	12 Control	Small	+ Con.	+ 3.6	+ 2.7
1951	Fear of 'cold war', desire for peace	3 Foreign	Small	+ Lab.		
	Attlee as successful PM	5 Candidate	Medium	+ Lab.		
	Churchill as inspiring alternative leader	5 Candidate	Large	+ Con.		
	Cost of living, unemployment	6 Govt. record	Large	– Lab.		
	Housing shortages	11 Redistribution	Large	+ Lab.		
	Nationalisation	12 Control	Small	+ Con.	+ 3.6	+ 2.7
1955	Eden as successful government minister	5 Candidate	Medium	+ Con.		
	Attlee as successful former PM	5 Candidate	Large	+ Lab.		
	Economic prosperity	6 Govt. record		+ Con.	+ 4.5	+ 0.9
1959	Post Imperial defence. Unilateral disarmament	4 Defence	Small	+ Con.		
	Macmillan's confidence and performance since became PM	5 Candidate	Medium	+ Con.		
	Economic growth and prosperity	6 Govt. record	Large	+ Con.		
	Pensions increases	11 Redistribution	Large	+ Lab.		
	Nationalisation	12 Control	Small	– Lab.		
	Tax reductions	14 Initiative	Small	+ Con.	+ 6.3	+ 1.8

Year		Issue	Salience	Direction		
1964	Deployment east of Suez	4 Defence	Small	+ Con.	+ 1.8	+ 2.7
	Wilson as inspiring alternative PM	5 Candidate	Medium	+ Lab.		
	Balance of payments	6 Govt. record	Medium	– Con.		
	Legislation on immigration	8 Ethnic	Large	+ Con.		
	Housing shortages, pension extensions, health, education	11 Redistribution	Large	+ Lab.		
	Nationalisation	12 Control	Small	– Lab.		
	Trade union powers	13 Intervention	Small	– Lab.		
1966	Entry to the EC	3 Foreign	Small	+ Lab.	0	+ 7.2
	Wilson as sound PM	5 Candidate	Medium	+ Lab.		
	Aversion of immediate balance of payments crisis	6 Govt. record	Large	+ Lab.		
	Social service improvements	11 Redistribution	Large	+ Lab.		
	Trade union powers	13 Intervention	Small	– Lab.		
1970	Opposition to the EC	3 Foreign	Small	+ Lab.	+ 3.6	+ 1.8
	Wilson as best PM available	5 Candidate	Small	+ Lab.		
	Price rises, wage freeze	6 Govt. record	Large	– Lab.		
	Control of immigration	8 Ethnic	Large	+ Con.		
	Housing shortages, shortfalls in social services	11 Redistribution	Large	+ Lab.		
	High level of taxation	14 Initiative	Small	+ Con.		
1974 (Feb)	'Who governs Britain?'	2 Constitutional	Medium	+ Con.	– 3.6	– 3.6
	Entry to the EC	3 Foreign	Small	– Con.		
	Heath as confrontationist maladroit PM	5 Candidate	Medium	– Con.		
	Industrial relations, rising prices, wage freeze	6 Govt. record	Large	– Con.		
	Disunity of Labour Party	6 Govt. record	Small	– Lab.		
	Nationalisation	12 Control	Small	– Lab.		
	Miners' strike	13 Intervention	Small	– Lab.		

Table 4.4 (Cont.)

Election date	Specific issues important in campaign	Broad policy area*	Extent of impact	Party favoured	Estimated net gains from issues Conservative (% vote)	Labour (% vote)
1974 (Oct)	Entry to the EC	3 Foreign	Small	– Con. – Lab.		
	Heath as unsuccessful PM	5 Candidate	Medium	– Con.		
	Settlement of industrial troubles, prices: higher wages	6 Govt. record	Small	+ Lab.		
	Housing shortages and promised remedies: social legislation	11 Redistribution	Large	+ Lab.		
	Nationalisation	12 Control	Small	– Lab.	– 2.7	+ 1.8
1979	Reform in law on picketing: fighting increased crime	1 Civil order	Large	+ Con.		
	Fair deal for UK from EC	3 Foreign	Small	+ Lab.		
	Competence and moderation of Callaghan (Lab. PM)	5 Candidate	Small	+ Lab.		
	Firmness of Mrs Thatcher (Conservative leader)	5 Candidate	Small	+ Con.		
	Breakdown of incomes policy; government vacillation: unemployment and inflation	6 Govt. record	Medium	– Lab.		
	Extension of government bureaucracy and regulation	12 Govt. control	Small	+ Con.		
	Power of trade unions, need for reform	13 Intervention	Small	+ Con.		
	High level of taxation, increase in individual initiative	14 Initiative	Small	+ Con.	+ 6.3	0

removed children more and more from parental control.

Electors are being reasonable, therefore, in expecting proposals for change, except where they produce immediate material benefits, to carry adverse consequences for their security. Their fear of change points out an obviously desirable goal within each area. Law and order should be maintained, the constitution respected, Britain continue to be strong and respected abroad, living standards guaranteed, traditional moral values upheld, government interference resisted, personal freedom defended, and so on. With its emphasis on maintaining the established structure of society, the Conservative Party has generally been associated with these 'obvious' policies in most areas and has gained the electoral advantage when they become important.

This is not true of all issue areas, however – otherwise Britain would not have a competitive party system. In the field of welfare and redistributive legislation (i.e. policies which take money and resources from the more wealthy to spend for the benefit of those less well off), the electors who stand to gain constitute a large majority of the population. Since the material benefits are concrete and immediate, electors on the whole favour more redistribution and more welfare. When these issues have been important, they have pushed electors towards the Labour Party which is clearly associated with such policies.

No one party has a record of consistent success in foreign affairs or in smooth running of government, nor do they have a monopoly of attractive candidates who might become the Prime Minister. Hence these issue areas are not permanently associated with either major party but are credited to one or the other depending on the particular circumstances of each election. The fourth column of Table 4.3 shows which parties are credited with the best policies in which area and the possibility both have of gaining credit on foreign affairs, candidates and government record. Of course, such assignments are changing with the growth of other political alternatives. Nevertheless since the SDP and Liberals are not yet associated with a clear record, electors even in the 1980s will still make their main decisions on the basis of Labour and Conservative appeals, voting Liberal or SDP if they find the major parties equally unattractive.

Since Labour and Conservatives have been evenly balanced electorally, the crucial winning votes have gone to the one most favoured by the important issues of the campaign. As Table 4.4 shows, the balance of issue advantages has swung fairly consistently between parties over the post-war period. Although the majority of issues which might potentially emerge favour the Conservative Party, the record shows that redistributive and welfare questions are so centrally important that they appear in most elections, thus redressing the situation in favour of Labour. Over the last fifteen years, failures in economic policy have produced assessments of government record unfavourable to the ruling party and/or favourable to the Opposition, whenever the incumbents have had a fair run in office. The difference now is that such assessments may be unfavourable to both.

What contribution to change is made by electors' reactions to important issues? Overall, a large-impact issue such as civil order, or welfare, or redistribution, when it emerges in an election, produces a net change of about 2.7 per cent in favour of the party to which it 'belongs'. This is a net change, concealing reciprocal movements of votes between the major parties themselves, and between each major party and the non-voters and third parties. A medium-impact issue (for example one affecting the constitution) produces a net change of about 1.8 per cent, and a small-impact issue a net change of about 0.9 per cent.

Using these figures we can actually state what overall changes in voting will be produced by a given set of campaign issues, by adding up the net changes which each issue salient in the election will produce. These overall gains and losses are shown in Table 4.4. In 1979, for example, the Conservatives gained 6.3 per cent out of their vote of 43.9 per cent from the issues prominent in the campaign.

In spite of their crucial strategic importance, it remains true that only a minority of electors are sensitive to campaign issues. Personal and social circumstances render one policy area of paramount and enduring importance to most of them. For example, an unskilled labourer in the North of England, hovering on the fringe of the poverty line, is likely to be concerned with welfare benefits to the exclusion of all else. Unswayed by any issues coming up in a particular election, such a person votes Labour consistently, since in all conceivable circumstances Labour will extend welfare more than the Conservatives, and this is crucial to the well-being both of himself and his family. For equally understandable reasons, a high-status professional in the South of England tends to vote Conservative all the time.

Social circumstances may in this way give such a clear indication of the type of policy beneficial to the family that choice between public alternatives becomes relatively simple. The enduring concern of most electors with a particular policy area explains two notable features of British elections. One is the relationship between voting choice and class: in 1983 a plurality (38 per cent) of manual workers voted Labour and 58 per cent of non-manual workers voted Conservative. These proportions were higher in earlier elections. As we have noted, much of this is a regional rather than a pure class effect. The importance of both factors, however, stems from their influence in 'fixating' most electors on certain policy areas by rendering these of prime importance for the individual and his family.

Such electors then cast a consistent vote for a particular party, thus explaining a second feature of elections: the great stability of voting choice revealed by all election surveys. In May 1979 86 per cent of Labour voters recalled voting Labour in October 1974 and 67 per cent of Conservative voters recalled voting Conservative at that time. Such electors were choosing in terms of a consistent policy preference which endured regardless of the particularly circumstances of each of these years. In this way they contribute to a stable basic vote which each major party can expect to receive even in the absence of issues from a particular campaign. This was at the level of 42 per cent of the vote for Labour and 41 per cent for the Conservatives up to the beginning of the 1970s. In the course of the last decade it has declined to 37 per cent for each party – a radical 'dealignment' of major party support. This reflects the influence of greater affluence, the break-up of old class divisions, and the greater importance of regions. These changes have altered personal and family circumstances to the extent that enduring policy interests are no longer apparent to so many electors, whose sensitivity to the effects of issues in each campaign is thus greatly enhanced.

The fall-off in these basic votes also means that many more electors are volatile in the sense of being willing to contemplate support for the Liberals, SDP or the various nationalist alternatives, which in turn makes it more likely that third parties will in the future hold the decisive Commons votes, as in the Parliament of 1974–79.

Other British elections

So far we have confined our discussion to general, i.e. national British electors, ignoring the two other types of regular election held in Britain. These are local elections (held every three years to elect district and regional councillors respectively) and elections to the Parliament of the EC. In both, voters react in essentially the same way as in general elections. The British government indeed is more visible and familiar to the majority of electors than either the local or European bodies, about whose exact powers they are unclear. This is partly due to the prominence given in the British press and television to the doings of the national government, which is true even for local newspapers and programmes. It is also due to the fact that practically all the candidates in these elections are associated with the parties represented in the British Parliament.

As a result electors react to candidates in local and European elections very much in terms of how their party is performing in the national government (or in opposition to it). Since most British governments are buffeted by economic circumstances and have to impose restrictive measures, elections at the local and European level tend to go against the governing party. Increasingly during the lifetime of a British government, control in the localities passes into the hands of opposition parties, adding to its difficulties in getting compliance with its policies and enhancing the desire of the local authorities to pursue an autonomous course of action. We shall discuss this phenomenon in the next chapter.

National issues thus push electors sensitive to campaign circumstances into changing their previous vote. Many electors, as in general elections, always vote for the party pointed out by their social circumstances as best on the issue most important to them. The salient issues at local elections – in spite of the efforts of Liberals and Nationalists to inject other concerns – centre round increases in rates (the local property tax) and extensions to welfare by providing more subsidised housing for those less well-off. The basic vote for the Conservatives thus consists predominantly of ratepayers who own their own homes, and the basic vote for Labour of the tenants of council-owned and subsidised housing. In the major cities this has given Labour an advantage, while in rural and sub-urban areas with a predominance of owner-occupiers, the

Conservatives have been permanently in power.

The directly elected European Parliament established in 1979 is relatively unknown to most electors. This is particularly so as its relationship to the executive bodies of the EC is unclear. Reactions to candidates tend to be shaped by reactions to national parties and governments. This widespead confusion about what the parliament is and what it does led to most electors not bothering to vote in the two elections of 1979 and 1984. Local elections also have a low turnout. This compares with the more than three-quarters of electors who vote in general elections when the issues are well publicised and the outcome seems important.

The different reactions at the various levels may disappoint the local patriot and the fervent European. They are perfectly understandable given the information electors have and the varying importance of the outcomes. Local and European elections are less likely to lead to significant change than the general election.

It does, therefore, seem that the British make sensible and understandable decisions when presented with the opportunity of choosing between political parties in elections. Admittedly this involves some simplification of the complex realities. Specific policies are overlooked, long-term linkages are made between particular parties and broad issue areas, and interconnections between the latter are ignored. Choices are made in terms of the importance of the issue area, either its enduring importance to the individual or (for a minority where the importance of an issue is not obviously determined by their personal situation) its centrality in the campaign itself. Nevertheless such simplifications are not necessarily wrong, and they are closely related to the way the parties choose to present themselves.

Elite manipulation or electoral autonomy?

This very fact has produced criticism that the parties mislead electors to their own advantage, by persuading them to oversimplify politics and ignore radical solutions to the real problems facing the country. To see how far such criticism is justified, we have to consider several interrelated points. The first is that electors' concern with personal and family security itself causes them to distrust radical solutions which bring the possibility of disruption and change. Their reaction to Conservative and Labour extremism in the early 1980s was not to support it but to desert these parties. Distrust of radicalism is, moreover, based on a family-centred outlook which seems perfectly natural and not imposed on electors by media advertising or party propaganda.

Are the real political problems (in the Marxist interpretation, questions of the unequal distribution of power and wealth) hidden from electors by the fact that the parties never raise them? We have noted that socioeconomic redistribution is one of the commonest issues in British national elections (see Table 4.4). And the Labour and Conservative parties do differentiate themselves noticeably on this and other issues (cf. Table 4.2). It is understandable and not 'false consciousness' on their part, that many electors concern themselves with general prosperity, rising crime rates or immigration – issues which can have an immediate concrete impact on family circumstances – rather than with remote and problematical questions of the distribution of power.

The issues which have been important in elections of the post-war period are, moreover, closely related to central problems or achievements of the time. The restrictions and controls of the immediate post-war period, along with the threat from the cold war, were replaced by reactions to the growing prosperity of the 1950s, and then by concern with Britain's faltering economic progress and the social problems of the affluent society over the last twenty years. Major decisions, such as the questions of union power and entry to the EC, are fully emphasised (see again Table 4.4). Thus real questions of pressing importance do seem to be raised by the parties and voted on by electors.

Given all this, does party propaganda nevertheless lead electors to oversimplify and miss the connections between different areas of politics, such as a link between the present power set-up, economic sluggishness, and bad social conditions? The problem is that the existence or non-existence of such a link and its exact form is hotly disputed by theorists and specialists. No obvious connections between policy areas exist, even for sophisticated decision-makers. So action on one area has to be planned without regard to its effects on another, since it is not known what the effects will be. Electors who simplify by dividing policies into broad areas which they assume to be sharply separated, are not stupid nor are they necessarily misled. It is difficult to see what other basis they could use for evaluating public policies comprehensively and easily, or for holding decision-makers accountable.

The election victory of one British party over the others does, on this evidence, genuinely mirror electoral reactions to issues of central importance. It is not decided on the basis of a 'politicians' ramp' which leaves all major questions to be decided elsewhere. Whether such reactions then get translated into effective government policy is another matter, related to the institutional arrangements discussed in the two preceding chapters.

Chapter 5
The other governments of Britain

Representatives and constituents

Parties and elections do not form the only way in which individuals can make their views felt or get government to solve their problems. We have already examined the activities of interest groups. Besides relying on representations made by such groups to civil servants and ministers, individuals can also go to courts or administrative tribunals (Ch. 7) for formal decisions about their grievance.

An immense variety of personal problems are raised by, or involved in, administrative processes. Many of them are too idiosyncratic and personal to impinge on parties or interest groups and are not suitable for court rulings (e.g. whether a lamp-post could be situated outside a dark entry for the convenience of an elderly invalid, or whether a decision about the award of a pension could be speeded up, or neighbouring waste ground cleared). Such matters not falling clearly into the remit of any organised body (along with many which do) are commonly taken up with political representatives, usually the MP or a local councillor, but sometimes a member of the European Parliament or of the House of Lords. Since these problems are ones which press directly on individuals – much more so than general questions of state policy or economic strategy – the importance of political responses to them can hardly be exaggerated, both for making British democracy work and for making it better liked.

Since each Member of Parliament represents a defined territorial area, within which his name is reasonably well known, individuals unfamiliar with politics tend to approach him on any pressing matter which seems to have a political bearing. Over half the cases many MPs handle are primarily local, falling within the competence of district or county authorities. A quarter or a third will be purely administrative, usually involving tax or welfare benefits. On most of these MPs can do nothing directly. Usually the matter is dealt with by telephone calls or correspondence with the appropriate local officials or civil servants. The MP's intervention is usually enough to get the matter dealt with promptly and sometimes where there is ambiguity or discretion it secures a more favourable decision.

So keen are MPs on this kind of contact with their constituents that almost three-quarters actively solicit cases. The usual way in which this is done is by advertising regular sessions or 'surgeries' in which the MP can see constituents and discuss their problems. More than a quarter search for cases even more actively by visiting houses or pubs and having discussions. All this is on a non-partisan basis as the MP generally tries to respond to all his constituents regardless of how they may have voted.

There is ample evidence that MPs take even the cases in which they are indirectly involved very seriously. In the late 1970s more than half of MPs spent over 40 per cent of their time on constituency work. Most dealt personally with purely local cases and did not simply pass them on to a councillor, though sometimes they collaborated with councillors of the same party in the locality.

A minority – a quarter or less – of an MP's cases fall more directly within his competence. For example, pensions or compensation may not have been paid even though payment seems to be justified by the rules, or through an anomaly a particular group is excluded from some benefit although obviously deserving. On these the MP can see ministers or party leaders, lay down questions in the House of Commons or even try to initiate a short debate. At the extreme he may try to make it the subject of a private Bill.

Members of Parliament can also refer cases which they feel to involve maladministration (very broadly defined) to the Parliamentary Commissioner for Administration, popularly termed the Ombudsman after the corresponding Scandinavian official. The Commissioner indeed can only act in response to MPs' complaints, but can then powerfully supplement them by detailed administrative investigations which the MP would not have the standing or resources to carry through. In another capacity the Commissioner can investigate the Health Service as well as the major central ministries. Since individuals often write directly to the Commissioner he also acts as another channel of communication by forwarding these to appropriate MPs. Local commissioners perform the same functions in regard to local and regional administration; they can, of course, be consulted by both MPs and councillors.

Broadly the same type of work is done by elected local councillors within their smaller constituencies. An enormously important source of help to individuals with problems is also provided by the local council or county offices and their associated staff. At the end of the 1970s local councillors were trusted by substantially more people to look after their interests than MPs (and local officials were preferred to civil servants by even more). Those who had actually gone to administrators and politicians for help were also better satisfied with the response made by representatives of local authorities.

These judgements testify to a general feeling that local governments are closer to the people and better aware of their needs than the central government, whether the executive or Parliament. It underlines the often neglected role of local authorities in tailoring administration to personal needs – an important aspect of representative democracy and perhaps crucial in maintaining its popular support.

In addition to a representative role which stands comparison with that of

Parliament, local authorities also undertake the bulk of the administrative business of the country. As they are charged with implementing most central decisions, their part is crucial in determining whether these are going to be effective or not. Enjoying a certain independent status *vis-à-vis* central government, they can negotiate with it on many matters as near equals. All this points to the need to consider local governments not simply as an additional element of representation but also, perhaps even more crucially, as major actors in the processes of policy-making.

The other governments of Britain

The conventional picture of Britain is of a unitary state, with a single Parliament, government and Civil Service, deciding on policy for the whole country and applying it throughout the national territory. Local elected councils and their supporting administrations exist, but they are concerned with important and necessary but mundane and technical functions (e.g. street cleaning). There are no local or other autonomous bodies which even compare in authority with national government.

It follows from what we have just said that almost every one of these assertions is misleading. As Chapter 2 demonstrated, central government is not particularly unified. On closer inspection it dissolves into a collection of departments and ministries (see Table 2.1 p. 23) with diverse views and considerable autonomy in their areas of operation, bargaining more or less as equals on the basis of established policies. If changes are to be effectively implemented they have to be negotiated rather than imposed.

What is true of ministries staffed by regular civil servants is even truer of the management of nationalised industries; and of the numerous nominated boards and committees entrusted with the regulation of particular groups and areas of life. Technically these are termed 'Quasi-autonomous non-governmental organisations' – the famous 'quangos'. The term is rarely used with any precision and encompasses a range of bodies from agricultural marketing boards with powers to fine producers (the Milk Marketing Board is a prominent example) to the BBC, the Jockey Club and Trustees of National Museums, as well as the nationalised industries. The Government can force these bodies to comply in general with its policies by giving or withholding grants, but often it faces resistance and the policies can be effectively modified, often by a coalition of various 'other governments' with recalcitrant departments of the central government itself.

It would be misleading therefore to describe British government as unitary even before examining the activities of the European Community in Britain (empowered by law to act without reference to the British government in certain areas: see Ch. 6). The idea of a unitary state becomes even less adequate when we consider local governments, particularly the large district authorities in the English conurbations, counties in England and Wales, or regions in Scotland. With independent sources of revenue and often under the control of parties out of office at Westminster, these have both the ability and the will to challenge central policy as it applies to their area. Dramatic examples are found in the areas of comprehensive education and subsidised public housing. Fifteen years after a Labour Government adopted the policy of closing selective schools or changing them into comprehensives which admit children of all levels of ability from their neighbourhood, many councils still have selective schools. In the area of subsidised housing, Labour-controlled councils have resisted pressures either to raise rents or to sell council houses to their occupiers. In the case of Clay Cross, a district in Derbyshire, the local councillors in 1973 refused to raise council rents as required by the Housing Finance Act of 1972. Although the councillors were suspended, attempts to fine them and enforce the rent increase were thwarted by local resistance. To provide a less controversial example, Hertfordshire County Council in the late 1960s had an informal arrangement with (i.e. it had struck a bargain with) the Department of Education and Science to increase its preschool educational provision even though, officially and publicly, there was a moratorium on such an increase.

The regular alternation of national parties at Westminster buttresses local authorities, since they can count on controversial policies being reversed in three or four years at the most. Thus after legislation in 1976 which forced local authorities to submit plans for comprehensive reorganisation, various Conservative-controlled counties submitted unacceptable plans which, when returned, were resubmitted in another unacceptable form. They were thus able to hold out until the election of 1979 ensured the demise of the policy for the time being.

Dealings between the Cabinet and Whitehall departments on the one hand, and the more peripheral central departments, nominated bodies and elected authorities on the other, are better characterised as intergovernmental relations than as hierarchical domination, as bargaining rather than as control. Britain does not have a federal constitution and differs from countries like West Germany and the United States in that the powers of local bodies are not specially reserved in law. But in practice the 'other governments' of Britain can have almost as much power as their equivalents in federal countries.

One significant difference from a truly federal set-up is nevertheless the essentially defensive and reactive position of the 'other governments' *vis-à-vis* the central government. Imposed policies can be slowed and occasionally defied outright. Nonetheless they will be adopted in most areas eventually, as with comprehensive education in the 1970s or the expenditure cuts exacted by Michael Heseltine, the Conservative Secretary of State, in the early 1980s. Even such a controversial matter as the sale of council housing (local public housing) to sitting tenants, enjoined by the Thatcher administration and fiercely opposed by Labour councils, was reluctantly accepted after a Court of Appeal decision in 1982 authorising the Secretary of State to take over the administration of council houses from Norwich Council, which was judged to have been slow in effecting the policy. (For other examples of Court decisions on central–local relations, see Ch. 7 below.)

The point is, however, that governments, with only four years between elections to carry their policies through, cannot afford too many delays or prolonged disputes, especially with the bodies on which they rely to implement many of their programmes. At some point they must compromise, as even the unusually determined Thatcher Government had to over the matter of imposing local referenda on high-spending councils who wished to increase their rate demands.

Inevitably the existence of elected bodies with independent resources and practical powers makes governing complex, even before we take into account the independent jurisdictions of the European Community institutions, the courts, the police, and the military. In view of the importance of these relationships, it is surprising that no introductory description exists which covers all the species of sub-national government. This chapter repairs the omission by first, presenting a general picture of the variety of governmental institutions in the United Kingdom; second, comparing the different local government systems to provide a detailed illustration of institutional diversity at regional and local level; and third, by identifying some of the major differences that can arise between the different governmental bodies. Finally, attention is focused on the problems posed by governmental pluralism – both central and local – particularly the obstacles it presents to the implementation of policy and to clear accountability to the population.

Varieties of government

The 'British Isles' contain two independent governments recognised as sovereign in international law: the Republic of Ireland and the United Kingdom of Great Britain and Northern Ireland. Relationships between the two are intimate and indeed the two areas were united under the British government until the violent secession of the Republic between 1918 and 1922. Northern Ireland is still disputed territory. Economically, until recently, Britain was the overwhelming supplier and customer of the Republic. A million Irish citizens live and work in Britain and cast votes in British elections. The Republican government remains a complicating feature of internal British affairs.

Within the United Kingdom itself there exist the four traditional areas each of which has its own distinctive governmental features: England, Wales, Scotland and Northern Ireland. There are also island groups, some of which like Anglesey and the Isle of Wight are governed under the arrangements prevailing in the adjacent mainland. Others, however, such as the Outer Hebrides, Orkney and Shetland have more extensive powers than county, district or metropolitan county councils. For example, Shetland controls oil developments in its own territory, and its council has spearheaded a strong movement towards complete internal autonomy.

The Isle of Man and the bailiwicks of Guernsey and Jersey in the Channel Islands already enjoy autonomous legal status, as crown dependencies, with their own parliaments and governments which effectively control domestic, fiscal and economic policy. Table 5.1 illustrates the territorial diversity of the British Isles, which in effect already has some federal arrangements if only for small peripheral parts.

Table 5.1 The constituent areas of the British Isles: by population size, 1976

	Population ('000s)
The British Isles	**59,089.1**
United Kingdom	55,927.6
Republic of Ireland*	2,978.0
Crown Dependencies:*	
Channel Islands	
Bailiwick of Jersey	69.3
Bailiwick of Guernsey	53.7
Isle of Man	60.5
United Kingdom	**55,927.6**
Great Britain	54,389.5
Northern Ireland	1,538.1
Great Britain	**54,389.5**
England	46,417.6
Scotland	5,205.1
Wales	2,766.8

Sources: *Population Trends* No. 9 Autumn 1977, except *UN Statistical Yearbook 1977*

Within each of the constituent areas and within the United Kingdom as a whole, the powers of government can be divided in a variety of ways. Territorially, authority can be *delegated* to civil servants, working locally, to make administrative decisions on behalf of the central administration. Alternatively it can be *devolved*, that is the right to make policy in certain areas can be given by law to local or regional bodies. These can be elected by the population of the area, as in the case of district or regional councils, or they can be nominated by the central government. A further possibility is that the powers which are delegated or devolved cover only a single area of policy (e.g. health) or cover a range of functions as in the case of local governments (see Fig. 5.1)

Each of these types of decentralisation can be found in the UK. An example of the administrative delegation of a single function is the Department of Health and Social Security with ten regional offices for social security, 900 local offices and approximately 1,000 employment exchanges (or job centres).

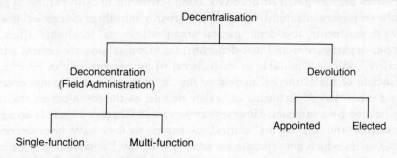

Figure 5.1 Forms of decentralisation

The best example of multifunctional delegation is the Scottish Office, which has had different responsibilities transferred to it piecemeal since its establishment in 1885. In 1976 it had fourteen separate departments accounting for votes in Supply Estimates. These included the Scottish Development Department, the Scottish Home and Health Department, the Department of Agriculture and Fisheries for Scotland, the Scottish Economic Planning Department and the Scottish Education Department, as well as lesser luminaries like the Trustees for the National Museum of Antiquities of Scotland. The Secretary of State for Scotland is responsible to the British Cabinet and Parliament for the work of the Scottish Office. He has been described as 'Scotland's prime minister' but the description is misleading because executive authority resides in British not Scottish governmental institutions.

Perhaps the best example of the devolution of functions to appointed or nominated bodies is the National Health Service (NHS). When the NHS was reorganised in 1974, fourteen Regional Health Authorities (RHAs) and ninety Area Health Authorities (AHAs) were established. The Department of Health and Social Security retained overall responsibility for finance and planning. Within the Department's guidelines the RHAs planned the services and allocated the resources within their own areas, whereas the AHAs operated and controlled the service. Both the RHAs and the AHAs were controlled by members appointed by the Secretary of State. Thus, for the RHA the chairman and approximately fourteen members are appointed by the Secretary of State. (In 1982, the AHAs were abolished and replaced by 193 District Health Authorities.)

The most important current example in the UK of the devolution of functions to elected bodies is local government, the organisation and structure of which are described in the next section. It is not, however, the only example. Prior to the imposition of direct rule in 1972, Northern Ireland had its own elected parliament (Stormont) responsible for nine departments. Throughout the 1970s successive British Governments tried to return to this arrangement, through an elected 'executive' in 1974 and an elected advisory body scheduled to take over administrative responsibilities on a 'rolling' basis in 1982. A return to quasi-federalism has been prevented only by the inability of local politicians to agree. Other examples of devolved elected governments are the Isle of Man and the Channel Islands.

Powers are delegated or devolved along territorial lines to various types of public sector organisations. They divide broadly into three categories: government departments, non-departmental organisations and local authorities.

Both departmental and non-departmental organisations are central administrative bodies accountable to Parliament, whose responsibilities cover either the whole of the United Kingdom or one or more of its traditional areas. It might seem that departments are easily defined as the set of offices traditionally headed by a minister. However, as we saw in Chapter 2 there is no agreed list outside the 'big twenty' central ministries, so they have been defined as the agencies which get separate allocations voted by Parliament in the annual Supply Estimates.

Problems in the definition of government departments pale into insignificance when it comes to examining quangos or non-departmental organisations. Broadly speaking they can be defined as 'organisations other than central goverment departments (including the judiciary and armed forces) and local government departments which deliver services on behalf of government' (Hogwood, 1979). Such a general definition encompasses a multitude of organisations. There have been many attempts to classify this throng but none are satisfactory. Simply to illustrate the variety, the scheme put forward by the Kilbrandon Commission will suffice. It classified such bodies by major function as follows: (1) executive bodies providing personal or social services (e.g. regional hospital boards); (2) industrial or commercial boards (e.g. gas, electricity); (3) advisory bodies (e.g. regional economic planning councils); (4) appellate bodies (e.g. rent assessment panels); and (5) consumer protection (e.g. gas consultative council) (Commission on the Constitution 1973: 226). Both departments and non-departmental organisations have decentralised structures and functions, on either a regional or local basis, or both.

There is no generally accepted definition of local government, although there is at least some agreement as to its major characteristics. These include a limited areal jurisdiction, election, and independent powers of taxation.

The sheer number of definitions and distinctions (and this account is much simplified) itself illustrates the complex structure of territorial differentiation in Britain. The point is further illustrated by Tables 5.2–5.4 which show the number of public sector organisations in the UK and their patterns of expenditure and employment (see chapter appendix p. 133, for sources and assumptions).

There are problems with this exercise. For example, because there is no agreed definition of non-departmental organisations, estimates of their numbers vary considerably. From reading the literature, it might appear that there

Table 5.2 Numbers of public sector organisations: by type and area, 1976*

Area	Departments	Non-departmental organisations (range)	Local governments (range)
England (including some UK-wide organisations[†])	54	159–2,559	412–8,359
Wales	1	10–99	45–727
Scotland	14	46–661	65–1,408
Northern Ireland	1 (9)[‡]	165	26 (73)
Totals	70	380–3,484	548–10,520

Notes
* For a discussion of sources see Appendix, p. 133
[†] The figures for non-departmental organisations in this row include some whose terms of reference cover the whole of the UK and for which there was no information on their areal organisation; twenty-eight non-departmental organisations which covered England *and* Wales and an unspecified number of such bodies which cover Northern Ireland
[‡] The figures in brackets for Northern Ireland refer to the situation before direct rule

Table 5.3 Identifiable public expenditure: by area

Country	Total £ per head		As % of total for England	
	1974–75	1976–77	1974–75	1976–77
England	543	754	100	100
Scotland	659	949	121	126
Wales	583	875	107	116
Northern Ireland	763	1,111	141	147

Source: *Social Trends* **9** (1979) adapted from Table 7: 16

Table 5.4 The distribution of UK public employment: by area and type, 1977 ('000s)

	England	Scotland	Wales	Northern Ireland	United Kingdom
1. Local government	2,471	293	156	87	3,007
2. Nationalised industries and publicly owned companies	1,694	196	140	37	2,067
3. National Health Service	952	135	60	37	1,184
4. Civil Service	629	72	42	36	792
5. Armed Forces	203	19	7	16	337
6. Others	345	50	15	20	430
7. Total public employment	6, 294	765	420	233	7,817
8. Total employed workforce	20,965	2,230	1,106	576	24,878
9. Percentage of employed workforce in public sector	30.0	34.3	38.0	40.5	31.4

Source: R. Parry (1980), Table 1, pp. 4–5

is some agreement on a total of 250–350 but this figure greatly underestimates the total. Taking note of these disagreements by indicating the range of estimates of non-departmental organisations, Table 5.2 still shows that the total number of public sector organisations could fall between 998 and 4,102, excluding all the delegated levels of administration in England. If parish and community councils (often important as local pressure groups) are included, the possible total becomes a staggering 14,074.

The simple fact that there are a large number of public sector organisations does not necessarily mean that they are important for the government of the country. They may have limited responsibilities, delivering few services to citizens. However, Tables 5.3 and 5.4 show that institutional variety *is* important, as the various types of public sector organisations account for a substantial proportion of public expenditure and public employment. It is significant that the level of public expenditure per head of population is greater in the other areas of the United Kingdom than in England, as is the rate of increase in expenditure. Nor is the money disbursed solely by central departments: local authorities account for 27 per cent of total public expenditure or 14.8 per cent of gross domestic product (or the value of all goods and services produced in the country). Unfortunately, reliable figures are not available for the other types of public sector organisatoins, with the estimates for non–departmental organisations displaying remarkable variation. Nonetheless, it is clear that the attitudes and behaviour of local governments are of great significance for the economic plans of central government. Cuts in public expenditure can be thwarted because local authorities are responsible for a large proportion, may not accept the government's economic and social priorities, and have their own sources of revenue which they can increase to offset reductions in central grant. However, local autonomy in this area may be diminishing as a result of firm central government action in 1981–82.

The importance of 'other governments' is also illustrated by the figures for public employment (Table 5.4). Public employment accounts for approximately 30 per cent of the employed workforce and again it is of far greater importance in the other areas than in England, reaching 40 per cent in Northern Ireland. Of the 10 per cent of public employees who are civil servants, 32 per cent are in local offices and 19 per cent are in the Scottish, Welsh and Northern Ireland offices. Local government remains prominent, accounting for 38.5 per cent of total public employment and 12.1 per cent of total employment. In other words, whether judged by the number of institutions or the distribution of resources and employment between these institutions, the structure of government in the UK can only be described as complex. It will appear even more so as flesh is added to this abstract skeleton, even though the next section only compares the overall pattern of local government in England with that in the peripheral areas. The different patterns will not be described individually. Although it is possible to construct a description of any one system from the following section, the emphasis has been placed on a *comparison* of the various local government systems. Local government is examined because it constitutes the most important form of decentralisation in terms of both public expenditure and public employment. It is also the type for which most information is available.

Systems of local government: an illustration of government variety

The reorganised structure of local government which came into operation in 1974 aimed at producing a fairly uniform pattern throughout the United Kingdom. Most major functions such as education, social welfare, police and planning were to be placed with large authorities. These were based either on the urban conurbations or on the former counties in England and Wales; and on amalgamations of counties and cities into 'regions' in Scotland. District authorities outside the conurbations were based on cities and large towns, or groupings of small towns and villages, and given only minor functions apart from housing. The major types of local authority created by the 1974 reorganisation are shown in Table 5.5.

Typically, this neat administrative pattern was complicated by a variety of political pressures and local circumstances. As noted earlier the remoter Scot-

Table 5.5 Major types of local authorities created by reorganisation: area and numbers

England Conurbations (excluding London)	England and Wales (rest)	Scotland
Metropolitan Counties (6)	County councils (39 + 8)	Regions (9)
Metropolitan Districts (36)	County districts (296 + 37)	Districts (53)
	Parishes (7,947 + 682)	Islands (3) Community councils (1,343)

tish island groups acquired substantial autonomy. With the help of their MPs, traditional counties like Fife asserted their status and became regions. In any case, owing in part to the preference of the Scottish Office for dealing with a limited number of authorities, and in part to the resistance put up by the traditionally Conservative English counties to amalgamation, the regions in Scotland are much larger than their counterparts in England and Wales; for example, Strathclyde Region, based on Glasgow, comprises half the population of Scotland.

Local government in Northern Ireland was dealt with very differently because the UK government, in an attempt to defuse the local 'troubles', took almost all its functions into the Northern Ireland Office. In England district councils in metropolitan, built-up areas were large enough to take over education and some social services as well as housing. The exemplar of this process was London, where the Conservative Government of the early 1960s abolished the old Labour-controlled London County Council and created thirty-two powerful new boroughs, extending the capital's boundary to include the Conservative suburbs. Thus the present Greater London Council has only general planning and co-ordinating powers: education is shared between the outer boroughs and the Inner London Education Authority (a unique, special-purpose indirectly elected body); and the boroughs are responsible for the remaining functions. An anomaly in London is the City of London, governed by its medieval constitution. It has vast rateable resources and a miniscule population – its survival being further testimony to the triumph of political pressures and tradition over administrative rationalism.

The original neat administration pattern was thus transformed into a number of distinct local government systems by a combination of specific circumstances and political pressures. These systems are examined in this section, as a concrete illustration of diverse governmental arrangements. Inevitably the description has to focus on some aspects of these and cover others only in passing. Since traditional descriptions have concentrated mainly on the formal constitutional position (stressing, for example, the *ultra vires* rule which prohibits local authorities doing anything they are not expressly empowered to do by Parliament), this section redresses the balance by concentrating on the variety of relationships between governmental institutions and the variety of resources underpinning these relationships.

As a starting point, it is clear that central government does not exercise effective, detailed control over local authorities. It is more accurate to describe the relationship in terms of bargaining: that is, central and local government are interdependent. Central government has resources which the local authorities need if they are to achieve their goals. Conversely, local authorities control resources which central government needs. Hence, central–local relations take on the aspect of a 'game' with both levels of government employing strategies within known rules in order to realise their goals. In this game, the resources of the participants have a marked influence on their chances of success. It is commonly argued that central government can control local authorities because it provides a substantial proportion of their income: 'He who pays the piper calls the tune.' However, money is not the only relevant resource. It is possible to identify at least five, as follows:

Constitutional and legal resources: The mandatory and discretionary powers allocated between central departments and other government units by statute and constitutional convention.

Hierarchical resources: the authority to issue commands and to require compliance which goes with the position of an actor in an organisational hierarchy. Although the authority to obtain compliance will have a legal basis, hierarchical resources do not rest purely on law. Habits of compliance can provide an alternative foundation for actual behaviour.

Financial resources: the money raised by a public sector organisation from services provided, from taxes, and from borrowing.

Political resources: the access to decision-making in government units bestowed on elected representatives by political office; the legitimacy deriving from the fact of election and the right to build public support.

Information resources: the information and expertise possessed by actors.

Thus, a government unit dependent on central government for money can still negotiate because it can exploit the centre's need for information and expertise.

The relationships between central government and the various types of local government can now be considered in terms of the different resources they deploy.

Constitutional and legal resources

The constitutional and legal resources of local authorities differ in that the statutory definition of their functions varies throughout the United Kingdom. There are two important aspects to the legal rules: first, the distinction between what is and what is not a local government function; and second, the distribution of functions between different types of local government units. Thus, employing the first dimension, one would separate the system of local government in Northern Ireland from that of the remainder of the United Kingdom, because housing is a function of the Northern Ireland Housing Executive whereas elsewhere it is a local government function. Similarly,

Table 5.6 Allocation of functions in UK local government

Function	England				London				Wales		Scotland						
	NMC	NMD	MC	MD	GLC	ILB	OLB	COL	NMC	NMD	MLR	MLD	PR	PD	ISL	NID	SCILL
Education	X		X	X	C	X	X	X	X		X	X	X	X	X	O	X
Housing	A	X	X	X	D	X	X	X	X	X	X	X	X	X	X	O	X
Libraries	X		X	X		X	X	X	X		X	X	X		X	O	X
Transport	X	B	X	B	X	B	B	B	B	B	B	X	X	X	X	X	X
Refuse collection	X	X	X	X		X	X	X	X	X		X		X	X	X	X
Refuse disposal	X		X		X			X	X		X	X	X	X	X	X	X
Social work	X		X	X	X				X		X	X	X		X	O	X
Leisure, recreation and museums	X	X	X	X	X	X	X	X	X	X	X	X	X	X	X	X	
Police	X		X		O		O		X		X	X	X		X	O	F
Fire	X		X		X				X		X	X	X		X	O	F
Burial grounds	X	X							X	X					X	X	G
Consumer protection	X		X						X	E	X		X		X	E	X
Environmental health	X	X	X	X	X	X	X	X	X	X	X	X	X	X	X	X	X
Water and sewerage	O	O	O	O	O	O	O	O	O	O	O	O	O	O	O	O	O
Gas	O	O	O	O	O	O	O	O	O	O	O	O	O	O	O	O	O
Planning	X	X	X	X	X	X	X	X	X	X	X	X	X	X	X	X	X
Building regulations	X	X	X	X	X	X	X	X	X	X	X	X	X	X	X	X	X

Key
NMC = Non-metropolitan county
NMD = Non-metropolitan district
MC = Metropolitan county
MD = Metropolitan district
GLC = Greater London Council

ILB = Inner London boroughs
OLB = Outer London boroughs
COL = City of London
MLR = Non-peripheral regions
MLD = Non-peripheral districts
PR = Peripheral regions

PD = Peripheral districts
ISL = Scottish islands
NID = Northern Ireland districts
SCILL = Scilly Isles

A = Reserve powers to provide housing subject to a request by a district council and/or the approval of the Secretary of State
B = Certain transport functions such as provision and maintenance of footways. For more detailed breakdown for England and Wales see Committee of Inquiry into Local Government Finance Report, p. 372
C = Education in inner London is provided by the Inner London Education Authority which is a special independent committee of the Greater London Council
D = The Greater London Council maintains housing stock inherited from the London County Council
E = Certain minor powers
F = Police and fire in the Scilly Isles are administered by Devon and Cornwall
G = No expenditure on burial grounds 1977–80
O = Not a function of local government

education and social work are functions of regional boards, in contrast to the practice in mainland Britain.

Taking the range of functions as one important criterion for distinguishing between local authorities, there are five broad groups in the United Kingdom: England and Wales, Scotland, London, Northern Ireland and the Scilly Isles. Each of these groups is also differentiated by the fact that they were constituted by separate legislation. Using the English and Welsh group (created by the Local Government Act 1972) as a basis for comparison, the Scottish group, created by the Local Government (Scotland) Act 1973, has additional functions such as water, sewerage and valuation of property for local taxes (rates), functions not exercised in England and Wales. The London group, created by the London Government Act 1963, has no direct responsibility for police since police services in London are administered by the Home Office. The Scilly Isles, the functions of which are outlined in the Local Government Act 1933, and not superseded by the 1972 Act, has water and sewerage functions. Local government in Northern Ireland, created by the Local Government Act (Northern Ireland) 1972, offers the strongest contrast to the remainder of the United Kingdom since it is now principally confined to cleansing, environmental health, leisure and recreation, burial and cremation.

The second dimension to local government's legal resources is the distribution of functions between levels of government. This, for example, distinguishes the metropolitan and non-metropolitan areas of England where the division of functions between county and district is different (see Table 5.6). Although seventeen different types of local authority could in theory emerge when the constitutional and legal dimensions are combined, there are in actual practice eleven local government systems with a differing range and distribution of functions. The smallest of these systems is the Scilly Isles, with a population of 2,000, and the largest is the non-metropolitan English system with a population of over 28 million (divided of course between numerous distinct non-metropolitan authorities).

The importance of variation in the constitutional and legal position can easily be demonstrated. The best way to predict the spending of any particular local government unit is to consult the distribution of functions shown in Table 5.6. With the exception of the City of London and Inner London, the spending figures for the Scottish systems tend to be grouped together, as do the English and Welsh systems, while the Northern Ireland system spends far less than any other, simply because it has fewer statutory functions. Similarly, an examination of the individual types of local government reveals that Scottish regions spend more than English and Welsh districts simply because they do more expensive things, such as providing education and social services (see Table 5.7).

The final difference in the constitutional and legal resources of the several local government systems stems from variations in the legislation affecting local governments. For example, the legislation on education or social work in Scotland is not identical to that in England and Wales. There is a large amount of specifically Scottish and Northern Irish legislation and corresponding differences in the scope and content of local services, a point illustrated by Table 5.8.

Table 5.7 The groups and systems of local government in the UK

Group/system	1976 population ('000s)	Percentage of the United Kingdom population	Expenditure per head 11976–77 (£)
English and Welsh group	**42015**	**75**	**257.63**
1. Non-metropolitan English system	27675	49	241.69
2. Metropolitan English system	11664	21	287.81
3. Welsh system	2766	5	290.41
London group	**7112**	**13**	**371.80**
4. Outer London system	4559	8	310.80
5. Inner London system	2548	5	470.18
6. City of London system	5	*	5,822.63
Scottish group	**5206**	**9**	**326.87**
7. Scottish mainland non-peripheral system	4715	8	326.98
8. Scottish mainland peripheral system	425	1	316.12
9. Scottish Island system	66	*	388.78
Northern Ireland	**1538**	**3**	**22.37**
10. Northern Ireland system	1538	3	22.37
Scilly Isles	**2**	*****	**290.28**
11. Scilly Isles	2	*	290.28
Whole United Kingdom	**55963**	**100**	**272.03**

Source: See Appendix, p. 133
* indicates less than one per cent

119

Table 5.8 Territorially specific Acts in Scotland and Northern Ireland

	Northern Ireland			Scotland		
	Specific Acts	Total Acts	Specific (%)	Specific Acts	Total Acts	Specific (%)
Amended	12	17	71	101	253	40
Repealed	67	92	73	99	173	57
Total	79	109	72	200	426	47

Sources: Local Government (Scotland) Act 1973; Local Government Act (NI) 1972
See also Appendix, p. 133

Hierarchical resources

Hierarchical resources vary between the local government systems in two important respects. First, they vary in terms of the internal organisation of the relevant 'central government' and second, in terms of the relationship of the government of the traditional areas to the UK central government. The relevant central government for Scotland, Wales and Northern Ireland exists in the multifunctional Scottish, Welsh and Northern Ireland Offices. In practice, and belying the Supply Estimates, the Northern Ireland Office consists of seven major departments: Finance, Agriculture, Commerce, Education, Environment, Health and Social Services and Manpower Services, with the Department of the Environment for Northern Ireland having general supervisory responsibilities for local government.

The Scottish Office's Scottish Development Department has general responsibilities for local government affairs, although on matters of specific concern, contacts with local government are maintained by the other Scottish Office departments, e.g. the Home and Health Department (health, fire and police), and the Education Department (education and social work). In so far as the terms have any meaning, the Welsh Office has no formal departments with the exception of the Health and Social Work Department. Instead it is divided into groups, such as Local Government, General and Housing Groups; Economic Planning; Land Use Planning; Finance; Transport and Highways, and Education.

These structures are significant for at least two reasons. First, instead of the range of local government functions being the responsibility of a number of ministers, they are largely, in the peripheral areas, the responsibility of one: the Secretary of State for Scotland, Northern Ireland or Wales. Second, the groupings of functions are different. For example, in England the responsibility for education and social services lies with two separate ministries whereas in Scotland it lies with one department of the Scottish Office.

Furthermore, it should not be assumed that the definition of the 'relevant' central government is a problem only for non-English parts of the United Kingdom. The major Whitehall departments have some form of regional organisation and much of the day-to-day contact between local and central government passes through regional offices of Whitehall departments. The

Department of the Environment (DoE) has general supervisory responsibility for local government in England. It has nine regional offices and they represent an important focus for the bargaining activity between centre and locality not only because they have important discretionary powers (such as examinations of Housing Investment Programmes in the finance of housing) but also because they are important routes of access to Whitehall itself. Other departments concerned with local government activities have regional organisations; the Department of Health and Social Security has nine regions for social services in England and the Department of Education's Inspectorate of Schools is organised into seven English and Welsh regions. However, 'the significance of the regional office of the DoE in comparison to other government departments and agencies in the region, is a reflection of the range of functions represented in the regional office' (Keating and Rhodes 1979: 10).

The importance of the Scottish, Welsh and Northern Ireland Offices, as well as the English regional offices, lies in the complexity they introduce into the pattern of intergovernmental relations in the United Kingdom. Not only do they increase the sheer number of public bodies, but they also differ from each other in terms of their structures and the discretion formally granted to them. Although all are bound by the conventions of cabinet and ministerial responsibility, the three offices in the peripheral regions differ from English regional offices because they have responsibility for a wider range of functions; they are funded through separate budgetary procedures; and they are headed by ministers of cabinet rank with formal responsibility for the provision of services for defined territories.

The nature of hierarchical resources can be illustrated by looking at one which is particularly outstanding: the circulars issued by government departments to local authorities. The functions of these are varied. Often they provide advice, but they may also direct local authorities to take particular courses of action, sometimes with backing from an Act of Parliament. There are four routes for this hierarchical resource of central government. The first is direct from London. Most circulars in England are issued by the central office of the London-based department. Some of the circulars in Scotland and Wales flow directly from London; for example, since consumer protection is not a function of the Scottish and Welsh Offices, these circulars come from London. Second, a circular may originate in a London-based department and merely be passed on to non-English local authorities, with the Scottish and Welsh Offices acting at most as a partner in the consultations which led to the circular and often merely as the distributor of circulars. For example, most DoE circulars are issued as Welsh Office circulars under a joint letterhead. Similarly, in Scotland, many circulars from the Department of Agriculture and Fisheries for Scotland came from the Ministry of Agriculture, Fisheries and Food a few days earlier. Circulars issued by the Public Works Loan Board, the public borrowing institution for local authorities, are issued in identical form by the Scottish Office Finance Division.

Third, some circulars which are issued in England are issued in Wales and Scotland in an amended form. For example, a Scottish Office Finance Division circular of 1975, 'The Attack on Inflation', contained a similar message to that issued in England and Wales but included specific references to patterns of finance in Scotland. Finally, circulars issued in England are not always issued in Wales or Scotland. For example, the circular giving guidance to local authorities on the interpretation of the Housing (Homeless Persons) Act 1977 was issued in England and Wales but, after a protracted debate, no equivalent guidance has yet been issued in Scotland.

On the other hand, some circulars emanate almost wholly from the sub-national offices. In Scotland, most circulars from the Scottish Education Department have no direct counterpart in the circulars of the Department of Education and Science, because the two educational systems are so different. These examples help to illustrate Madgwick's terse summing up of the role of the Welsh Office, which may act as 'the centre of government, or on behalf of, or as an Agency or intermediary for, a London central department; or may be bypassed when a central functional department deals directly with a local authority' (Madgwick and James 1979: 3). This summary can be applied, to a greater or less extent, to both the Scottish and Northern Ireland Offices.

Financial resources

Students of local government tend to stress the financial resources of local government, arguing that local dependence on central grant underpins central control of local authorities. The argument is often overstated, however, and it is useful to distinguish between locally raised resources which consist of the rate, that is the local tax levied upon property; charges for local services such as school meals and rents for local authority housing; and intergovernmental transfers, that is the grants paid to local government from central government funds. It is one of the peculiarities of the British system of intergovernmental finance that for the most part little attention is paid to the amount that local authorities actually spend. The main focus is on 'net' expenditure, that is expenditure net of income from service charges. Hence it is often assumed that local authorities in the United Kingdom receive more support as a percentage of their expenditure than is actually the case.

The most recent reliable figures for *comparing* gross expenditure refer to 1974–75. These figures show that Scottish local authorities receive 55 per cent of their total current income from central government grants, 22 per cent from rates and 23 per cent from charges and other sources of revenue. In England the figures are 45 per cent, 24 per cent and 31 per cent respectively. In Wales they are 56 per cent, 17 per cent and 27 per cent. The strongest contrast is provided by Northern Ireland where only 21 per cent of expenditure comes from government grants, 45 per cent from rates and 34 per cent from fees and charges.

The diverse nature of the financial resources of local authorities can be further illustrated by looking at the distribution of grant between the several local government systems (see Table 5.9). In terms of total grant, the City of London has the highest per capita receipts, while Northern Ireland has the lowest. Elsewhere in Britain, the level of grant ranges from £226.43 per head in inner London to £138.12 in outer London. In terms of the way in which grants are

Table 5.9 Grants receipts of UK local government systems, 1976–77

	Needs element RSG per head £	Resources element RSG per head £	Specific grants per head £	Housing revenue account grants per head £	Total grants per head £	Total grants as percentage of expenditure
1. Non-metropolitan English system	68.35	39.25	17.00	14.11	138.71	57
2. Metropolitan English system	84.89	47.91	23.03	22.47	178.30	62
3. Welsh system	80.36	72.44	24.06	19.38	196.24	68
4. Outer London system	84.36	9.02	9.24	35.50	138.12	44
5. Inner London system	132.78	7.25	16.56	69.84	226.43	48
6. City of London system	350.37	1.57	574.54	192.10	1,118.58	19
7. Scottish mainland non-peripheral system	126.08	29.95	11.90	26.58	194.51	59
8. Scottish mainland peripheral system	136.64	44.38	11.93	27.95	220.90	70
9. Scottish Island system	198.02	86.09	16.60	33.82	334.53	86
10. Northern Ireland system		4.43	1.57	0	6.0	27
11. Scilly Isles	153.00	16.43	5.49	18.54	193.46	67

Source: see Appendix, p. 134

provided to local authorities there is also great diversity; outer London receives 61 per cent of its grant through the needs element of the rate support grant (which is intended to reflect the expenditure needs of the locality) while in Wales only 41 per cent of the grant comes through the needs element and 37 per cent through the resources element (which is intended to equalise the different tax bases of local authorities).

In terms of the percentage of net expenditure financed by grants, peripheral Scotland receives the highest percentage support, while the City of London, with its large rateable value per head of population, receives the least. In Northern Ireland the percentage support through grants is comparatively low, due to the fact that the heavily grant-aided services such as police, education and social services, are no longer functions of local government. Elsewhere in mainland Britain, the percentage support ranges from 68 per cent in Wales to 44 per cent in outer London.

The variations in local dependence on central grants caution against any easy generalisation about the dependence of local governments on the centre. If grants are an important means of central control, the extent of such control will vary considerably between the different types of local government system. And even this generalisation assumes that weakness in the control of financial resources cannot be made up by deploying other resources. The consequences of financial dependence are unlikely to be as obvious as 'he who pays the piper calls the tune'.

Political resources

The political resources of local governments are extremely diverse. Those available to Scottish local governments, for example, are affected by the presence in the Scottish Office of a minister of cabinet rank, and by the existence of a relatively coherent community of Scottish Labour and Conservative politicians and party activists. Both these features of the Scottish political system may provide local authorities with easier and more effective access to 'national' politicians. However, this argument should not be taken to imply that a relatively coherent community is absent in all the English regions. The political resources of a local government may also be affected by such factors as the standing of its Member of Parliament, the marginality of the constituency in which it is located, or by more specific factors. For example, it has been argued that the opposition of MPs in the North East of England to the precarious devolution legislation from 1977–79 brought benefits to local authorities through promises of additional regional aid and grants.

Party control of local governments also affects the political resources available to them. The number of authorities controlled by the different parties in 1976 is shown in Table 5.10. While party control of specific authorities has changed markedly since then, the general pattern remains relevant. The non-metropolitan English districts and outer London boroughs are predominantly Conservative controlled, as are the counties in non-metropolitan areas, whereas in metropolitan districts and inner London Labour has the upper hand; the Conservatives, however, control a majority of metropolitan counties.

Table 5.10 Political control of UK local authorities, 1976

	Conservative	Labour	No overall control	Independent	Other	Total
Non-metropolitan districts (England)	163	30	49	53	1	296
Non-metropolitan counties (England)	20	6	12	1	0	39
Scottish non-peripheral districts	3	17	12	4	1	37
Non-metropolitan district (Wales)	4	11	8	13	1	37
Metropolitan districts	13	20	3	0	0	36
Northern Ireland districts	0	0	6	0	20	26
Outer London boroughs	11	8	1	0	0	20
Peripheral Scottish districts	1	0	1	14	0	16
Inner London boroughs	2	10	0	0	0	12
Non-metropolitan counties (Wales)	0	4	1	3	0	8
Metropolitan counties	2	4	0	0	0	6
Scottish non-peripheral regions	1	2	3	0	0	6
Peripheral Scottish regions	0	0	1	2	0	3
Scottish islands	0	0	0	3	0	3
City of London	0	0	0	1	0	1
Scilly Isles	0	0	0	1	0	1
GLC	0	1	0	0	0	1
Total	220	113	97	95	23	548

Source: *Local Government Trends 1976; Municipal Year Book 1977*; and D. Birell and A. Murie (1980): 188

Wales and Scotland both show the weakness of the Conservative party in local government and the strength of Labour and independents. The party system of Northern Ireland differs from that of the remainder of the United Kingdom; hence the 'others' column in Table 5.9 includes ten districts with a single unionist party majority, seven with a unionist/loyalist majority and three with an SDLP/Nationalist/Independent majority. And it should be added that the figures for mainland Britain still showed the influence of the Conservatives' climb to power at local and national levels at the end of the seventies. Under a Conservative government, Labour extended their control in the early 1980s.

Nor is the full extent of the differences between local authorities revealed by this analysis of variations in political control. It does, for example, ignore the extent and type of party influence. Jones (1975: 19–22) identified several kinds of political system and, simplifying his typology, the following major variations in local politics can be identified:

1 *The non–party*: predominantly in the hands of non-partisan independents although the council may contain some (or one) small minority parties.
2 *The partially party*: the parties contest the elections but, once elected, members behave as independents.
3 *The emergent party*: both independents and parties contest the election and members on the council are organised into socialist and antisocialist groups.
4 *The wholly party*: parties both control elections and form the basis of organisation within the council. This category can be further subdivided into:-
  (a) the one-party monopolistic;
  (b) the two-party competitive; and
  (c) the multi-party.

In a similar vein, Stanyer (1976: 152–6) distinguishes between non-partisan, semi-partisan, partisan and 'secret caucus' systems. Both typologies simplify complicated situations, as their authors fully recognise, but they do demonstrate that local government contains many varieties of local politics, differences which encompass both elections and the ways in which the council makes its decisions. The difference between the 'squirearchy' of some shire counties and the party-controlled local authority in the conurbations, with its model standing orders, group meetings, whips and party patronage, is great indeed.

A number of consequences can arise from this but one is of overriding importance: no national government can rely on the support of like-minded local politicians. Where the two levels of government are controlled by different parties (and every minister will face some local authorities controlled by opposition parties), disagreements over policy can be exacerbated. Conservative controlled councils will be reluctant to implement a Labour Government's comprehensive education policy, and even members of the minister's own party may disagree with him. Whichever party is in control at the local level, it will have its own views about local problems and priorities. Accordingly, it will be willing to debate the merits of a policy with the minister either within the party, in Whitehall, or in the media. Variations in party control of localities can be seen, therefore, as an indication of diverse local policy preferences. And the existence of 'other' parties in the peripheral areas simply compounds this variety by interweaving religious and nationalist ideologies with those of the three major parties. Not only do variations in party control at the local level put a premium on the political support available to the minister, but they increase the range of political pressure to which (s)he is subject.

One final political resource should be mentioned. Each type of local authority in England and Wales has formed a national association to represent its interests. Thus county councils in England and Wales have formed the Association of County Councils (ACC); the Greater London Council, the London boroughs, the metropolitan districts and the metropolitan counties have formed the Association of Metropolitan Authorities (AMA); and county districts have formed the Association of District Councils (ADC). In Scotland, however, all types of local authority are represented by the Convention of Scottish Local Authorities (COSLA). Welsh local authorities are members of the appropriate English associations. However, the Local Government Planning and Land Act 1980 placed the responsibility for grant negotiations on the Welsh Office, and this development may strengthen the separate identity of the Welsh arms of the associations. These local authority associations have been described as part of the constitution of the country; it is certainly difficult to underestimate their influence. At the very least, they are an important channel of communication between the two levels of government, even if, like the other 'peak' associations considered in Chapter 2, they are unable to guarantee the behaviour of all their individual members.

Information resources

One of the peculiarities of British government is that 'central government does not concern itself directly with executant activities' (Sharpe 1979: 44). For example, the DoE does not build houses; they are built and the estates are managed by local authorities. One consequence of this is that the local authorities possess information and expertise which is essential to central departments if they are to evaluate and make policy. And the control of information, particularly when it is so treasured and guarded as in Britain, is one lever for persuading central departments to introduce, modify or withdraw a particular policy. One way of assessing local government's advantage in this area is to compare the numbers of people employed at each level of government. Table 5.11 shows the number of people in employment in both the civil service and local government for each constituent area of the UK. Clearly, local authorities employ a far larger number of people than central departments. The partial exception is Northern Ireland where the major local government services were transferred to central government with the introduction of direct rule. Even there, local authorities still employ twice as many people.

Comparing the number of employees can be misleading. Local government employees could be performing routine tasks or manual work under central direction: the major policy and managerial decisions could be taken by civil servants. However, one of the most prominent characteristics of local government is 'professionalism'. In other words, local authorities are divided into

Table 5.11 Civil Service and local government employment: percentages of total public employment in each area, 1977

	Civil Service	Local government
England	10	39.3
Wales	10	37.1
Scotland	9.4	38.3
Northern Ireland	15.5	37.3
United Kingdom totals	10.0	38.5

Source: R. Parry (1980), Table 1, pp. 4–5

departments each of which is responsible for a major service or services and each of which is staffed by professionals. These professionals undergo prolonged training to obtain the requisite qualification and they exercise a major influence on central as well as local policy-making. Frequently, they have national organisations which advise both central departments and the local authority associations – for example, the Society of Local Authority Chief Executives (SOLACE) and the Chartered Institute of Public Finance and Accountancy (CIPFA).

Some indication of the professionalisation of local government can be obtained by looking at the distribution of employment by services. Thus, of total local government employment in England, 48 per cent is accounted for by the education service and 27.1 per cent of these are teachers. A further 9.5 per cent are in the social services and 12.9 per cent in miscellaneous services (a category covering such central service departments as treasurers). Those services where one would anticipate a high proportion of manual workers (e.g. refuse collection) account for a small proportion of total employment (2.5 per cent). The proportions for all these services are of the same order in Scotland and Wales. White collar workers outnumber manual in full-time local government employment by two to one, although no separate figures are available for professionals and managers (*Department of Employment Gazette* 1977).

Local government control of information and expertise, as measured by the number and type of personnel employed, is particularly important for showing that central departments can be dependent on local authorities for information at the same time as local authorities are dependent upon central departments for finance.

Consequences of institutional diversity

The comparison of local governments adds further weight to the conclusion derived from the analysis of central decision processes, that policy-making in Britain is fragmented. The seeming ability of politicians to impose complete reversals of policy, enshrined in the doctrine of parliamentary and (through party majorities) governmental supremacy, is greatly undermined by the ability of nominally subordinate bodies to persist with their own organisational goals. Such recalcitrance may limit the damage which 'U-turns' might otherwise inflict, and it certainly ensures that local preferences are represented (particularly where elected local councils are involved). But it imposes even more constraints on the 'rational' planning and co-ordination of national resource allocations.

The existence of this underlying diversity is often overlooked – for example, in the assertion that lócal autonomy has been eroded by central government's fiscal policies. By focusing on the many resources that may be deployed, it has been shown that relationships cannot be analysed solely in financial terms. And relationships differ between the traditional areas of the United Kingdom and between individual types of local authority. Some of this variety has been illustrated by the examples given earlier. Although any typology of behaviour in intergovernmental relations must necessarily be tentative given the limited amount of research which has been done, it is possible to identify some of the strategies employed:

1 *Authoritative allocation*: through its command of resources, especially constitutional and legal resources, the government can determine the relationships between public sector organisations (e.g. the reorganisation of local government; Local Government Planning and Land Act 1980).

2 *Co-option*: incorporating local government into central decision-making (e.g. Consultative Council on Local Government Finance).

3 *Consultation*: central government initiates discussion of its proposals with local government without committing itself to any modifications (e.g. Green Papers, White Papers).

4 *Bargaining*: each unit of government commands resources required by another or others and they attempt to agree the terms of any exchange (e.g. nursery education).

5 *Competition or disruption*: the units of government cannot agree on goals (policy), so each deploys its resources to achieve its own goals, ignoring the other party(ies) (e.g. comprehensive education).

6 *Non-compliance or confrontation*: local authorities defy central government and break the law by refusing either to terminate an illegal policy or to implement a statutorily prescribed policy (e.g. Clay Cross).

This list of strategies is by no means complete nor is it clear how frequently the various strategies are employed. Certainly Griffiths (1966: 515) has argued that central departments have very different attitudes towards local government, distinguishing between laissez-faire, regulatory and promotional departments; and Regan (1977: 33–4) has argued that the self-same differences exist *within* particular departments. There can be little doubt, therefore, that there is considerable variation in patterns of behaviour in central–local relations. The problem is to systematise such information and develop adequate generalisations. Ideally, it should be possible to compile an empirical taxonomy: that is, identify the dimensions along which intergovernmental relations vary; compare actual variations in behaviour; and ultimately explain such variations by reference to such factors as the type of local political system. The importance of such an exercise cannot be overestimated because the study of intergovernmental relations is pervaded by inaccurate descriptions. For example, it is commonly asserted that the Scottish Office is more corporate in its dealings with local authorities, has closer relations with them, and exercises more effective control than English Departments (*Report of The Committee of Inquiry into Local Government Finance* 1976: 87). This description is misleading. Although there are many differences between central–local relations in Scotland and those in England, the available evidence does not support the hypothesis that there is more centralisation in Scotland (Page 1978: 69). Given the continuing pressure to produce a better co-ordinated response to economic difficulties, it would be as well for any reform proposals to be grounded in an accurate description of the existing situation. Academic concerns and public policy problems do not always coincide, but they do here.

A second consequence of variations in intergovernmental relations is that citizens receive different services and varying levels of service, depending on their physical location. Expenditures reflect but do not adequately capture this variation. To take just one example, the content of educational policy in Scotland is not the same as in England. To the extent that this differentiation more sensitively matches local needs, the responsiveness of governmental institutions is enhanced. One danger, however, is that accountability is obscured. So many bodies are involved in the delivery of services that none can be held precisely responsible for their non-delivery or poor quality.

There are of course strategic advantages for politicians and administrators in this situation. It leaves them more freedom of action and scope for manoeuvre in negotiations with other bodies. A local authority faced with the task of cutting services can blame central government. Central governments trying to control inflation in the economy can blame their lack of progress on overspending by local authorities. This problem is not peculiar to local authorities in their relations with central departments. The minority report of the Kilbrandon Commission criticised the profusion of *ad hoc* nominated bodies and called for them to be subject to democratic control by elected regional governments (Commission on the Constitution 1973: II, 83). The National Economic Development Office report on the nationalised industries commented:

In current conditions in Britain the management of any large industrial concern is a complex and difficult business. Attitudes to the social responsibilities of companies are changing; the role of the employees and trade unions in decision taking is being widely debated.

In the nationalised industries these problems are accentuated; because they are not subject to the same market disciplines as the private sector there is more scope for argument about their proper role and objectives.

Our enquiry has left us in no doubt that the existing framework of relationships, developed under governments of both main political parties, is unsatisfactory and in need of radical change . . .

— there is a lack of trust and mutual understanding between those who run the nationalised industries and those in government (politicians and civil servants) who are concerned with their affairs;
— there is confusion about the respective roles of the boards of nationalised industries, Ministers and Parliament, with the result that accountability is seriously blurred;

— there is no systematic framework for reaching agreement on long-term objectives and strategy, and no assurance of continuity when decisions are reached;

— there is no effective system for measuring the performance of nationalised industries and assessing managerial competence (NEDO 1976: 8).

This could be taken as a summary of the problem for all species of sub-national government. Ambiguity in the allocation of responsibilities has led to confused lines of accountability which is tantamount to there being no accountability at all.

Such a situation of course further compounds problems of implementation. The blurring of responsibility not only makes it more difficult for ordinary individuals to hold decision-makers to account, it also makes it difficult for decision-makers themselves to know precisely whose co-operation or compliance is required. As a result it is much easier to prevent action than to take it: a consequence that applies to all British governmental bodies in their dealings with each other.

There has been a growing awareness of these problems, particularly on the part of central government, which has become concerned about its inability to control local expenditure. The first major manifestation of this concern was the appointment of the Committee of Inquiry into Local Government Finance (Layfield) in 1974, followed by the creation of the Consultative Council on Local Government Finance (CCLGF) in 1975. While the former was to identify the means to improve the financial relationship between central and local government, the latter was to provide a forum for discussing common problems and, more importantly, it represented an attempt to create a local government 'peak' association at the national level. Neither achieved major changes in the relationship, although both made a positive contribution, but such gradualist (or incremental) improvements were swept aside by the maelstrom of a new Conservative Government in 1979. Committed to reducing public expenditure, the new Government posed perhaps the most serious threat to local autonomy in the post-war period: a threat known unprepossessingly as the Local Government Planning and Land Act 1980. With this Act, the Secretary of State for the Environment, Michael Heseltine, abolished the needs and resources elements of the Rate Support Grant and introduced the controversial Block Grant. To simplify, the most significant innovations were the introduction of grant-related expenditure (GRE) and the grant-related poundage schedule (GRPS). In future, the Secretary of State will estimate for *each* local authority how much it needs to spend (GRE). He will also specify the 'price' (in terms of the rate to be levied) for the various levels of expenditure (GRPS). Thus 'all authorities should face the same "price" if they incur expenditure equal to their GRE, and ... they should all face the same "price" for any particular deviation in expenditure from their GRE' (Bramley and Evans 1980: 5). The amount of grant actually paid will be the difference between the total expenditure of the local authority and the amount of income raised (notionally) 'by applying to the authority's total rateable value the scheduled poundage corresponding to the deviation from GRE' (Bramley and Evans 1980: 7). Crucially, these changes will penalise 'overspending' authorities. A local authority with a high level of expenditure (i.e. a high deviation from its GRE) will find that the corresponding poundage demanded by the GRPS will, at a certain threshold, lead to a reduction in grant. To summarise these changes in a few words, for the first time central government has direct rather than indirect controls over the level of expenditure of the individual local authority.

Its ability to specify such controls testifies to the considerable constitutional resources that British central government enjoys under a formally unitary system. Effectively imposing them, or preserving them from erosion, may be another matter, particularly in the light of local governments' technical expertise and control over much necessary information.

Efforts at central control are made more difficult by the fact that local authorities are themselves strongly differentiated internally, between their major departments. To a considerable extent it is not a question of central government dealing with a recalcitrant local council, but the various departments of central government dealing with separate departments locally. Each may know more about the views and activities of its contact at the other level of government than they do about the position of other departments and specialists at their own level. Confusion and ambiguity, as well as bargaining, conflict and downright imposition, are the stuff of intergovernmental relationships in the United Kingdom.

If the mace has been the central political metaphor of the British system of government for most of the twentieth century, then the 'maze' seems the more appropriate metaphor for the remaining years. The mace, or the myth of parliamentary sovereignty, fosters a distorted picture of the reality. The maze, or the complex interdependencies of public sector organisations, presents a simplified but nonetheless more realistic picture of events. Britain does not have a federal constitution. However, a formally constituted federal system is not the only form of government that allows sub-national units of government to influence the outcome of the policy process. As Finer (1947: 21) argued:

'We have not decentralisation, but a small sphere of almost complete freedom side-by-side with an organised integration based on a national will, mitigated by free discretion to adapt and apply it to the local circumstances. What name to give it we do not know.'

And no matter what term is ultimately preferred – whether it be unitary, federal or some variant of these – nonetheless it remains clear that:

'It is an illusion to pretend that government as a whole represents a cohesive or comprehensive totality or that its range of activities and the distribution of responsibilities among the various arms and tiers of government represent a designed and manageable system related to the present day needs of the community. In reality, government is an agglomerate of innumerable accretions that have compounded over the centuries and which are now controlled by a series of somewhat unrelated processes and arrangements supported by an even more detached, yet complex and ambiguous, financial mechanism' (Committee of Inquiry into Local Government Finance 1976, Appendix 2, 281–2).

Appendix: Sources for Chapter 5

Compiling the statistics for this chapter was an exercise fraught with difficulty and it is particularly important to note both the sources of information and the assumptions underlying the compilation of the tables. Where possible, a single source has been placed at the foot of each table and this source provides the requisite information. For a number of tables, however, the data was less readily available and this appendix provides a *brief* guide to sources and assumptions.

Table 5.2

As indicated in the text, particular problems surround non-departmental organisations. The figures are taken from Bowen (1978) and Holland (1979). Neither source is accurate and the range given must be seen as a rough approximation. The operational definition of departments is taken from Hood, Dunsire and Thompson (1978). The data on local government is from the *Municipal Year Book*.

Table 5.3

Identifiable public expenditure is that expenditure which can be identified from public records as having been incurred in each country, but excluding expenditure on defence, overseas services, and debt interest. Identifiable public expenditure was approximately 80 per cent of total public expenditure in 1976–77.

Table 5.7

There are numerous sources for this table. Population figures are from Chartered Institute of Public Finance and Accountancy, *Local Government Trends 1976*. Expenditure figures are from Chartered Institute of Public Finance and Accountancy, *Return of Rates 1976–77* (some of the population figures are also from this source); Department of the Environment, *Local Government Financial Statistics 1976–77*; Chartered Institute of Public Finance and Accountancy (Scottish Branch), *Rating Review 1976–77*; Chartered Institute of Public Finance and Accountancy, *Housing Statistics. Part 2. Housing Revenue Account 1976–77*; Department of the Environment for Northern Ireland, *District Councils: Summary of Statements of Accounts Year Ended 31 March 1977*.

Population figures differ slightly from those presented in Table 5.1 since both sets of figures are estimated upon a different basis.

Expenditure figures refer to net expenditure only on the Rate Fund account plus *gross* expenditure on the housing revenue account. Rate Fund contributions to the Housing Revenue Account have been subtracted from the Rate Fund account to avoid double counting. Gross figures broken down by individual authorities are unavailable for the Rate Fund account. For Northern

Ireland, net expenditure is defined as total expenditure on the Rate Fund account minus income from fees and charges.

Table 5.8

The appendices to the Acts noted under sources list the legislation amended or repealed by the constituting legislation. The extent to which a particular local government system is subject to specific legislation can be estimated by the number and percentage of these amended or repealed Acts. The analysis could not be extended to England and Wales because territorially specific Acts are not clearly indicated.

Table 5.9

The sources are the same as those for Table 5.7.

The general grant in Northern Ireland is allocated on a different basis from the RSG in the remainder of Britain.

Specific grants includes specific grants included in the RSG, supplementary grants (such as the Transport Supplementary Grant) and mandatory student award grants.

Total grants per head includes only those grants to the rate fund revenue and housing revenue accounts and excludes, for example, capital grants and grants for rent rebates. The table does not include the domestic element of the Rate Support Grant which is given in aid of domestic ratepayers.

Total grants are here expressed as a percentage of the total rate fund net expenditure plus housing revenue gross expenditure as given in Table 5.5.

General sources

Birrell, D. and Murie, A. (1980) *Policy and government in Northern Ireland*, Gill & Macmillan, Dublin.

Blackstone, T. (1971) *A fair start: the provision of pre-school education*, Allen Lane, The Penguin Press.

Bowen, G. (1978) *Survey of fringe bodies*, C.S.D.

Bramley, G. and Evans, A. (1980) *SAUS/ADC block grant training package*, School for Advanced Urban Studies, Bristol.

Commission on the Constitution (1973) I *Report*, Cmnd 5460; II *Memorandum of dissent*, Cmnd 5460–I, HMSO.

Commission of Inquiry into Local Government Finance (1976) *Report*, Cmnd 6453, Appendix 2, *Evidence by the local authority associations*, HMSO.

Department of Employment Gazette, November 1977.

Griffith, J.A.G. (1966) *Central departments and local authorities*, Allen & Unwin.

Hogwood, B. (1979) The tartan fringe: quangos and other assorted animals in Scotland, *Studies in public policy* **34**.

Holland P. (1979) *Quangos, quangos, quangos*, Adam Smith Institute, London.

Hood, C., Dunsire, A. and Thompson, S.K. (1978) 'So you think you know what government departments are?' *Public administration bulletin* **27** (August): 20–32.

Jones, G.W. (1975) 'Varieties of local politics', *Local government studies* (1) **2**: 17–32.

Keating, M. and Rhodes, M. (1979) 'Is there a regional level of government in England?' *Studies in public policy* **49**.

Madgwick, P, and James M (1979) 'Government by consultation: the case of Wales' *Studies in public policy* **47**.

National Economic Development Office (1976) *A study of the UK nationalised industries*, HMSO.

Page, E. (1978) 'Why should central-local relations in Scotland be different to those in England?', *Public Administration Bulletin* **28** (December): 51–72.

Parry, R. (1980) 'The territorial dimension in United Kingdom public employment', *Studies in Public Policy* **65**.

Rhodes, R.A.W. (1981) *Control and power in central–local government relationships*, Gower, Farnborough Hants.

Regan, D (1977) *Local government and education*, Allen & Unwin.

Sharpe, L.J. (1979) 'Modernising the localities: local government in Britain and some comparisons with France', in J. Lagroye and V. Wright, eds, *Local government in Britain and France*, Allen & Unwin.

Stanyer, J. (1976) *Understanding local government*, Fontana/Collins, Glasgow.

Chapter 6
The European Communities

Community Institutions

Accepting the analogy with a maze, has membership of the European Community added another element of confusion to British decision-making, blurring the lines of responsibility and accountability still further? Or has the necessity of producing a single British view to put to the other members helped straighten out the tangles? As we shall see, there is something to be said on both sides of this question.

We should note at the outset that the Community itself is not a single institution. At least four separate bodies are involved in the Community relationship with British governments. The best known is the European Commission, a body of fourteen technocrats located in Brussels; two nominated by each of the four big countries in the Community (Britain, France, Italy and West Germany) and one nominated by each of the smaller countries (Denmark, Ireland, Netherlands, Belgium, Luxembourg and Greece). The job of the Commission is to initiate all Community legislation, and send its policy proposals for decision by the Council of Ministers (which we describe below). In making proposals, the Commission consults with the various national governments, interest groups, etc. It also mediates Council decisions. In addition, the Commission has the task of implementing numerous regulations emanating from the Treaty of Rome (the original agreement which set up the Community) and from previous Council decisions. The Commission sees that the Treaty is observed by member states, and any infringements may be reported to the Court of Justice of the European Communities, the second major community body which affects Britain and which sits in Luxemburg. The Court, consisting of one judge from each of the member states, ensures the observance of Community laws. Its decisions are made by majority verdict, and are binding on member states.

The Commission is often viewed as the community institution most likely to interfere in British affairs. It is certainly true that in the implementation of policy it is vested with authority that is independent of national governments. But the Commission is still tied by decisions made by the Council of Ministers. The more significant development is the supreme authority of the

Court over British courts and over Parliament. Traditionally, courts in Britain have seen themselves as merely interpreting Acts of Parliament. To what extent this view is correct we shall see in Chapter 7. The explicit task of the European Court, however, is to ensure that the Acts of national parliaments or governments do not conflict with the founding agreements of the Community embodied in the Treaty of Rome. For the first time Britain has in this Treaty a written constitution that limits the supremacy of Parliament, a fact that renders the position of the Court very important.

The third major Community body is the Council of Ministers, which again meets in Brussels. The Council consists of a General Council and various technical councils. The foreign ministers of member states meet in the General Council, while ministers for particular policy areas such as agriculture meet in the technical councils. Associated with the ministerial councils is the Committee of Permanent Representatives (COREPER in Community jargon). COREPER I 'shadows' the Foreign Ministers and consists of the national ambassadors to the Community. COREPER II consists of the deputy ambassadors. Associated with it are numerous committees and working parties of appropriately qualified national civil servants. All these bodies carry out detailed preparatory work for the meetings of corresponding ministers.

The single-chamber European Parliament (whose members were first directly elected for 'Euro-constituencies' in June 1979; Britain has eighty-one such constituencies) is the fourth major community body. It meets for one part of the year in Strasbourg and for another part in Luxembourg, often holding committee hearings in Brussels. It does a great deal of its work in specialised committees like the select committees of the British Parliament. Although its members belong to six major party groups (Socialist, Liberal, Christian Democrat, Progressive Democrat, Conservative and Communist) and some small groupings, party divisions do not dominate its life as they do the House of Commons. This is partly because its competence is limited, so there is little as yet to divide over. Its major powers – to dismiss the Commission and reject the Budget – can be wielded only with a two-third majority. Its main influence is through publicity and investigation where it has extensive and increasing scope, particularly in regard to the Commission. Apart from the Parliament the main representative body is the Economic and Social Committee, but this is merely a consultative meeting of business and union interests with no formal powers.

Figure 6.1 graphs relationships between the European bodies. The outcomes of Community deliberations are expressed in directives, regulations, opinions and resolutions emanating from the Council of Ministers, and in judgements and opinions of the European Court. We shall consider later how these impinge on British governments and in turn are influenced by them.

Community membership as a political issue

Most people would agree that Community membership has far-reaching implications for British politics. It is interesting however, that by far the most visible have been connected not with the detailed provisions of the Treaty of

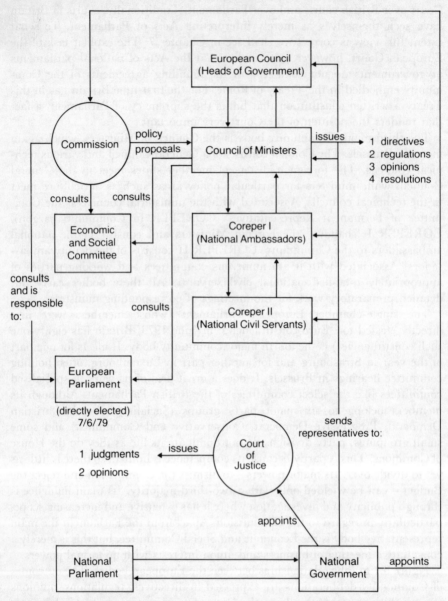

Figure 6.1 European Community institutions and their relationships with each other and with national bodies

Rome but with the conflict over membership itself. The significance of the conflict lies in its cross-cutting of party lines. Only the Liberals have been consistently united (since 1958) on a pro-Community stance. The Labour and Conservative parties have both been deeply divided. In the parliamentary vote on the terms of accession which took place in October 1971, thirty-nine Conservative opponents voted against their own party whip. Heath's Conservative Government was dependent for its victory on the pro-Community vote of sixty-nine Labour MPs and the handful of Liberals in the House. A futher twenty Labour MPs abstained. By the end of the decade, the Conservative Party was relatively united in support of the Community. At least, the party did not seriously contemplate withdrawal. The Labour Party, on the other hand, remains seriously divided over Community membership, with overwhelming approval of a motion for British withdrawal at the National Conference of 1980. Broadly, the division over Community membership matches the division between the right and left wings of the party. Though there are many other issues which divide them, passions have run higher on the European issue than on almost any other issue. Prominent members of the pro-Community right have threatened to resign from the party in the event of a future Labour Government withdrawing Britain from the European Community. Indeed, many have already left in response to the Party's current position. One of the major questions on which the Social Democrats withdrew from the Labour Party to form their own party was their support of EC membership against the Conference Resolution.

The question of membership was also associated with two major constitutional innovations in 1974–75. In the general election of 1974 the Labour Party had kept the debate over EC membership alive by making a commitment in the Party manifesto to renegotiate the terms of entry and hold a popular referendum on the new terms. Following the defeat of the Conservatives, the new Labour Government kept its word. Terms were renegotiated, and in June 1975 a referendum was held which confirmed Britain's membership of the Community. In the process, two established political conventions were broken. First, the referendum itself challenged the traditional notion of parliamentary sovereignty. Though parliamentary sovereignty has long ceased to mean that political power resides only in Parliament, it does at least mean that Parliament is the supreme law-making body. Certainly, in this sense, the electorate has never been considered sovereign. In declaring that the Labour Party would be bound by the results of the referendum, the Prime Minister effectively usurped the sovereignty of parliament. In the absence of a party position on EC membership, MPs were being told to vote, not according to their unbiased opinions, mature judgements and enlightened consciences, but according to the 'will of the people'. Four years later, the precedent of the EC referendum was called upon to hold a referendum in Scotland and Wales on the Government's devolution Bill. On any future constitutional change we can clearly expect strong pressures to emerge for the electorate to express its views directly.

The second long-standing political convention to be challenged by the conflict over EC membership was the doctrine of 'collective cabinet responsibility'.

In an attempt to keep the Labour Party and the Labour Cabinet 'united', the Prime Minister temporarily relaxed the convention whereby ministers are expected to defend the majority decisions taken in Cabinet. An 'agreement to differ' was allowed, and Cabinet ministers publicly opposed one another during the referendum campaign. In 1978 on the question of direct elections to the European Parliament, Cabinet ministers were once again allowed to differ in public speeches.

An important underlying factor in the membership debate has thus been the growth of political participation, which has both stimulated debate and been fostered by it. The EC is clearly too important an issue to be determined unilaterally by governments in terms of their own assessment of the public good. It has thus acted as a catalyst for political change, which may have important effects on the traditional aloof style of the British executive.

Much British hostility to the EC appears to be based, at first glance, on economic grounds. There have been the perennial complaints about the costs of the Common Agricultural Policy (the use of a Fund financed by levies on imports of foodstuffs, to keep up prices for Community produce) and about the effect of EC membership on the competitive position of British industry. More recently, the size of Britain's budget contribution has become an issue of controversy. At the root of most opposition, however, is concern over the political and/or constitutional implications of EC membership. The main issue has been the loss of sovereignty by national political institutions to the European Community. Given the controversies over this point, discussion is too often superficial and couched in political rhetoric. Inevitably certain structural constraints are imposed by membership on British domestic and international policies. What is usually not mentioned is Britain's considerable influence over Community policy through government participation in its decision-making bodies. In the remainder of this chapter we shall examine both aspects of the present situation.

The European Communities and British government

In acceding to the Treaty of Rome in January 1973, Britain was accepting a body of law which formally committed governments to certain common European policies, and to defined procedures for reaching decisions on these policies and enforcing their implementation. The Treaty of Rome, however, cannot always be taken at face value. Like many national constitutions, it often deals with prescriptions and intentions rather than hard realities. It is, too, a document that is subject to various interpretations, at least in areas where the European Court has not been asked to pronounce. It is difficult, then, to pin down the precise characteristics of the European Community and the ways in which Community membership affects national governments. The EC is also an evolving organisation, moving when it can into new policy areas or those areas of common action designated by the Treaty of Rome but not yet implemented. In some policy areas, the progress has been smooth and straightforward; in other areas, innumerable setbacks to common action have occurred. Equally difficult to describe generally are the decision-making structures. Sometimes, it is all too easy to point to the dominance of national governments in the making of common policies. But there are certainly instances in which Community institutions such as the Commission and the Court of Justice exercise considerable authority. Despite these problems in generalising about the characteristics of the European Community, it is useful to examine the effects of the EC on British Governments in terms of (a) the substantive areas of EC policy and action; (b) the EC policy-making process; and (c) implementation of EC policies.

Substantive areas of EC policy

The EC has moved with varying degrees of success towards the creation of a customs union, then a common market, and finally the harmonisation of social and economic policies. The final stage implies full political union. It is in the creation of a customs union that EC policies have been notably successful. Under the terms of the Treaty, the British government ceded its authority to fix quotas or taxes on imported goods (tariffs) and to subsidise exports independently. The General Agreement on Tariffs and Trade (GATT) is the international organisation under which tariffs and trading agreements are fixed. But GATT negotiations are now conducted by the Commission on behalf of Britain and other EC member states. Thus what was once an area of national competence has become an area of EC competence. The British government is not excluded completely from taking action on tariffs. But that action must be approved by the Commission and fit within the framework of GATT provisions negotiated by the Commission. Thus, in February 1980 the British government sought and gained permission from the Commission to fix import quotas on certain US synthetic textiles. The Commission allowed the British government to freeze 1980 imports at the level of the average volume for the previous two years. A similar request, however, to limit the import of tufted carpets into Britain from the United States was not allowed.

Though trading agreements for tufted carpets seem a world away from the controversies of high politics they are, nonetheless, part of a range of tariff questions which have vital importance for the British economy. As tariff negotiations have become the responsibility of the Community, so have national governments lost an important weapon in their armoury of economic policies. Governments ignoring tariff regulations and taking unilateral action can soon find themselves at odds with the Community and legally bound to pursue policies in accordance with the Rome Treaty. Where governments have in fact ignored Community directives, as in the case of France in the 1975 'wine war' with Italy and the 1980 surcharge on British lamb imports, there is strong Community pressure on the recalcitrant state to bring policies into line with common practice.

While the EC is firmly established as a customs union, progress has not been so rapid in the building of a common market. A common market implies a higher stage of co-operation than a customs union. It involves the free movement of labour and capital and the elimination of barriers to competition. The

Treaty of Rome is quite clear in setting out the various provisions for the creation of a common market. But these provisions have been enforced quite haphazardly. Take the case of the free movement of capital. Throughout the 1970s, the British government placed limits on the amount of money that British citizens could send abroad either for investment or consumption. Though the limits placed on money sent to EC member states were higher than those for non-EC states, such limits were not sanctioned by the Rome Treaty. Yet the Commission did very little to force British compliance with the Treaty provisions. When in 1980 the Conservative Government finally abolished exchange control regulations, it was presented as an act based on economic doctrine (and probably North Sea Oil wealth) rather than on a desire to comply with the Rome Treaty. Such a conclusion seems even more justified when we remember that all exchange control regulations were abolished, not merely those that applied to capital transfers to the European Community.

Progress towards eliminating the barriers to competition has also been haphazard. Fiscal harmonisation has proceeded to the point where there is a common turnover tax (VAT) throughout the European Community. But the British government, like other EC governments, has still retained its prerogatives in many other areas of taxation, such as income tax. Even where VAT is concerned, each government remains free to fix the rate at which tax is charged. Community control of certain discriminatory taxation policies has been more evident. British whisky producers, for instance, were pleased to see the European Court's outlawing of discriminatory taxation on certain kinds of alcoholic spirits. In some EC member states, such as Denmark and Italy, it had been government practice to impose lower duties (taxes) on home-produced spirits than on those produced elsewhere.

Other areas of competition policy also show uneven development. The granting of subsidies by national governments, for instance, is illegal under EC competition rules, except within the (officially defined) less developed regions. In Britain, these regions consist of Scotland, Wales, Northern Ireland and much of the northern part of England. The EC, through a ruling of the European Court, was able in 1978 to prevent the British government from giving a subsidy to pig farmers. But, over the same period, there seemed much less willingness on the part of the EC to control the activities of the National Enterprise Board in giving preferential loans to British industry. British Leyland and British Steel are notable examples of firms receiving government aid which might be construed as illegal under the terms of the Rome Treaty.

The Commission has also been eager to achieve agreement on rules for awarding public sector contracts. While national governments continue to give preference to domestic firms in awarding government contracts, a common market cannot be said to exist. Understandably, perhaps, governments of the various EC member states have shown some reluctance in formulating a common policy. As a consequence, progress has been slow. The Commission has had more success in achieving agreement on Community-wide specifications for manufactured products. So long as each national government issues its own specifications, markets are defined by national boundaries. British electric fires, for instance, could not be sold in France because they did not meet French safety specifications for such appliances. Firms could compete throughout the EC only through the costly business of gearing production to meet the specifications of each member state. In such circumstances, home firms are distinctly advantaged in their domestic markets. Much of the energy of Community administrators is focused on common product specification and over 2,000 directives have been issued on this point.

Legal directives of this kind stand rather outside the usual practice of British courts or the British Civil Service. Certainly government ministers issue (or have issued in their name) administrative or statutory instruments of various kinds, which are in effect directives. They are usually more general in both application and style, however, and are designed to fill in the details, or alter the scope as circumstances change, of the Act of Parliament which empowers them to be made. Moreover the text has usually to be laid before Parliament in some way (if only in the sense that the instrument applies if no objection is lodged within a fixed number of days).

Stemming from continental traditions of administrative law, the Community directives are much more detailed. They do not base themselves on Acts of either the British or European Parliament but on the independent responsibility of the Council of Ministers to enforce the Treaty of Rome. In framing technical directives the Commission has of course consulted various interests, as the British Civil Service would do in its own sphere. After such consultation the legally binding form of the directive represents a direct imposition of state authority on the regulated interest. The British tradition, particularly with the professions and business, would be to reach an informal understanding with interest group representatives and leave its enforcement in their hands (as with the General Medical Council for doctors, or the Milk Marketing Board).

The effect of direct governmental imposition is heightened in the British case by the fact that many directives framed in the 1960s before Britain became a member, and hence without consultation with British interests, were imposed en bloc on her accession to the Community. This is an area where Community practices are introducing new procedures into Britain. Given government impatience with long processes of consultation in the face of what they see as a mounting crisis, there may be a temptation to emulate the authoritative style of the Commission directives within their own sphere, particularly as these impinge on wider and wider areas of life.

The trade and industrial policies reviewed above represent only some of the directions in which the EC has moved in order to develop a common market within Europe. In the industrial sector, as we have seen, the process is by no means complete. There is a dual problem: first, that of reaching agreement on common policies, and then in enforcing those common policies. In the commercial sector of the economy, there has been still less progress. National laws, for instance, still prevent French and Italian citizens from purchasing life insurance, or indeed any other form of insurance, on the British market. It is only in the agricultural sector that the EC has made major progress towards the creation of a common market, through the Common Agricultural Policy

(CAP). In this case, the common market has been achieved by an EC price support system covering most agricultural products. Prices are fixed at the Community level.

The CAP represents one of the few instances of the successful harmonisation of national policies at the European level. It is criticised in Britain because of the effect of the price support system in raising consumer food prices. Nonetheless it provides, or is intended to provide, basic income security for large numbers of poor agricultural producers throughout western Europe. Britain is unusual in having the smallest agricultural population in western Europe. The tiny inefficient farms found in many parts of continental Europe and Ireland are rare in Britain. Thus Britain gains little from the redistributive impact of the CAP. Since the early 1970s, the EC has been keen to promote other redistributive policies. On the initiative of Willi Brandt, then Chancellor of the German Federal Republic, the October 1972 summit of the EC heads of government in Paris called for vigorous Community action in the social field. The summit demanded a programme of action on employment training, work conditions, workers' participation, consumer protection and regional development. In 1974 a programme was approved signalling a more interventionist phase in the Community's development. Since then, further grants have been available for the restructuring of industry and the development of infrastructure, channelled through such bodies as the European Regional Development Fund and the various funds of the European Coal and Steel Community. Loans at preferential interest rates have also been made available through the European Investment Bank and similar facilities.

The supporters of these new initiatives hoped that the EC would cease to be identified merely as an organisation facilitating trade and investment for European businessmen. They hoped also that agriculture would cease to be the only major area into which EC resources were channelled. Such hopes have not been realised. The CAP still accounts for some 70 per cent of the EC's budget. Spending on other areas remains tiny by comparison, and common policies have been slow to develop.

This overview of the substantive areas of EC activity reveals the spasmodic and uncertain development of the Community. In very few areas have EC policies effectively replaced national policies. There have been interminable delays in formulating common policies, and also inconsistencies in their enforcement once they have been agreed. As far as British government is concerned, there are some areas of policy, such as tariffs and agriculture, which were once dealt with at national level and are now almost exclusively handled at Community level. This means that government departments like MAFF (Ministry of Agriculture, Food and Fisheries) have a very important European dimension to their work. But such has been the range of EC initiatives that there is hardly a government department that is not in some way involved in EC activity. Certainly, departments such as those of Trade and Industry are affected by EC membership: both are concerned with tariff policy, and must clearly bear in mind EC legislation when considering, for example, policies involving government aid to industry. Even the Home Office is affected by EC membership. As the department responsible for the issue of visas and work permits, it has been very much affected by the EC policy on the free movement of labour within the member states. Treasury policies are affected by EC policies on spending and fiscal harmonisation, etc. The list can go on. The Foreign and Commonwealth Office (FCO) is also heavily involved as the main liaison between national ministries and the EC organisations.

In terms of substantive policies, there can be little argument that Britain has become deeply enmeshed in the European Community. Though the depth of involvement differs among various policy areas, it nonetheless covers an extremely wide range of government activity. How, though, have the *processes* of British government been affected by EC membership? To answer this question, let us look now at how policies are made in the Community.

The EC policy-making process and British politics

One of the persisting doubts (among the doubters) about British membership of the EC concerns the extent to which the British government has ceded its authority in important areas of national policy to a *supranational* organisation. When Britain joined the EC, she was already a member of several other international organisations: the United Nations, The North Atlantic Treaty Organisation (NATO), the Organisation for Economic Co-operation and Development (OECD), the International Monetary Fund (IMF), etc. All these organisations involved, to some extent, an international commitment by the British government, even to the point of declaring war. The perceived difference, however, between the latter organisations and the EC is that they are *intergovernmental*. Decisions within these international organisations are made by agreement among national representatives. No government is obliged to agree to a policy that it does not want to accept. The British government, therefore, could not be told what to do and be obliged to comply. In the EC, it could be told what to do. In principle, the EC has authority over the British government.

A supranational authority was exactly what the original founders of the EC had wanted. In practice, however, the way in which policy is made in the Community shows that national governments have lost very little of their authority. The EC's founding fathers had envisaged that the *Commission*, which is the executive body, would share authority with the *Council of Ministers*, which is the decision-making body representing the various member states. One of the jobs of the Commission is to initiate all EC legislation. It formulates various policy proposals by consulting with national governments and interest groups, and then submits these proposals for consideration by the Council.

As noted above the Council consists of a General Council and various technical councils. The foreign ministers of the various member states meet as the General Council, while ministers for particular policy areas, such as agriculture, trade, social security, etc., meet in the technical councils. The decisions of the Council are issued in the form of regulations, directives, recommendations, and resolutions. Regulations have the immediate force of Community law. Directives, on the other hand, though binding on member states, leave national governments free to determine the means of carrying out the policies concerned. Thus the Community directive on direct elections to the European Parliament necessitated the British Government putting its own Bill on the elections through Parliament.

Though the above outline approximates to the formal procedures for EC policy-making, it conceals the developments since 1966 which have brought about a considerable increase in the power and authority of the Council. The Rome Treaty neither provides for the effective voting system used in the Council, nor for the growth of two important institutions linked to the Council: COREPER (The Committee of Permanent Representatives) and the European Council.

Under the terms of the Rome Treaty, a weighted voting system is used in Council decision-making, which allows policies to be determined by majority decision. In practice, however, ever since the Luxembourg Compromise in 1966, which ended a French boycott of Community institutions, any member state has been able to exercise a technical veto on a policy which it feels will threaten its vital national interests. In such cases the veto works simply by not putting the proposal to a vote. The veto powers enjoyed by each member state are extremely broad for there is no precise definition as to what constitutes vital national interests. Few governments would presume to define the vital national interests of another, or be prepared to have others judge their own. On more than one occasion the British government has successfully argued that the mesh size of fishing nets is a matter of vital national interest to Britain.

The only occasion when the Luxembourg compromise has broken down and 'vital national interests' have apparently been ignored was during the May 1982 meeting of Community agricultural ministers. The British Government was the last one to hold out on the 1982 farm price increases, already agreed by the other nine community members. Amidst growing frustration with British intransigence, the farm deal was put to the vote by the Belgian President of the Council, receiving the support of all but the British, Danish and Greek representatives. Accordingly, the price increases were approved by qualified majority.

At the time of writing, it is difficult to assess the long-term implications of this vote. Clearly there are important interests both within the Commission and in the Benelux group of nations who would like to see more issues put to the vote. This would decrease the power of individual nation states, increasing the power of the Commission and making the Community more of a supranational organisation. It is surely significant that at the time of the vote, Belgium held the presidency of the Council of Ministers (each country takes it in turn for a six-month period), and could take a certain initiative. Had the presidency been in other hands, the question might well not have been put to the vote.

What seems most likely is that the vote effectively denying Britain's 'vital' national interests will be treated as a one-off phenomenon. A majority of member states, including all the large ones, seem unwilling to see the vote as setting any kind of precedent. They point to the particular circumstances surrounding the vote. First, and most important, Britain had no objection in principle to the proposed price increases. By holding out on the issue, Britain was hoping to obtain agreement on completely different and unrelated issues, namely her budget rebate for 1982 and trade sanctions against Argentina; thus it could be claimed that on the question of farm price increases there was no threat to British interests. Second, Britain had delayed agreement on the farm deal far longer than in previous years. Governments in the other member states faced considerable political pressure at home to bring the issue to a speedy conclusion.

On the whole, the particular way in which decisions are made within the Council has meant that Britain and the other member states have increasingly viewed Community decision-making as a bargaining process. It has been in the interests of the British Government to define its national interests carefully and then engage in horse-trading both within and across policy areas. The result has been an enormous expansion of the number of bodies in which trading takes place. When a Commission proposal arrives at the Council, it is immediately sent to one of the committees or working parties attached to COREPER. These committees and working parties consist of civil servants representing each member state. Some are permanent, such as the Article 113 Committee which assists the Commission in trade and tariff negotiations, and the standing committees on agriculture and employment. Many of the working parties, however, are set up on an *ad hoc* basis; during 1979 there were approximately fifty of these working parties in operation. It is in these committees and working parties of national civil servants that the major part of Council business is handled.

It is only when a proposal cannot be agreed at the level of COREPER's working parties that it is passed up for negotiation at a higher level. In such cases, the function of the working parties will be to determine the major points at issue between the various parties. From the working parties, the proposals go first to Part II of COREPER, consisting of the deputy permanent representatives of the member states (i.e. the deputy ambassadors). If necessary, it will go to Part I of COREPER, consisting of the full permanent representatives. It is only when a matter has not been agreed at this level that it will go for discussion in the full session of the Council of Ministers.

It is in the nature of the EC bargaining process that disputes between parties tend to involve trade-offs across a whole range of issues. Such bargains can be struck most effectively by those at the centre of the policy-making process. It was a natural progression, therefore, that the European Council should have been set up in the early 1970s. The European Council is the thrice-yearly meeting of the European heads of government. Each member state takes its turn in hosting the meeting. Though having no formal basis in the Treaty of Rome, the European Council is the forum in which agreement can best be reached on the most intractable issues within the Community. It is rarely concerned with the fine details of an issue. These are left to the various technical councils and the working parties of COREPER: the Council instead seeks to influence the broad direction of EC policy and to iron out disputes among the member states. In 1979–80 the European Council discussed, among other items, Britain's budgetary contribution to the EC, which the British government claimed was disproportionately large compared to the budgetary contributions of other members. The deal that was eventually worked out to solve this problem involved the British government's agreeing to an increase in EC agricultural prices (something unpopular with British consumers), and also the rechannelling of Community money to Britain through the regional aid programmes. In this instance, then, a bargain was struck which involved three major areas of policy.

It could be said that the bargaining over Britain's contribution broke down in May 1982 when the British Government was outvoted on the farm price increases. Farm prices could no longer be kept as a bargaining ploy in negotiations over budget contributions and economic sanctions against Argentina. More to the point, however, is that Britain overestimated the strength of her bargaining hand. The fact that unlimited sanctions were agreed by eight members of the Community and that a budget compromise was also agreed just a few days after the farm vote, suggests that bargaining still has an important place to play.

As things stand, there is little doubt that the Council of Ministers and the other institutions representing member states dominate the EC decision-making process. Though the Commission has been eager to take initiatives on common policies, it has usually found itself playing a mediating role. The Commission has been obliged to accept a much more gradualist view of European integration than the one it had adopted in the early days of the Community. As studies of EC policy-making have indicated, the formulation of common policy has depended far more on the strength of support among national governments for a particular policy than upon the activities of the Commission. Even where strong member state support is forthcoming, determined opposition from another member state can effectively stifle the legislative process. It is for this reason that we are likely to see a continuation of the existing constitutional practices within the Council of Ministers.

The direct election of the European Parliament (the first elections were held in June 1979) has also made little difference to the policy-making dominance of the Council of Ministers and its associated organisations. Like the appointed European Parliament before it, the present parliament has few powers with which to challenge the authority of the Council.

What consequences, then, has the EC policy-making process had for the processes of British government? First, it is clear that the *executive branch* of British government is very closely involved with the Community decision-making process, at all stages. It is consulted by the Commission when the latter formulates its policy proposals; it is also, with the executives of the other member states, at the centre of the Council decision-making process. As a consequence, British government ministers and civil servants now make frequent trips to Brussels, engaging in meetings both with the Commission and their counterparts from other member states. Prime Ministers meet in the European Council, ministers in the Council and its technical councils, and civil servants in working parties of COREPER and other committees.

Besides the home civil servants making frequent trips to Brussels, there are also significant numbers based for longer periods at the United Kingdom Permanent Representation to the European Communities. Though this office is headed by officials from the Foreign and Commonwealth Office, approximately two-thirds of its staff consist of home civil servants from other government departments. In its own way, the Permanent Representation is a mini-Whitehall, and is thus quite different from the usual British embassy abroad. The home civil servants are seconded for approximately two-year periods. They make up many of the regular staff of COREPER's working parties. Though formally accountable to the FCO, they maintain close liaison with their home ministries.

The close involvement of the executive branch of British government in the EC policy-making process stems, of course, from the fact that policy is determined by a process of bargaining between national governments. These circumstances in turn affect the way Britain's EC policy is formulated. Clearly, in many areas of policy, British officials do not think of their role in terms of formulating a bargaining position. Relationships between the British government and the EC are very much an ongoing process, day by day and minute by minute. In this way, relationships between departmental civil servants and their opposite numbers in Community secretariats are rather like those they enjoy with some domestic interest groups (Ch. 2).

From the British point of view, much EC legislation and activity is entirely non-controversial. However, the fact that policy is decided through negotiations between national governments and that there are, on occasion, questions which arouse considerable controversy, pervades the entire policy-formulation process. The British government thus tends to define its interests in relation to the Community as a whole and the other member states. The politicisation of the EC issue in Britain is a further stimulus to think of EC policy-making in the sense of defending British interests. The simple result of these perceptions is that the Foreign and Commonwealth Office, which traditionally represents British interests abroad, has become the central co-ordinating ministry for EC policy. It organises the UK Permanent Representation in Brussels and acts as the link between the home civil servants based in Brussels and their counterparts in the Whitehall ministries. The European Communities Section in the FCO is responsible for most of the co-ordinating work; it consists of several desk-men covering different EC policy areas.

European Community membership has meant that the FCO has come to play an important new role in the domestic policy process (so far as the latter is influenced by the EC dimension). The importance that the FCO attaches to this new role is illustrated by the fact that in 1982 the Permanent Under-Secretary and the Deputy Permanent Under-Secretary of the FCO were Britain's last two ambassadors to the European Community. It might well be argued that the FCO has found a convenient new *raison d'etre* at a time when Britain's influence in the world, and therefore the role of the Foreign Office, was declining.

Though the FCO plays a co-ordinating role in formulating Britain's EC policy, it does not have the technical competence to determine that policy by itself: in discussing, for instance, the specifications of an industrial product, it is hardly within its competence to make an effective contribution. Thus there is considerable reliance on the functional ministries which do possess such expertise. Departments closely involved in formulating British EC policy in their areas of competence are the Treasury, MAFF (Agriculture and Fisheries), DoE (Environment), Trade, Industry and Energy. Most of these departments have EC sections co-ordinating their involvement with the Community. Departmental representatives liaise with the FCO, but also participate directly in meetings of specialists held under the aegis of the Commission; in the working parties and associated committees of COREPER; and also in *ad hoc* committees shadowing Council and European Council meetings. In 1979–80, for instance, the Permanent Secretary of the Treasury participated in a series of meetings with his counterparts from the other eight member states to discuss Britain's EC budgetary contribution. The functional departments also play a major role in the preparation of briefs for Council meetings.

Co-ordination of British policy is achieved for the most part through a series of informal telephone contacts among officials from interested government departments. But there is also a committee system through which EC policy can be discussed. At a basic level, there are a series of interdepartmental committees in the major policy areas. There is also considerable scope for the creation of *ad hoc* committees, bringing together the people most immediately concerned with a particular policy issue. Usually, these *ad hoc* committees are organised at the instigation of one of the functional departments. Its composition might vary widely. A committee meeting on shipbuilding subsidies, for instance, would be chaired by a representative from the Department of Industry, and include officials from the Treasury, the Department of Employment, the FCO, and possibly the Welsh, Scottish or Northern Irish Offices. Only the FCO would be represented on every committee.

Above the specialist policy committees is a European Communities Committee that oversees the preparation of briefs for the Permanent Representation and the Council meetings, and is generally responsible for the co-ordination of Britain's EC policy. There has also been an even higher level committee of top civil servants who have discussed the longer-term issues involving Britain's membership of the European Community. Almost certainly, in the light of the Labour Party's proposals to withdraw Britain from the EC, there has been high level discusion of the implications (economic, political, etc.) of withdrawal.

In its capacity as a central co-ordinating body, the Cabinet Office also plays a significant role in the formulation of Britain's EC policy. Officials from the Cabinet Office attend the regular committee meetings on the EC, and are very closely involved in the more controversial Community issues. They also play a mediating role in ironing out differences between government departments: such a mediating role is especially important in EC policy, where the government tries to present its views in Council meetings in terms of a national consensus.

Besides all the interdepartmental civil service committees concerned in formulating Britain's EC policies there are, too, political interministerial committees. These include a Cabinet Committee composed of the ministers most affected by EC activities, which regularly discusses EC issues and which is chaired by the Foreign Secretary.

Many of these arrangements for co-ordinating policy form an extension of the interdepartmental committees and negotiating sessions already described in Chapter 2. What is new is the central co-ordinating role of the Foreign and Commonwealth Office, and the opportunities for civil servants from different Ministries to work closely within the same organisation in Brussels, at the British Permanent Representation. With the additional complexity of the Community bureaucracy to contend with, we might have expected the existing fragmentation of British administration to increase. In fact, the negotiation of additional Common Market agreements seems to have been assimilated into the existing structure with considerable ease.

This may of course stem from the ability of a loose-jointed structure to adapt comfortably, but still loose-jointedly, where a tighter-knit organisation might have had to recast its entire procedures. And as we have seen, change towards greater co-ordination in British administration might have been no bad thing. It is typical that Community membership has not strengthened the hands of the Treasury, the traditional co-ordinating department; nor has it produced a notable expansion in the role of the Cabinet Office, which might have been expected to plan centrally for all the activities of government. Instead a third co-ordinator has arisen in this specialised area, one without much technical expertise and with a traditional, rather cautious, attitude. With this development the fragmentation at lower levels of British government is also reflected among the co-ordinating agencies.

The Community structure also adds substantially to the points at which agreements from other parties have to be obtained in the process of making policy. This increases the already large number of bodies with inherent blocking abilities which exist inside Britain and which we examined in the last chapter. The greater the number of decision points, the less likely is a policy to be agreed and implemented – though conversely the more extended opportunities are for affected interests to make their views heard. In light of the much greater complexity of the Community structure it is surprising and reassuring that British administrative processes have adapted to it with relative efficiency. While membership has done nothing to reduce fragmentation in British government, it has not notably increased it.

One reason for this lies in the tendency of British interest groups to work directly with departments in London rather than negotiating at one remove with Community agencies in Brussels. It is certainly true that such groups, whether employers' associations, trade unions or others, have developed links with European organisations representing their respective interests, but co-operation still seems minimal. Some interest group representatives are formally involved in EC organisations through their membership of such bodies as the European Economic and Social Committee. The latter, however, has only consultative functions. Other British interest groups have sent delegations to the Commission and the European Parliament when they have wanted to have their say on a particular issue. The problem is that policy is made in the Council through the process of bargaining between member states. Thus interest groups have found it to their advantage to focus their attention on their own national government and, indeed, on the particular government department responsible for their own policy area. The National Union of Farmers therefore seeks to influence the Common Agricultural Policy through the Ministry of Agriculture. At best, the Commission or the European MPs will be viewed as an important ally in obtaining the desired outcome. There is no doubt, though, that in the ordering of priorities the Whitehall department most immediately concerned is the first group that needs to be convinced of a particular policy. The focus of interest group activity, then, has changed little since Britain joined the Community.

The picture that emerges from our analysis of British involvement in EC policy-making is one of the dominance of the national government. For the British Parliament, the picture is not so satisfactory. Indeed, it could be argued that one of the major consequences of EC membership has been the burgeoning power of the British executive. There has certainly been a problem in exercising public control over decisions made by national governments in the Council of Ministers. From the point of view of the British Parliament, the mere fact that decisions having the immediate force of law can be made in the Council of Ministers means that Parliament is no longer the supreme law-making body in all areas.

The best that Parliament can hope for in controlling EC legislation is to exert control over the British government's negotiating position within the Council, the European Council, or COREPER. In practice, the experience of Parliament in trying to exert this control has been less than happy. When Britain joined the European Community, the Foster Committee in the House of Commons and the Maybray-King Committee in the House of Lords were set up to report on appropriate methods of scrutiny. In the Commons, the Committee on European Secondary Legislation was formed in May 1974; it consisted of sixteen members. From the beginning, it was clear that the Committee would be hard pressed to fulfil its functions of scrutiny. The Committee has the right to examine draft proposals submitted by the Commission to the Council of Ministers. These documents are supplied by the relevant Whitehall departments. However, the Committee has extremely limited powers once it has received the documents. It is *not* empowered to debate the merits or demerits of a Commission proposal; all it may do is to recommend that a particular proposal be referred for debate to a standing committee or, in certain important cases, to the House as a whole. With thirty to forty documents arriving at the Committee every day, there are few that either merit or can be given further consideration.

Once an issue has been earmarked for debate, there still remains the problem of how Parliament is to influence the government's Council negotiating position. No specific amendments are allowed to be made to the Commission proposals, and the House or standing committee may only debate on a 'take note' motion. Additional problems arise from the fact that a maximum of ninety minutes is allowed for a debate, and even this small amount of time is not made available until two hours before midnight.

From 1974 to 1976 the government was prepared to listen to the views of parliament on EC legislation, though it would not submit its own views to scrutiny. By 1976, however, the government was no longer prepared to grant even this meagre concession in all circumstances. Michael Foot, then Leader of the House, stated on behalf of the Government:

Ministers will not give agreement to any legislative proposal recommended by the Scrutiny Committee for further consideration by the House before the House has given it that consideration, unless the Committee has indicated that agreement need not be withheld, or *the Minister concerned is satisfied that agreement should not be withheld for reasons which he will at the first opportunity explain to the House.*

(The italic type emphasises the considerable freedom of action which the British government has been able to reserve for itself). The Committee faces further scrutiny problems when the Commons is in recess. No debate can be called and the Committee cannot even meet. The Chairman cannot act on his own initiative to scrutinise legislation. The fact that the parliamentary time-table is not co-ordinated with the timetable of the Council of Ministers means that the Committee is often in a position where it cannot carry out its functions. When an instrument is adopted in Council before it reaches the Committee, the limit of the government's obligation is 'that the Committee should be informed, by deposit of the relevant document and by submission of an explanatory memorandum, of instances where fast-moving documents go for adoption before scrutiny can take place'.

In view of the unfavourable procedures for adequate Commons supervision of EC legislation, it is hardly surprising that there is little rush among MPs to serve on the Scrutiny Committee. There have also been persistent calls by those serving on the Committee for an improvement in the scrutiny procedures.

The House of Lords provides a far more successful example of parliamentary scrutiny of EC legislation. Like the Commons Committee, the Select Committee on the European Community in the House of Lords was set up in 1974. It has twenty-three members on the main committee, and some eighty peers who are involved with the seven specialist subcommittees. Unlike the Commons Committee, the Lords Committee is able to call expert witnesses and debate the merits of the proposal before it. The Chairman can decide which issues to put before the Committee, and in addition the various subcommittees allow the Committee time to deal with the more important business. As in the Commons, however, debates held in the Lords on Commission proposals are limited to 'take note' motions.

The limited influence of Parliament over EC legislation cannot be laid entirely at the door of the European Community. To be sure, the fact that ministers go to Brussels to bargain in the Council of Ministers means that it is difficult to tie them down to a particular line. The policy that emerges in the Council will almost certainly be a compromise, and Parliament cannot anticipate precisely what it will be.

Denmark, in contrast, provides an interesting example of a national parliament (the Folketing) exerting considerable authority over EC legislation. The Folketing secured its position during the debate on EC membership. Under the Danish Act of Accession, the government is required to make an annual report to the Folketing and keep parliament informed of Council business. General debates on the EC are held at regular intervals, and special debates also take place. The main mechanism, however, by which the Folketing controls the government's negotiating position in the Council of Ministers is through the Market Relations Committee. The committee system is extremely well developed within the Folketing, and committees enjoy considerable authority. The Market Relations Committee is the most authoritative of all the Folketing's Committees. It is also the most prestigious. Its seventeen members, elected proportionately from the various political parties, include many former Cabinet ministers. Under the rules of procedure, the government is committed to consult with the Market Relations Committee on all Council business. The Committee meets weekly and may question ministers and civil servants involved in EC policy. The government is obliged to seek mandates from the Committee before important Council decisions. In many council sessions, Danish ministers have had extremely narrow mandates, and have, on some occasions, had to seek new mandates from the Committee before reaching agreement on a particular issue.

In the light of Danish experience, the inability of the British Parliament to control its government's negotiating position should perhaps be put down to the more general decline discussed in Chapter 3, and attributable to the dominance of a single party in government at any one time, government control of the parliamentary agenda, the poor access of parliamentarians to information and the growth of direct consultation with interest group representatives. What seems also to be the case, however, is that in Britain EC membership has allowed the executive even greater rein to escape legislative scrutiny. It seems unlikely that Parliament will be able to regain its authority. In the case of EC legislation, the European Parliament will very likely inherit it. Already, that body is a growing thorn in the side of the Council of Ministers as it attempts to exert authority over the Community budget.

As things stand at the moment, there is neither European parliamentary control nor British parliamentary control over the EC policy-making process. As a result, British EC membership has resulted in a considerable increase in executive power. It might even be said that the increase has been in bureaucratic power. It is surely significant that the only British representatives permanently based in Brussels are civil servants.

The implementation of EC policies

The last of the ways EC membership has affected British government is in regard to the implementation of policy.

Once the Council of Ministers has made a decision, it may issue a regulation or a directive. The matter then passes out of the hands of the Council. In its capacity as guardian of the Treaty, it is now the Commission's task to ensure that Community law is observed, and that national governments carry out the obligations agreed in Council. Where a directive has been issued, the Commission may find itself in the position of having to cajole a government into enacting the necessary national legislation. This happened with regard to a 1976 Council directive on the use of tachographs in the cabs of long-distance lorries. Faced with British unwillingness to enact the directive, the Commission took the British government to the European Court which ordered the British government to comply.

In enforcing the observance of Community laws, therefore, the Commission can call for a judgement from the European Court. It also has the power to impose sanctions directly on firms that violate EC competition laws. In December 1979 Pioneer was fined $6.2 million for operating a discriminatory pricing policy within the European Community. This fine amounted to 4 per cent of the company's turnover. This powerfully illustrates the point made above about the change from informal to legal enforcement of policy with Community membership.

It is, indeed, the role of the European Court in this process that may be of most significance for domestic politics. In acceding to the Treaty of Rome, EC law immediately became supreme over domestic law. For Britain, this change was particularly dramatic. Britain has never had a written constitution and Parliament has always been regarded as the supreme law-making body. There were no British courts formally empowered to consider the 'constitutionality' of a law passed by Parliament. As part of the EC, Britain is subject to the rulings of the European Court which has the authority to determine the 'constitutionality' of a British Act of Parliament (although paradoxically an Act abrogating British adherence to the Treaty would not be subject to review).

The supremacy of the European Court has made it an important influence on social and political change in the member states (including Britain). In the case of *Smith* v. *Macarthy* a Mrs Wendy Smith employed by a pharmaceutical company brought a case against her employers who were paying her £10.00 less than a man who had previously been employed in the same job. The firm was found in violation of article 119 of the Treaty of Rome. No doubt the firm would also have been in violation of the EC's 1975 directive on equal pay. An interesting aspect of the case was the claim by the advocate-general that a woman should be paid the same as a man even where only a hypothetical comparison could be made. As was noted at the time, a finding of this type would go further than Britain's own equal pay act. Not just on equal pay but also on consumer and environmental protection, action in the European Court may well represent a route whereby individuals and special interest groups can effect change. Accordingly, the European Court, in a similar way to the Supreme Court in the United States, is well able to take an important part in British politics. The slowness of the decision-making process within the Council of Ministers may actually push it into doing so.

Chapter 7

Judicial decision-making

British governments have complied not only with judgements of the Court of Justice of the European Communities (to give the 'European Court its full name), but also with the more controversial rulings of the Commission and Court of Human Rights. This was set up at Strasbourg under the European Convention on Human Rights to which the British Government is a signatory. Its doubts on the validity of terrorist interrogations in Northern Ireland in the early 1970s moved governments to amend procedures and instructions on this point to provide more safeguards for the suspect, even though the court has mainly moral authority on its side rather than the economic sanctions of the Community. In 1982 the Court ruled that children whose parents disapproved of their corporal punishment should not be caned or strapped in British schools – a decision which materially affected the structure of authority in education and was followed by government circulars designed to restrict the practice so severely as almost to extinguish it.

In all, the British government was found in the wrong on no less than eight occasions by the Court of Human Rights in the period 1975–82, on matters ranging from the retention of flogging in the Isle of Man to restrictions imposed by the Home Office on prisoners' rights to communicate with their lawyers. In all cases the condemnation prompted some action by the government – sometimes a substantial modification in the offending practice if not its outright abolition (though there was little it could do to get the Manx Parliament to comply).

One reason for the unusually high number of cases in which Britain has been cited is the activity of British interest groups in bringing cases to the Court. Otherwise weak groups have recognised it as a highly effective means of influence and publicity. In view of their success it is possible that not only European courts but also domestic courts will become regular targets for interest group activities during the 1980s.

Is the political influence of the European courts matched by the British courts within their own domestic jurisdiction? We have already referred to the courts as an 'alternative government' with a very extensive jurisdiction and areas of independent decision-making. Given the division of power between central departments on the one hand, and quangos and local governments on the other, it would be very surprising if the courts did not have similar scope. We shall examine this point below, along with the criteria used to decide cases; and how far this contributes on the one hand to the fragmentation of policy-processes, and on the other to the protection and representation of the individual.

Court structure and work

First, however, we shall summarise the way in which courts are organised and the broad nature of the work they do. As with local government, there are different court systems in different areas of the United Kingdom: one for England and Wales, one for Northern Ireland and one for Scotland. The English system (also covering Wales) is by far the most important in terms of numbers of cases and people dealt with. Table 7.1 summarises its main features. The bottom tier consists of a fairly unique institution, the magistrates' courts, where men or women without legal training (justices of the peace: JPs) have basic criminal jurisdiction (involving violence against people and offences against property such as theft) and some social and family cases (involving disputes between husbands and wives, for example). The magistrates are unpaid and work part time. Local notables such as doctors, clergy and trade unionists are appointed through a secret committee for each area, but the quickest route is through nominations from local political parties. Partisanship on the bench is strongly disapproved, however, and almost unheard of. Since most political activists and local notables are middle-class, so are the magistrates. They deal with the vast majority of legal cases. As there is little central supervision of their actual work, other than the small numbers of cases appealed to higher courts, there is considerable variety in their decisions between different areas, notably on sentencing and fines. Above the magistrates' courts are the crown and county courts, staffed by professional judges, which hear more important civil and criminal cases.

Although the magistrates' and crown courts deal with most people, they are not important enough nor central enough to affect policy. This is the sphere of the higher courts located in London. They are collectively known as the Supreme Court of the Judiciary.

The first of these is the High Court, comprising about one hundred judges sitting in three different divisions and dealing both with criminal and civil cases of the greatest importance. The first of these is the Family Division, which covers matters like property settlement after divorce, adoption, child care and so on. While decisions in these areas are not what is usually seen as 'politics', making and applying rules governing our behaviour in such intensely private and sensitive areas can plausibly be seen as an exercise of power that has more real or potential impact on the lives of ordinary people than anything that an ordinary backbench MP could ever expect to have, and perhaps an impact of greater force than more clearly political matters such as the budget. The best example of this power is the way Lord Denning, one of the Chief Justices, managed over the years to ameliorate conditions for women deserted

Table 7.1 The modern English court system in outline

Court	Functions		Number of courts	Annual case load	Composition	Additional comments
	Criminal	Civil				
Magistrates Courts	Petty crime	Very limited	Several hundred	Vast	Part time lay JPs	Apart from trying minor crime, these courts vet all prosecutions in remand hearings
County Courts	None	Extensive case load for all civil cases subject to financial limits	Over 100	Nearly 2 million cases started each year; less than 5% come to trial	Circuit judges and Recorders (more than 500)	Most civil cases start and finish here, and much of the work is small claims business
Crown Courts	All	Some limited areas	Technically one court, with 97 centres	Approximately 60,000 cases put down for hearing	High Court and Circuit judges and Recorders	This is the main criminal court. It has three tiers; in the first High Court judges sit to try the most serious crimes, in others circuit judges try more minor offences. It also hears appeals from magistrates' courts and passes sentences on certain cases where conviction has taken place before magistrates
The High Court A: Chancery Division	None	Trusts, wills, tax law, company law, property, etc.		Approximately 700 trials	12 High Court judges under the Vice-Chancellor	
B: Family Division	None	Family law in general		2/3,000 defended cases	17, under the President	All divorce cases start in the County courts but defended ones may come here, as with adoption procedures

Court	Criminal jurisdiction	Civil jurisdiction	No. of cases	Composition
C: Queen's	Some appeals, mainly in public law from tribunals and magistrates courts	All civil law not dealt with else-where, especially contract and tort	1,500/2,000 full trials	44 judges under the Lord Chief Justice
Court of Appeal				The Master of the Rolls and 16 Lords Justices of Appeal. Usually operates in 3 man benches
A: Criminal Division	Most criminal appeals	None	6/7,000	It consists usually of one or two judges from the court of appeal sitting with judges from Queen's Bench Division in a bench of three.
B: Civil Division	None	Most appeals from anywhere which are not strictly criminal law	c. 1,500	
The House of Lords		Appeals from any court in England and Wales on any matter, and from Scotland and Northern Ireland in many cases. Most of the work consists of civil appeals from the Court of Appeal	50/60	Between 10 and 12 Lords of Appeal, under the Lord Chancellor (who will very rarely sit). Usually works in five-men benches
The Judicial Committee of the Privy Council		Basically this is a group of Law Lords acting as a Supreme Court of Appeal from some parts of the Commonwealth		

Note A. Case loads are very difficult to estimate because the bulk of civil cases are resolved either before coming to trial at all, or before the trial is over. The figures given are rough estimates of the number of cases that actually do come to trial, whether they are actually brought to judgment or not.

Note B. The various divisions of the High Court all play some appellate role over cases in their areas from lower courts and from tribunals. This is particularly so for the QBD which has an overall responsibility to supervise all inferior courts and tribunals.

by their husbands, by his personal interpretation of their rights, doing more in this direction than any Act of Parliament passed this century.

The Chancery Division deals with tax matters. While it may make decisions from time to time which run counter to government policy, these can be rapidly changed in the annual financial legislation passed by Parliament.

Politically, the most important part of the High Court is its biggest division, the Queen's Bench Division (QBD). This owes its importance to three roles. First, it essentially guides the development of the criminal law, both in the definition of crimes and of rules of evidence (which are usually left to common, judge-made, law) and in sentencing patterns. Second, it deals with most important cases in civil law, and even where these are actually controlled by statute (i.e. Acts of Parliament) rather than common law rules, the statutes are usually based on existing common law traditions. If this sounds innocuous, consider how vitally political is the question of when you should be liable for injuries your carelessness causes strangers. It was, for example, a civil law case coming from QBD that did more than any government managed to do up to 1982 to make the wearing of seat belts compulsory. Because of that decision, anyone injured in a car crash who was not wearing a seat belt would get damages much reduced from what he would otherwise have received, however much the other driver was at fault. No government ever contemplated a fine for not wearing a seat belt that would be anything like so punitive.

Thirdly, the most important reason for regarding the Queen's Bench Division as politically crucial is that it is the nearest thing in Britain to an Administrative Law Court of the sort found everywhere in Europe and modelled on the French Conseil d'Etat. Administrative law, the very existence of which in England is a moot point, is that branch of law which controls the behaviour of officials towards the ordinary public. Thus it is deeply involved in civil rights problems of all sorts, and also in the question of how, in a democracy, one makes sure that governments only do what they have been authorised to do by Parliament. England lacks, for example, a Bill of Rights, and there are no courts specially charged with ensuring that civil rights are observed. But the Queen's Bench Divisional Court will hear cases arising from alleged improper behaviour by governments and their agents under the traditional protection of common law rights.

What rights? They can be very trivial or very vital, and are usually somewhere between: important for the individual concerned but of no earth-shaking consequence, *taken singly*, for most of us. Cumulated, however, the public law decisions of the QBD and the Appeal Courts set the pattern of democratic rights against public authorities. For example: a market trader urinated against a wall in the market place, and promptly had his trading licence taken away by the local council. The court gave it back to him. (Should a man's livelihood be put at risk by the arbitrary reaction of local authorities to his natural functions?) In 1976-77 a Cabinet minister gave instructions to the Civil Aviation Board not to allow Mr Laker to fly people cheaply over the Atlantic, in a way that Mr Laker claimed the enabling legislation did not allow. (Should ministers be able to interfere with entrepreneurial spirit so easily unless the legislature is very clear that it wants this restriction? The courts agreed with Mr Laker.) The Home Secretary found out that people, knowing their TV licences were going up in price soon, were rather sensibly buying their next licence early at the lower cost. The BBC was losing money by this, so he tried to stop them doing so, and indeed to claim back extra money from those who had got away with it. The court did not let *him* get away with it. In these ways the court sometimes protects, sometimes opposes, the private individual against the state.

Such decisions do not go unchecked as any politically novel and potentially influential case will be appealed to a higher court. Appeals, moreover, are often granted; indeed a counter-appeal after the appeal is often granted too, returning the situation to base. There are two levels of appeal. A case decided in the High Court can be appealed first to the Court of Appeal, in either its criminal or civil division. The civil division, presided over by a senior judge known as the Master of the Rolls, hears about 1,000 cases a year, sitting in benches of three. All but a tiny minority of cases stop here; the next stage of appeal is to the Judicial Committee of the House of Lords which is entirely separate from the House of Lords as a legislative body. The Court of Appeal has usually only about thirty members, the Lords about twelve. We have a tiny judicial élite: counting the whole of the High Court, less than 200 important judges.

It is interesting to note that the recruitment area is similarly restricted. All senior judges must have been barristers and usually Queen's Counsel; and we have possibly less than 3,000 practising barristers in this country at any one time. Britain is peculiar in distinguishing between solicitors, charged with routine legal business, and the barristers (advocates in Scotland) whom they brief for major cases and who alone are entitled to appear in important courts for the opposing sides. Queen's Counsel are the most senior and successful barristers; the number with the age and experience to consider themselves suitable for judgeships in any generation is naturally much smaller.

It is in the Court of Appeal and the Judicial Committee of the House of Lords that the vital decisions are made which often have political bearings. Though the decision of course may merely ratify a decision of the High Court, which itself may ratify a decision of a magistrates court or a special tribunal, it may alternatively mean overthrowing a decision that has been agreed on by all the previous tiers.

There are in addition two other legal structures which give to English judicial officers a potential impact on politics. At a level lower than the High Court are innumerable tribunals and appeal tribunals, dealing with matters as diverse as income tax appeals, industrial injury cases, immigration and equal opportunity appeals. Though undeniably important in their own right, especially because they are partly staffed by laymen, they feed into the main court system. Appeals can be brought from such tribunals to the High Court divisions and ultimately to the House of Lords. As the courts are charged with the general supervision of this area as well as deciding the leading precedents for them, we can safely ignore them here.

Finally, there exists something called the Judicial Committee of the Privy

Council. In fact this is the Law Lords under another name. This committee acts as a final court of appeal from certain commonwealth and colonial countries. As such it often acts as a fully fledged supreme court interpreting a written constitution. The Privy Council has, for example, decided on the constitutionality of the death penalty in Singapore. But it is of little importance in British politics.

Courts in Northern Ireland, though separate, closely resemble the English, with less of an emphasis upon lay magistrates and juries. The law administered there derives largely from English common law, modified for Irish conditions and shaped to some extent by Acts of the former Northern Irish Parliament between 1922 and 1972. There is an Appeal Court in Belfast, but the judicial House of Lords has ultimate jurisdiction.

The Scots system is more distinctive. While there are district courts with lay magistrates, the major court of all work is the Sheriff Court, with jurisdiction over a considerable population and area, and powers to try all but major criminal and civil cases. The sheriff is a professional lawyer, like the judges in the Crown Courts in England. At the centre of the system are the eighteen senators of the College of Justice in Edinburgh, who man both the chief civil court, the Court of Session, and the chief Criminal Court, the High Court of Justiciary. Other senators than those who tried the original case sit as a Court of Criminal Appeal, which is the final authority in criminal cases. There are also appeals in civil cases from the Outer to the Inner House of the Session, but the final authority here is the (judicial) House of Lords, sitting with two Scottish Lords of Appeal out of the five judges.

These institutional differences are reflected in the different nature of the law administered in Scottish courts. This diverges from the English system in two major ways. The actual law, in the sense of the legal rules applied by courts, is often different from equivalent rules in England. Property law, for example, retains much more of the feudal inheritance than does the English law of real estate. Secondly, the sources of law, and the general theory of law is different. Although this difference can easily be exaggerated it is still true that Scots lawyers operate under a system heavily influenced by Roman law, as is true in continental Europe. There is no room here to discuss Scotland separately. Much of what is said below will still be true of Scottish courts and judges, but not all. It will certainly be the case, however, that any conclusions about the autonomy and political importance of English judges will apply equally, if not more, to Scottish judges (and for that matter to Northern Irish judges).

A last general point about all the legal systems is the exceptional degree of autonomy which lawyers as a profession enjoy. With regard to the practice of their profession and its ethics, they are totally self-regulating under their elected councils. Since legal ethics determine the conduct of business in court, and much of the interpretation of law, the self-government of lawyers is even more important politically than the self-government of other professions like doctors; it reaches out to the substance of law in the proceedings of the (separate) Law Commissions for England and Scotland. These are quangos charged with revision of law, and composed wholly of lawyers. Formally they deal with technical revisions of law – cleaning up obscure language, consolidating and codifying branches of law, repealing obsolete statutes – and everything they recommend has to be approved by Parliament. In practice, the matters being technical and non-controversial, their recommendations are accepted with little debate. Although technical, such revisions can have enormous importance for individuals as when they changed the basis of Scottish landholding to absolute freehold from a form of tenure where the superior still retained certain rights (such as mineral rights) and could prohibit development, for example. In some areas the Law Commissions act like a mini-legislature, except that they are nominated, not elected bodies, and are responsive to legal opinion much more than to any other influence. Assessments of their role form a good introduction to the general role of courts – primarily as we cautioned earlier, under the English system.

The political role of courts in a system without judicial review

'Judicial review' means a system in which laws and other acts of the Legislature can be overruled by a court if they are held to conflict with constitutional rules, basic human rights, or any other laws treated as superior to ordinary legislation. In the United States the Supreme Court can invalidate Acts of the Federal Congress or the State legislatures if they contradict the constitution. Courts with similar powers exist in Canada, Australia and West Germany among other countries, and as we have seen the European Court has similar powers in countries of the Community.

When this sort of power belongs to a court, its judges are clearly of political importance. Most experts would agree that no such power belongs to English courts: no Act of Parliament can be brought before a court and challenged as to its basic lawfulness (Scottish courts have asserted vague claims to do this on occasion, but have never actually done so). This is part of the general doctrine that Parliament is supreme and knows no constraint at all. In practice this is being undermined. As British courts are subordinate to the European Court in matters concerning Community law, they might have to hold, if asked, that British statutes did not have legal force where it ruled that they were inoperable. However, this is as yet hypothetical and in matters of domestic law English courts could certainly not invalidate parliamentary actions.

This of course is also true of governments, quangos, local government, and all the other bodies considered in Chapter 5. Nonetheless these can by their actions render parliamentary or even governmental action more or less effective, and sometimes a dead letter. Thus it does not follow that, because the courts cannot overrule state law, they therefore lose their political relevance. It is useful in thinking about this to note a seldom mentioned fact about other national courts that do have the power of judicial review. They seldom use it. Only a handful of Congressional Acts have been overruled in America since the 1930s, and in Canada, Australia and West Germany the use of a court to veto legislation is even rarer. But no one will try to argue that these supreme courts have stopped being politically important.

The truth is that judicial review is only one of a series of powers that courts everywhere exercise, and arguably is not the really important one anywhere. Let us list briefly the possible areas of power of our courts, the better to consider this matter. To start with, the only thing the courts in England cannot do is to say that a parliamentary Act is not valid law at all. But how restrictive this is depends on another matter: how much of the work of governing England is carried out by parliamentary Acts? The detailed answer to that question is found elsewhere in this book. Here it is enough to say that much of the exercise of power and control by the state in Britain does not involve the application to a citizen of statutes passed by Parliament. For one thing, local authority bye-laws are controllable by the courts, who may overrule them if they do not fit with the parliamentary legislation authorising them.

For example, a whole series of important cases in England during the 1960s involved the 1961 Caravan Sites Act. Under this, local authorities were given great powers to plan and control the development of caravan sites, but their effective power to do so was severely limited by the (judicial) House of Lords, who used the empowering legislation, the parliamentary Act, to curtail and alter what the local authorities wanted to do. In this and similar ways the whole of England's planning law is subject to control by the courts, and planning law is hardly a trivial matter.

Next we ought to note that many parliamentary Acts do little more than empower ministers to make detailed regulations roughly in conformity with a (very often vague) general intention. This discretionary power is entirely subject to control by the courts, with the effect that though an Act may not be overruled, most of the steps necessary to make the Act *do* anything can be. One case to hit the headlines in the late 1970s shows this: the Tameside case, where the (Labour) Secretary of State for Education tried to stop a local authority changing from an original plan to go comprehensive in order to retain its grammar schools. The Act certainly gave him, in general, the power to intervene in such situations. But the local authority and parents took the minister to court and succeeded in getting a ruling that what the minister was trying to do was illegal. One might well ask 'who needs judicial review?' in situations like this! Very few Acts can be so specific as not to need ministerial discretion, or not to involve the passing of delegated legislation, both of which can be and are checked by the courts.

Next, although courts cannot overrule an Act of Parliament, that does not mean Acts do not come before the courts. The vast majority of law cases, whether they are between private citizens or between a citizen and the state (either as criminal cases or otherwise) involve statutes. No one asks a judge to say a law is not a law at all in Britain, as they sometimes do in America. What they ask is what the law actually means. This process is called interpretation, or 'construction'; it is in interpreting the meaning of the Act, often a matter of dealing with very vague or general phrases, that judges have most of their power. The whole thrust of a piece of parliamentary legislation can be changed or bent or reduced or increased in impact in this way, and all entirely legally, but without recourse to 'judicial review'. For example, the 1971 Race Relations Act was very considerably reduced in its ability to prevent discrimination between citizens of different racial backgrounds by two decisions of the House of Lords which were presented as simply matters of 'interpreting' what the words in the Act actually meant. In one case a local authority was allowed to refuse to give a council house to a man who had the legal right to live permanently in Britain, and who had done so for twenty years, and who was otherwise entitled to a house, simply because he was, in origin, a Pole. The court 'interpreted' 'race' to mean only colour, not nationality, so it was acceptable to discriminate between whites from different countries.

In another case a political club was allowed to refuse membership to a card-carrying member of the relevant party because he was black. They 'interpreted' a clause that forbade discrimination by anyone 'providing services to the public or a section of the public' in such a way as to allow this discrimination, though no one could possibly have thought Parliament wanted to let political clubs off the duty to be unprejudiced.

Finally our courts have enormous influence over the rules we all have to obey in our relations with each other, because much of criminal law and most of civil law does not come from parliamentary Acts at all, but from what is known as 'common law'. Common law is overtly made by the judges. It was the original law of the country before parliaments either existed or bothered much about regulating private activities. It is a matter of tradition, a slow developing of rules based on previous cases known as 'precedents.' Most of the law of contract, for example, which regulates business activities, is still common law; what rule shall govern a contract drawn up between two private parties is essentially up to the judge and his ability to understand or to change the rulings in previous similar cases.

In criminal law too this judge-made law is often important. When can a policeman break into your house and search it? Is someone who burns down a house in revenge without realising that there is someone in it who consequently dies, guilty of murder? The answers to questions like this cannot be found in any statute. Parliament has never legislated on the matter. But hundreds of judges over the centuries have made decisions which can be seen as containing rough and changeable rules on the matter.

All these powers go together to suggest that courts and judges in England are very important indeed; if the judges can create rules that we have to obey, or can alter rules created by Parliament, or can control the exercise of powers given to ministers and authorities *by* parliamentary Acts, are they not actually governing us? And is not governing precisely what makes an institution 'political'?

There is one (and only one) argument that says no to that question. At any time, if Parliament does not like what the courts are doing, it can change the law by passing a new, clearer, more specific Act which the courts will have to obey. The chapters in this book on parliament and the executive have shown why this is a less than powerful argument. How much time can be spared, how much attention can the Cabinet give, to checking what the courts do? In criminal law there has only been one major example since the war of Parliament passing an Act which was intended, partially, to change a ruling that the court had made. In 1963 a murder conviction was upheld by the House of Lords on a man who had killed a policeman by driving fast and dangerously as the officer, trying to arrest him, clung to the running board of his car. It was fairly clear that the driver (who, incidentally, was a personal friend of the policeman) had never intended to kill him, and had not realised he was likely so to do. This was thought so unfair that some years later an Act, the 1968 Criminal Justice Act, instructed courts to take more notice of what alleged violent criminals thought they were doing. It is interesting to note in passing that most criminal lawyers believe that the wording of that Act is still so vague that it probably does not prevent a court repeating the original decision that produced it

If this example, and the absence of other examples, means anything, it means that the role of the courts is not seriously constrained by Parliament's theoretical power to change the law and overrule them. Though there are certainly isolated examples of governments doing so, these are rare, and less important than the general point that Parliament is far too busy and preoccupied to monitor what judges are doing in their vast areas of discretionary power over our lives.

There is another, rather less formal aspect of the power of our judiciary. For many years now Home Secretaries, civil servants and eminent criminologists have tried to introduce reforms in sentencing policies in our criminal courts. Not only have they had pragmatic policy changes in mind, they have been more generally concerned to introduce a formal punishment theory accompanied by suitable training for new criminal court judges prior to their handing down their first sentences.

Despite the essentially non-partisan nature of this attempt, almost nothing has been achieved in the face of intransigent, if often well argued, opposition by the judges. This came to a very public head in the autumn of 1981. The Home Secretary was faced with desperate overcrowding in prisons, to such a point that his own prison governors had started writing letters of complaint to the press. To reduce the problem he was contemplating a reform of sentencing policy designed to cut the prison population by giving nearly all prisoners an automatic parole after they had served a part of their sentence.

The Lord Chief Justice called a meeting of all High Court judges. The Home Office proposal was dropped. Very simply the judges had told the Home Secretary that if he implemented his reform they would merely increase the sentences they handed down so that, even with the automatic parole, prisoners would be serving sentences as long as they had in the past.

This sort of judicial power is not inescapable. Other jurisdictions have much tighter control over what happens to criminals. But in Britain the very assumption of the non-political role of the judiciary in some ways increases their power. For where the official ideology of crime and punishment has for so long been removed from party politics and placed in the hands of men – the judges – clearly identified as politically neutral, they seem justified both to themselves and to the public in asserting their autonomy in their own sphere. This special public image has ramifications throughout politics. If the government wishes to neutralise a potentially serious incident, they appoint a judge to investigate it. Whatever he may find, few will dare to challenge or ignore his conclusions because to do so would appear as an unseemly intervention of power or politics into a 'professional' zone. The same Law Lord (Scarman) – just one example – was given the tasks of investigating the killing by British troops of thirteen Ulstermen in a riot, the death of a demonstrator in London, and the disastrous Brixton riots of 1981 in London.

As the judges are elevated to such an important role by governments, it is not surprising that they should be able to control many legal matters behind the scenes, whatever the executive might wish.

The ideology of English judges

The autonomy and political power of the courts render specially important the nature of the legal culture – the criteria according to which judicial decisions are made – corresponding to the administrative culture of bureaucrats discussed in Chapter 2. Specifically, how far does it reflect popular attitudes and interests, or how far act against them?

Judges themselves conceive the courts as neutral appliers of law, thinking of their function as 'deciding disputes in accordance with law and with impartiality'. The law is thought of as an established body of principles which prejudges rights and duties. Impartiality means not merely an absence of personal bias or prejudice in the judge but also the exclusion of 'irrelevant' considerations such as his religious or political views. In contrast it has been claimed that judges' real view of the public interest contains three elements: 'first, the interests of the state (including its moral welfare) and the preservation of law and order, broadly interpreted; secondly the protection of property rights; and thirdly the promotion of certain political views normally associated with the Conservative Party' (Griffiths 1977: 195).

This assertion has been buttressed by a demonstration that the family and social background of judges is extremely privileged and atypical of the population; they come from wealthy professional, upper-middle-class families, were predominantly educated at exclusive schools and Oxford or Cambridge, and are forty or fifty when first appointed and in their sixties before they attain a really powerful position in the House of Lords or Court of Appeal. With a more formal training system for barristers, and with adequate incomes to be earned soon after admission to the Bar, the system of recruitment should be less exclusive in the future, but most barristers and hence most judges are not even then going to be men of the people.

The same can be said of the personnel of all the key institutions in Britain, including the Labour Party. So a more exclusive background is not necessarily associated with Conservative opinions. In any case, the definition of the Conservative side varies. Upholding the right of neofascists to speak in public could be a Conservative, not to say reactionary, position; or it could proceed from a 'progressive' concern with civil liberties which also uphold a Communist's or homosexual's right to do likewise. But the main reason for background not affecting decisions is that it is such a remote influence. Decisions are more likely to be affected by intensive professional training, professional traditions, and the views of one's working associates.

If we accept this, what are the main tenets of the legal profession which influence judges? The first and perhaps most important is to stick to clear and unambiguous precedents. Judges themselves do not see themselves as free, and often give decisions that go against the grain. Hark to Lord Hailsham, who as a member of several Conservative cabinets can be unambiguously categorised politically. He was giving judgement in a case where a woman was being prosecuted for breaking regulations governing overcrowding in boarding houses, though actually she was running a refuge for battered wives:

At the beginning of this opinion, I said that my conclusion, though without doubt, was arrived at with reluctance ... This appellant ... is providing a service for people in urgent and tragic need. It is a service which in fact is provided by no other organ of our much vaunted system of public welfare ... When people come to her door, not seldom accompanied by young children in desperate states and at all hours because, being in danger, they cannot go home ... the appellant does not turn them away ... but takes them in and gives them shelter and comfort. And what happens when she does? She finds herself the defendant in criminal proceedings at the suit of the local authority because she has allowed the inmates of her house to exceed the permitted maximum, and to that charge, I believe, she has no defence in law. My Lords, this is not a situation that can be regarded with complacency by any member of your Lordships' House, least of all by those who are compelled to do justice according to the law as it is, and not according to the state of affairs as they would wish it to be (Lord Hailsham, at page 443 (1977) 2 All ER 432).

He then cast his vote against the side he undoubtedly favoured.

Similar examples are too numerous to mention; the extent to which judges do believe that they are restricted by precedent and by a duty to follow Parliament is something that could not be exaggerated were it not that the orthodox view in English law unfortunately has exaggerated it. Perhaps there is no better example of this role belief than the voting in one case in 1972, *Jones v. Secretary of State for Social Services*, which, as far as facts went, was a nearly identical replay of a case in 1967. In the Jones case at least two Law Lords voted for Jones, in order not to overrule the earlier case, *even though* they felt that both Jones and the earlier plaintiff were not entitled to win, and *even though* they acknowledged that the House has the right to reverse itself. So strong was their adherence to the principles of certainty and *stare decisis* (letting previous decisions stand).

The law, however, is often not clear, and judges have wide areas of discretion. What legal values guide them in this case, and are they systematically biased towards one political side rather than another? It is certainly the case that judges (and lawyers generally) are professionally trained into notions of restraint, caution, restriction, respect for property and family, and obedience for law. Possibly they also have a leaning towards conventional moral values. These are attitudes congenial to Conservatives in Britain and, as we have

Table 7.2 Voting records of certain Law Lords in 'difficult' cases*, 1965–77 (percentages)

Name	Votes for prosecution in criminal cases	Votes for Revenue in tax cases	Votes for state in public law cases	Votes for 'more powerful' side in unequal civil cases
Reid	49	38	71	70
Morris	64	55	65	40
Wilberforce	50	57	48	50
Pearson	77	46	56	53
Diplock	76	53	33	46
Dilhorne	74	65	44	37

Percentages are based on very small sample sizes and are not reliable in many cases: the table is intended only to be illustrative of an approach.

* By 'difficult' is meant cases where there has been some amount of judicial disagreement, either inside the Court of Appeal, inside the Lords, or between the two. It is a way of measuring the idea of the 'voluntariness' of a judicial decision, in that the result cannot be totally determined by the law, inasmuch as at least one pair of judges have decided differently.

shown in Chapter 4, they are also values cherished by most Labour supporters. In other words, to equate generally conservative attitudes (with a small 'c') with politically Conservative attitudes on the part of judges also implies categorising the British population as a whole as Conservatives, which is obviously not correct. The striking similarity between legal attitudes and those of the population suggests on the contrary that the courts may reflect rather well the underlying preferences of most citizens.

One can put the idea of a politically Conservative bias on the part of judges to a partial test by examining their actual decisions on a number of cases. Judges who regularly vote in a way that, for example, protects individuals against state intervention by holding against tax inspectors and planning bodies and so forth, but who very frequently vote to uphold criminal law convictions, might be seen as revealing pro-Conservative sympathies. If most judges voted in this way the bench collectively might be seen as Conservative. In fact even a partial check on decisions of a few leading judges (Table 7.2) reveals considerable differences between them. It is hard to explain why these should exist if we have a consistently pro-Conservative bench. Using the figures in the table to infer different judicial ideologies along the lines of pro-state/anti-state, pro-law and order/anti-law and order, Lord Pearson might be characterised as most Conservative in inclination (though his record in that respect is not consistent). In other cases there is either a balance with about 50 per cent of decisions on both sides, or a judge must be characterised as Conservative in some areas but not so in others (as for example Lord Reid on votes against criminal prosecutions, or Lord Dilhorne in upholding the weaker side in unequal civil cases). But if judges divide among themselves (or incline to different sympathies on different issues) they are doing no more than reflecting general tendencies among the population and can hardly be singled out as politically biased on that ground.

This is not to deny, of course, that judges decide on the basis of their own values at times and that these are generally conservative (with a small 'c'). However, rather than seeing this as a deliberate attempt to impose their own views on the rest of us, it can more usefully be seen as evidence of weakness in the structure of our laws. When a judicial decision is not strictly determined by the legal/factual material before a judge, he is not only free, but forced, to give a decision that will have ideological undertones. There is no such thing as a 'neutral' decision in these circumstances.

Consider, for example, a decision often taken as evidence of the Conservative bias of the Lords, in a case on the 1971 Race Relations Act. The court was required to determine whether a prohibition on discrimination in facilities that provided a service to 'any section of the public' included a private club. The judgement was criticised for using a restrictive definition that curtailed the reach of the Act. It has often been asserted that they should instead have extended the scope of the legislation. Perhaps they should. But had they done so, they would not have been acting neutrally, but demonstrating another ideological bias. Wherever choice exists, the choice made will be representative of some set of values. Neutrality is hardly to be obtained.

Judges' values and court decisions

We shall finish this chapter by discussing the way in which judicial political values, often conservative in a general sense, slip into the system via structural weaknesses in the law.

The following are the most important aspects of law that involve a judge's private ideology in his legal decisions:

1. The interpretation of statutes where they are unclear.
2. The inclusion within statutes of concepts which call for judges to decide an essentially unknowable thing; i.e. what a reasonable man would do, or whether a minister 'is satisfied that', or whether (more rarely) something is 'in the public interest'.
3. Statues that require the judge himself to use discretion with little in the way of guide lines. Typically these are family law cases where the judge must decide himself what is in the interest of the child.

Statutory construction

This is the most important, because the most frequently found, of these situations. When a statute is unclear in what it requires a court to decide, the judge must find some way of removing what is unclear. Although there exist a host of rules for statutory interpretation, they provide little real help. Like 'Interpretation Acts', they are best seen not as telling judges how to decide, but 'how to express what he has decided'.

Basically what judges have to do in such a situation is to try to work out what Parliament really intended when it passed the Act. They are allowed access only to the text of the Act, and may not even consult what was said in the relevant parliamentary debate, which hardly makes the job easier.

Although some of the difficulties of discovering parliamentary intent are pragmatic, in that it is probable that Parliament had some intention relevant to the case and expressed itself badly, most cases are not like this. The worst problems of statutory construction arise because no one ever thought of a particular problem at all during the legislative phase, and there is no intention to discover. And, of course, the whole idea of Parliament's intention is often metaphysical – who is Parliament? The best approximation is probably that 'Parliament' means the draughtsmen who composed the text and the Secretary of State.

These combined pragmatic and logical difficulties mean that where lack of clarity exists in a statute, the judge may resolve it only by setting himself in Parliament's place and deciding what he would himself have intended to do about a problem had he been a legislator. Indeed, this is precisely what judges are told to do by the Swiss rules for interpretation, which gain at least in honesty over our legal system.

Other rules of interpretation, notably the 'plain words' rule, help to point out a further essential weakness in the structure of statute law. One must follow the literal meaning of a statute unless to do so would either be clearly unjust or lead to a situation Parliament would not have intended. This is tantamount to saying that not only must the judge use his own initiative where there exists a lack of clarity, but also that it is up to him to decide when there is a lack of clarity. Statutory lack of clarity is not a practical problem that can, hypothetically, be got round. The judgement of when a statute requires interpretation is itself a political judgement; the law reports are full of cases where a statute that is the very model of linguistic clarity is deemed to require interpretation not because it is hard to see what Parliament *said it intended* but because a judge was unable to believe that it *could have intended* that thing.

It is in the decision to use such interpretative powers that political ideology can most often be seen to invade judicial impartiality. Consider the two following examples of statutory interpretation. The first demonstrates a conflict between judges where there does appear genuine uncertainty about the meaning of a phrase. In the second the conflict is really not about verbal confusion but about whether Parliament could possibly have meant what it said.

In *Suthendran* v. *Immigration Appeal Tribunal* the Lords had to decide the meaning of a clause of the 1971 Immigration Act, Section 14(1), which allows an alien 'who has a limited leave' to stay in the country to appeal against a decision of the Home Office not to extend that appeal. Suthendran, having entered as a student with a 'limited leave to stay' while he underwent a training course, defied the terms of his leave, took a job, and overstayed his permit. Various efforts were made, by him and by his employers, to get his leave extended and to get him a work permit, though none of these actions were taken until his original one-year permit had expired. He appealed against the Home Office's refusal to let him stay and originally his appeal was upheld but later was rejected by the Immigration Appeal Tribunal on the ground that the Act clearly only granted the right of appeal to those who *have*, not to those who *no longer have*, 'a leave to stay' and Suthendran's appeal had not been lodged until some time after his permit had expired.

Is the Act unclear here? Can one say that 'has a leave to stay' automatically includes those who 'have had' but do not now have a leave to stay? The Lords were divided three to two on the issue, the majority denying Suthendran's appeal and upholding the Home Office's right to deport him. Divorced of context it might seem that the debate is trivial but the political context introduces on both sides of the case important reasons for finding one way or another. The minority were worried at the potential injustice of the 'literal reading', for it would allow the Home Office to win dubious cases by delaying their decision on a request to remain until the original leave had expired and thus save themselves from a potentially embarrassing appeal. The majority felt it necessary to stick to the literal words of the Act. Although they did not say so, there was a political reason here too, in all probability. The reason is demonstrated by a case going on in the Court of Appeal at almost the same time; if an alien manages to remain in Britain for five years, he wins an automatic right to permanent residence. The court clearly feared that by indefinite delay and by using up all the various rights of appeal given in the Act, an alien could prevent himself ever being deported.

The majority in this case were 'strict constructionists'. Lord Simon, one of the majority, said, for example:

Parliament is prima facie to be credited with meaning what it says in an Act of Parliament . . . The drafting of statutes, so important to people who hope to live under the rule of law, will never be satisfactory unless the courts seek . . . to read the statutory language . . . in the ordinary and primary sense which it bears in its context without omission or addition.

He goes on to admit that this must not be done were it to produce injustice but that 'it would be wrong to proceed on the assumption that the Secretary of State would act oppressively'.

The minority simply invert this last argument. Lord Kilbrandon: '. . . faced with two interpretations of this somewhat perplexing statute, . . . neither of them altogether convincing, I prefer that which . . . at least avoids giving a statutory sanction to a possible injustice which I do not believe Parliament would knowingly have countenanced.' One thing is certain: no decision in this case would have been neutral, and nothing, other than a private feeling about what one would have done as a legislator oneself, can solve the problem presented.

Although in the American context one is used to the idea that strict constructionists are conservative, no simple lining up like that is possible in this country because strict construction may on occasion require the more liberal of two possible readings. The next case demonstrates this, for three of the judges – Wilberforce, Dilhorne and Kilbrandon – heard both cases. Whereas Dilhorne was a strict constructionist and conservative in the Suthendran case, in *Davmond* v. *SW Water Authority* he insisted that the words of the Act could *not mean* what they said and again produced a conservative judgement. Wilberforce, in the minority on Suthendran, now turns into a strict constructionist, to render a liberal judgement.

Mr Daymond complained that he ought not to be required to pay a sewerage charge in his water rates because he was not connected to mains drainage. The statutory clause in question provides that water authorities can fix such charges 'as they think fit' and Dilhorne says: 'This section is silent as to the persons from whom water authorities can obtain payment of their charges. I find this most astonishing.' After insinuating that the government deliberately left this section unclear so as to avoid controversy in Parliament, Dilhorne goes on to say that it is unthinkable that the intention was to allow water authorities to tax anyone in the UK, and proceeds to demonstrate that Parliament could only have intended to make those pay who actually benefit from a service. In so doing he rejects the argument, persuasive to Wilberforce and Diplock in the minority, that as local authorities had *always* had the right to pay for sewerage from a general rate, Parliament could not be seen as intending to remove this vital public health power from the new authorities, unless they said so. This second case, like the first, demonstrates that statutory interpretation necessarily involves private belief. How else could a judge first decide whether a clause was in need of interpretation and then go on to interpret it?

Inconclusive concepts

A second structural weakness of law is that statutes often require judges to interpret such notions as 'reasonable care', or others that, though having the appearance of 'hard law', are in fact empty. A good example is the task set by the law on obscene publications, where the jury has to decide whether a magazine 'has a tendency to deprave or corrupt'. In public law the vital questions refer to a minister's judgement of a factual situation. Courts may hold a minister to be acting *ultra vires* where a statute empowers him to act 'if he is satisfied that' something is the case. The judge has to decide whether the minister considered anything he ought not to have considered, or failed to consider what he ought to have done. By their own testament, judges *may not* replace the minister's judgement with their own – they are entitled only to decide whether or not the minister *could* be satisfied of something.

Now these examples are even more pernicious than statutory interpretation because they pose problems only soluble by the judge in fact doing what he is supposed not to do – replacing a minister's judgement with his own. The Tameside case is the most recent important public law example of this test. The 1944 Education Act authorises the Secretary of State, where he is satisfied that an education authority is acting unreasonably, to instruct them to desist. The House of Lords then had a double inference problem: what constitutes 'unreasonable behaviour' by an LEA, and could the minister be satisfied in this case that these constituent elements existed?

The case centred round the cancellation or postponement by a newly elected Tory education authority of detailed comprehensivisation plans due to go into effect in September 1976, the authority not being elected until the spring of that year. In particular the controversial point was whether or not the hastily reintroduced assessment procedures for the grammar school places that would now exist would be fair, given the shortage of time, and the possibility of a withdrawal of co-operation by teachers angry at the abandonment of the plans.

The Lords unanimously argued that the word 'reasonable' must be taken very extremely – it did not refer to mistaken behaviour but only behaviour so guaranteed to create chaos that no reasonable education authority could possibly undertake it. On these grounds it was further argued that the Secretary of State, who only had 'to be satisfied' that the authority was acting unreasonably, could *not* have been considering the situation correctly, because there were no grounds on which he could possibly believe Tameside's new plan to be literally unreasonable in this way. This, despite the fact that the authority in the end had to plan on doing the assessment of several hundred children, for only 200-odd places, in a few weeks, with a team of only a few teachers not joining the strike; and where, though there was testimony by some experts that it was possible, there was testimony by others that it was not.

Not only was the decision in the Tameside case conservative but it was conservative *because* the Lords had no choice but to put themselves in Mr Mulley's place. The only way they could possibly come to the conclusion that he was misdirecting himself in law was by considering the evidence available to him (and, actually, evidence *not* then available to him) and deciding that *they* didn't think the authority was acting unreasonably.

This, naturally, is not the only case raising similar problems. In the past the courts' tendency has been to treat ministers' statements that they were satisfied with something as sacrosanct except when there was objective evidence that they had cheated. So in the classic case of *Podfield* v. *Minister of Agriculture*, in the mid-1960s, a minister required to use his discretion in allowing or refusing a special investigation into the Milk Marketing Board was held to be acting *ultra vires* in refusing an investigation only because he had stupidly written a letter admitting that his action was dictated by party-political motives. However, over the last decade courts have increasingly felt able to say that a minister *could not* be satisfied, while at the same time insisting that they were not applying their own reasoning but objectively testing the minister's process of reasoning.

There are other structural weaknesses of this sort. Often statutes as well as common law rules involve the idea of 'reasonable behaviour', or rest on what a 'reasonable man' would do in some situation. For example, one branch of family law entitles a court to dispense with the consent of a parent to the adoption of his child where that consent is 'unreasonably' withheld. On this criterion the Lords, in a case in 1976 concerning a homosexual father, felt entitled to ignore the father's objection to the adoption of his son. Though he wished only to be allowed to visit the boy for a few hours a week, in the mother and stepfather's home, they argued that no *reasonable* father could fail to agree that a homosexual has nothing to offer his son. Certainly a conservative judgement by much modern opinion, but what could the court do but consult their own ingrained prejudices? Who else has a better right to have their prejudices consulted, after all?

Discretionary judgements

In a vein generally similar to the case considered above, one must separately add those cases where the courts are not so much called upon to vet another's decision as to make their own first-order decision. The examples are again taken from family law but only because it is an area where cases most ripely demonstrate the inevitability of judicial ideology having a role. The first example is more directly political than the second.

It is no dramatic case of the overthrow of a parliamentary statute by a powerful and independent judiciary. Merely the 'automatic' application of a written law in a civil case against a mere local authority. In 1979 elections to the Greater London Council were won by the Labour party which campaigned on one issue above all others: it would introduce cheaper fares on London Transport. It was therefore a manifesto commitment. As soon as possible after their election they introduced an extensive flat-rate policy of cheaper fares under the general label of 'Fare's Fair'. To cut the fares they had to increase rates, the property tax on London residents. The GLC did this by telling the

London borough councils to apply a supplementary rate. Most obeyed without question, and public transport fares in London dropped dramatically, though rates did go up. One Conservative borough council rebelled and appealed to the courts. The case did not come up until the London Transport Executive, under the instructions of the GLC, had completely restructured its transport plans and fare structures to fit the Labour party manifesto.

When the borough council's case came to the High Court it failed, but they went on to the Court of Appeal under the presidency of Lord Denning. It upheld the appeal on an interpretation (ultimately accepted by the Law Lords) of one word in the governing Act, the 1969 London Transport Act. This had a phrase which said that the LTE, under conditions set by the GLC, must organise the metropolis's transport 'economically'. Nobody in the country knows what, if anything, that was really supposed to mean. Most probably it was there as a caution against rampant inefficiencies. However, the courts saw it as very simple. It meant that London Transport must be run at least on a break-even basis. It could not adopt any policy known ahead of time to be sure to incur a deficit, even if the relevant political, elected authority asked it to do so and guaranteed to make up the deficit by a grant, financed from local taxation, which they had every right to levy. Whether or not such a policy is just, sane, politically admirable or whatever is no decision for us to make. But no more is it a decision for eight senior lawyers to make. This one decision had immediate and direct effects on a travelling population of nearly ten million people, involving, in the estimate of the transport experts, an average fare rise of 150 per cent, in a world where almost no mass public transport system breaks even and during a period when it would throw a large number of newly employed transport workers out of a job in a city which already had more than 300,000 on the dole. Right or wrong, this was an enormous power to be exercised by an odd interpretation of one word.

But cases of less public importance can also reveal the extent of the power wielded by judges through their interpretations. In one typical family law dispute a father wanted custody of his daughter, the girl's estranged mother having died. He could offer a home with a perfectly adequate income, a wife (the daughter's stepmother) and a stepsister for the daughter, with a generally suitable background in terms of parental and sibling age. But he was challenged by his wife's mother, the girl's grandmother, known to the social services as bitterly opposed to the father and determined to make the child hate him. The father, on the other hand, was accepted as doing his best to help the daughter continue loving her other relatives. The job of a judge in such a case is to choose whatever is in the child's best interest. The High Court and the Court of Appeal both decided the grandmother should have custody because the stepmother, now in her late twenties, admitted having been promiscuous as a teenager. Although most readers will agree with the social services report in this case, firmly on the side of the father and stepmother's right to custody, no one can complain that the judges unfairly exercised a biased opinion. Yet again they were given no choice but to rule as their private attitudes required because there *is* no other solution.

Instead of this harrowing family law case we might have quoted a more traditionally 'political' example from, say, the Restrictive Practices Court, where judges are required, off their own bat, to decide whether some complicated trade arrangement is or is not in the public interest. We chose the family case only because it has an immediate subjective meaning for most of us. The problem remains the same in that judges are required to decide what is or is not in X's interest, in a political system that supposedly decides 'interest' questions through a pluralist electoral representative system. It is hardly surprising that they consult their private views and decide, in the family case, that grandmother should have custody, and in restrictive practices cases readily accept high unemployment rates. Still, if Parliament insists on judges answering problems that legislatures and executives fight shy of, they can only blame themselves if the answers are not always in tune with recent fashion.

In conclusion we should note first, that the courts in England do have enormous political power, but secondly, that they do their utmost not to use it. Court cases involving industrial relations show this. Some judges in the lower courts, and notably, until his retirement, Lord Denning in the Court of Appeal, are clearly trying to tighten the law on secondary picketing (the right of strikers to penalise companies not party to the original dispute). The House of Lords, however, has resolutely upheld a narrow interpretation on the Acts supporting union immunities. The Law Lords may privately agree with Lord Denning, and perhaps with Mrs Thatcher, about what should be done to unions. But they know too well how quickly their own power would be destroyed were the courts actively to conflict with so large a sector of organised opinion, so they rely for safety on a passive view of their role.

This is perhaps the clue: like all courts they often have to rely on private values to make decisions because the law is actually silent on what the decision should be. In the absence of any clear public opinion they will be likely to hand down judgements reflecting their own class and career socialisation. This may on occasion be more conservative than the majority view in the population, though often as we have seen it merely reflects popular conservatism. Where they can see a real political conflict arising, or for that matter where there is enough public debate for there to be a clear majority opinion, they are unlikely to go against it. The US Supreme Court (often analysed in similar terms) has been called 'the least dangerous branch' of government. The House of Lords is no different. Perhaps this is why the two most brilliant and strong-minded men since the war to be appointed young to the Lords, Patrick Devlin and Alfred Denning, both became so bored and felt so ineffectual that they resigned, Devlin to write and lecture, Denning to head the lower-ranking Court of Appeal where he could at least try to influence legal thinking with vigorous dissents. Neither had the freedom to be effective in the highest court of the land.

Chapter 8
Coercive powers: the police and military

In the last few chapters we have examined various bodies and institutions in the British political structure which function autonomously of national government. Sometimes these directly hinder the implementation of central policies and thus contribute to the fragmentation discussed in Chapters 1 and 2. Sometimes they distance themselves quite carefully from overt political matters, like the English courts, but make autonomous decisions affecting a wide range of life. In these cases they may not increase fragmentation but they certainly contribute to the loose-jointedness of the system.

All the institutions examined up to this point have claims to some kind of representative role, alternative or supplementary to that of the British Parliament and government. Local authorities have elected councils, the European Community has its directly elected Parliament, courts are invested with legal authority, many quangos and interest groups have elected spokesman. The police and the military, who are discussed in this chapter, could on the other hand be dismissed simply as bureaucracies with little discretion or ability to pursue independent policies. Such an impression is strengthened by the fact – remarkable in a world where two-thirds of the countries are subject to recurrent military coups and half the rest are run by a bureaucratic and secret police apparatus – that the British police and military forces have never tried to take over, or even directly threaten, the civil government.

There is indeed a significant absence of this type of political ambition among police and military leaders. This is not to say that they do not have an important political role or make important political decisions. To a large extent, as with judges, these result from the failure of other authorities to make sufficiently detailed rules about the matters on which they have to act. As we saw in Chapter 7 the law is far from clear, even after court rulings (and these, after all, are given only after a case is raised – the matter may previously have lain obscure for many years). Police are bound to make their own interpretations. Given the immense mass of law that purports to regulate our lives, and their limited material and manpower, the police are also bound to set priorities: to decide what shall be given most priority and enforced most strictly, and what shall be left to enforce itself, if it can. The military too have to decide on priorities, as well as having at times absolute jurisdiction over a highly trained, disciplined, and centralised force of personnel with an effective monopoly of weapons. These considerations render an analysis of their leadership essential to any complete picture of British politics, though their disinclination to interfere outside their own specialised areas causes them often to be overlooked.

The constitutional position of the police

The constitutional position of the police in Britain is in one sense simple: there is only one important Act governing them; but in another it is extremely complex: they have no clearly defined role, and the mechanisms of political control over them are few and ill understood. The current structure and constitutional position of the police derive from the Royal Commission on the Police, which sat between 1961 and 1963. Most of its recommendations were put into the 1964 Police Act. Apart from the change in treatment of complaints against the police instituted by the 1976 Police Act, there has been no important legislation since 1964 (and before then there was hardly any legislation at all). It may well be that the Royal Commission on Criminal Justice set up in 1979 will recommend considerable changes. What these might be we discuss later. It is important to realise how scanty is the *statute* as opposed to the *common law* rules our political system has about policing itself, and how little of what there is exists in a simple codified form. Instead it is scattered in hundreds of precedents, bye-laws, and conventions accreted over time. So much is this so that it is extremely difficult to give any simple straightforward account of the powers, roles and duties of the police and of the way they are controlled. Even to attempt to do so can be misleading, because the very confusion and uncertainty about the matter is itself an important fact about our political system.

To make a really simple start we can say that there are four important types of actor involved in the system. These are: the Home Secretary (and Scottish, Welsh and Northern Irish Secretaries within their areas), the chief officers of each of the police forces, the other officers of the forces, and the Police Authorities. One thing we can be sure of is that the really important entry in this list is the chief officers, the chief constables of the police forces outside London and the commissioners of the Metropolitan and City of London police forces – to which we must add the head of the Royal Ulster Constabulary in Northern Ireland. Their importance arises from the fact that (by tradition, common law, and now by statute) they are the only police officers who in any way interact with the political elements, the Home Secretary and the corresponding regional Secretaries, and the Police Authorities. They also have total and sole command of all other officers in the police service.

The chief constable is wholly responsible for all operational, administrative, disciplinary and logistical decisions in his force. He cannot be given an order by any political authority on any such matter. (The position of the commissioner of the Metropolitan Police is somewhat different, as the police authority in his case is the Home Secretary himself; in theory the Home Secretary may have some slight power to give him orders, but in practice we can treat him as substantially in the same position as a chief constable. This also applies for the Royal Ulster Constabulary.)

The chief constable (and no other officer) is, however, 'responsible' to his Police Authority. The meaning of this responsibility and accountability will take us some time to analyse satisfactorily. The Police Authorities have the same structure now for every police force outside the metropolis, consisting of two-thirds of councillors from those local authorities covered by the force, and one-third from magistrates in the area. Before the 1964 Act there were a variety of police authorities depending on the sort of police force, i.e. county, borough or city force, and it is sometimes argued (for example by Sir Robert Mark, the ex-commissioner of the Met.) that they exercised much more detailed control than do the new Police Authorities. As well as being responsible to the Police Authorities, chief constables can be required to give reports to the Home Secretary or corresponding regional Secretary on any matter; the Home Secretary or corresponding regional Secretary can give certain orders to the Police Authorities, and has an ultimate influence on them by determining their grant from the Exchequer, and by failing to recognise a force as efficient.

There is much disagreement on the extent to which central government controls and influences local police affairs, though such disagreement is probably more a matter of what sort of local autonomy one regards as important, rather than differences of opinion over facts. One can, quite legitimately, portray central government as having crucial power. For they, through Her Majesty's Inspectors of Constabulary, must check the efficiency of police forces. They also have considerable control over the funding of the constabularies. Manpower targets, for example, are not solely a matter either for the chief constable or the Police Authority. The Home Secretary and his regional colleagues can affect such matters considerably, both indirectly and by fiat. General questions of the nature and abundance of police equipment are also most directly decided by the Home Office, or regional offices.

This question of relative autonomy in different spheres of policy-making was well demonstrated by the urban riots in Liverpool, Manchester and London in the summer of 1981. As soon as they broke out, MPs were demanding action and explanations from the Home Secretary. It was he who announced, rapidly, decisions about buying and authorising more effective riot control equipment. The central government was quite rightly seen as the overall authority for the range of tactics available for deployment and for the general police strategy to be adopted. But when it came to the level of just how streets were to be policed, given the existing material, of whether a 'low profile' or 'intensive policing' was to be adopted, neither the Home Secretary nor any other political authority was involved.

The range of strategies adopted by Chief Constables during these few weeks is the best measure of immediate police autonomy; the ultimate role of the Home Secretary and his regional counterparts in deciding how in the future similar situations should be handled, is the best indicator of a different sense in which the police are not independent.

Operational control of the police

This bald and deliberately simple setting out of the system we are to analyse, immediately demonstrates the typically British indirectness and pluralism of authority and power in the system – it is indeed reminiscent of the political system for controlling education in Britain, and for good reason. If there is any central ideological thread running through the history of British policing and education, it has been fear of allowing the central government to have any political control of the area. In the case of the police, the fear has extended to local political control. To judge from senior police officers' views, it is now local political control they dislike even more than central. Privately (and some-times publicly) chief constables express very scathing views of the calibre and political judgement of local councillors, which is one reason why the Police Authorities tend to be so difficult to analyse. The other is that they do so little of significance in any case.

It would be a mistake to assume that senior police officers are all alike, or that they necessarily share a closely knit ideology. Their perceptions of their role, duties and responsibilities vary a good deal. Perhaps more important, their perceptions of police tactics and strategies vary, and this leads to huge differences in policing policies even in situations where their political and social values may be identical. The former chief constable of one west country force, for example, is known as the darling of the National Council for Civil Liberties because of his commitment to something called 'community polic-ing'. This same concept is often on the lips of a Midlands chief constable, a young man known principally for his experience in counter-terrorist policing, who is the archetype of a neutral professional only concerned with the tech-nicalities of his job. The chief constable of a major northern city is a funda-mentalist Christian, known for giving speeches about the need to restore moral values to our society, who gave up 'soft policing' during urban riots only after he felt (soft) measures had failed. The deputy commander of the Metropolitan Special Branch publicly opposes any increase in police powers to deal with terrorist threats, because he thinks his job is to police society rather than to reorganise society to make policing easier.

These differences come about partly because policing *is* a technical pro-fessional matter, and because professional values vary with the different experi-ences and problems which police officers have faced. The whole doctrine of the 'professional' nature of police work is complicated and potentially dan-gerous. If one accepts the 'professional' thesis there is no good argument for political control. But who is to judge when some decision is a professional matter?

Even the examples given above over-simplify the variety of our police sys-tem, for not all forces are territorially organised in the way so far assumed. There are other police forces such as the British Transport Police with a very wide jurisdiction stretching throughout the United Kingdom. The Department of Defence has its own civilian police force for guarding such key points as research establishments. The lines of political control over such bodies are extremely hard to define. The most obvious example of a centrally controlled and politically highly relevant body with a police function is of course the security service and its more public counterpart in the Special Branch of the Metropolitan Police (about 500 highly trained men operating over the whole of the UK). Here even more than in other areas of police work it is difficult to find out enough to draw firm conclusions about power, control and police ideology. Certainly the wide deployment of the 'national' forces of police, supplemented by bodies such as Customs and Excise and Immigration Control, give the central government more potential to act directly at local level than is generally admitted. In terms of numbers on the other hand the 'national' police are eclipsed by the local forces. In discussing police work in general one must therefore focus on the latter, since they deal with the overwhelming bulk of cases.

The Royal Commission on the Police of the early 1960s profoundly shaped the nature of the service today and left one problem unresolved, the consequences of which are still with us. The most important practical consequence was the power the resulting Act gave to the Home Secretary to enforce mergers between police forces, which has drastically reduced their number, massively increased their size, produced much greater uniformity and rendered more serious the problem of political control. Before the amalgamations forced through by Roy Jenkins as the Labour Home Secretary in the mid-1960s there were over 150 separate and independent police forces in England and Wales outside London, many of them very small indeed, covering small areas. They tended to be highly individualist, with characteristics suiting the difference between, say, a sprawling, almost deserted rural county or a physically compact and densely populated urban centre. The Royal Commission evidently did not object to this, for it recommended as the best size for a force something in the region of 500 officers.

There are now only forty-nine forces outside London; the biggest is the West Midlands Constabulary, a force of 6500 officers, policing both Birmingham and rural areas miles from its centre. Partly as a result of the original amalgamations, and partly because of the subsequent local government reorganisation, these forces now cut across local authority lines, with no simple identity between them. Thus problems of co-ordination occur between, for example, police forces and social services, one of which may be organised round a metropolitan county, the other around district councils. Forces like the Thames Valley Police bear no relationship to any administrative or traditional community at all. The political consequence is clear: the old watch committees for forces like, for example, the City of Leicester police were staffed with councillors from that one council, and were aware of the city's problems as a unit, able to help and, if necessary, influence the chief constable to create a policy for an area for which they were already collectively responsible. The council members of the Thames Valley Police Authority are drawn from a whole series of different councils, have no permanent political unity or other collective responsibilities, do not know each other and are correspondingly both unable and perhaps unwilling to exercise the same sort of detailed control. It is in this sort of context that the potentially uncontrollable power of chief police officers becomes a serious problem.

Although it is not usually presented in this way, it can be argued that the current structure of the police service is a compromise between efficiency, sup- posedly served by amalgamations and greater size, and the need to keep the police independent of the central government. For the 1962 Royal Commission had, somewhat unusually, a minority dissenting report, in which a very dis- tinguished lawyer, Lord Goodhart, argued forcefully for a total change in the nature of the police service. Goodhart wanted a single national police force, directly under Westminster control. This was, and still is, opposed as being too dangerous an instrument. One chief constable recoiled in horror at what he saw as a massive force of 120,000 men under the control of one super-chief constable. His argument was that the power of a chief constable was much too great to put such a force in any one man's hands.

So it would be, but that was never what Goodhart, or other civilian advo- cates of the idea, had in mind, and the assumption that such would be the political shape of the force tells us a good deal about the actual police situation. The chief constable in question did not see himself as too powerful, though he commands a force which accounts for nearly one-fifth of those men and resources. His fear is unrealistic, though explicable on different grounds – such a force could not have the political independence, and therefore would not have the power, he enjoys. The point is that only by making the central state directly command the police force can it be politically controlled: Goodhart's plan would have given Britain a politically accountable force *with* whatever benefits there may be in size and uniformity. But it would do so at the cost of the hallowed British tradition of the impartiality and political independence of the police. Thus the scene is set to investigate the two vital questions that are so little understood or considered when the political role of the police is considered in this country. The questions are first, just how accountable or responsible are the chief constables; and second, what is meant by the police being politically impartial in our society?

Police accountability

Accountability is at best a complex matter, and the complexity allows simul- taneously for chief constables believing quite sincerely that there is a great deal of accountability to the political rulers of society, and for many others to believe there is virtually none. Two things are clear. Both the Home Secretary and, to a more limited extent, the Police Authorities may demand reports from chief constables about matters arising under their command, and indeed each chief constable has a duty to report about his force to his Authority every year. Only the Home Secretary (or the regional Secretaries) may demand reports on 'operational' matters, and the annual report to the Police Authority is under the chief constable's discretion. He can (and they sometimes do) refuse to divulge to his Authority information expressly requested, such as the size of the Special Branch component of their force. Whatever the Home Secretary demands as information can be made the subject of questions and debates in Parliament. Although there are problems, it is probably true that political authorities can extract enough information from the police after the event. At least, the Home Secretary can, and often does, while the Police Authorities may be able to, but hardly ever do. It seems common ground both to the police and to academic critics that the Police Authorities have in practice been extremely passive and made very little use of even those powers they have under the 1964 Act, despite the expectations and intentions of the Royal Commission.

If the ability to find out what someone is doing after he has done it (and if you know what to ask about in the first place) is accountability, then there is a considerable degree of accountability by the police service in Britain. For example, the 1981 national enquiry into the West Yorkshire force for its failure to catch a murderer, the 'Yorkshire Ripper', over a period of years, strongly criticised its procedures and produced major operational changes inside the force. But, as a distinguished constitutional expert once said, 'What we really mean by accountability is the power to say "Tell me what you are doing, and stop doing it".'There we have a problem, because no one seems empowered in Britain to utter the second half of the sentence. The only actual control over what the police do, as opposed to what they tell you about what they are doing, is the law: if a chief constable breaks it the courts exist, as they do for any citizen. Also a rampantly inefficient chief constable could be dismissed on the Home Secretary's order.

It may be difficult at first to see why this situation should not be enough. Policemen find it very difficult indeed to see why it is not adequate. Why should anyone control the chief constable in 'operational matters'? The problem is that under 'operational control', which sounds an anodyne matter of technical expertise, lie at least two major discretionary powers, the exercise of which involves fundamental policy questions which would appear, at least on the surface, to be more naturally the scope of democratically elected politicians than appointed and autonomous police chiefs.

The discretion arises from two obvious facts: the police do not have the men or resources to patrol everywhere fully, to investigate all crimes fully, or indeed completely to carry out all of their legal duty to 'cause the peace to be kept and preserved, and prevent all offences against the persons and properties of Her Majesty's subjects'. Choices have to be made about the distribution of these resources, and the choices will affect the lives of Her Majesty's subjects. Should major police resources be put into a campaign against drunken drivers at Christmas time? Should vandalism in huge anonymous council estates be a major concern, even if this may mean less protection against serious theft for richer sections of a city? Should pornography be swept off the streets, prostitution be kept tightly within the law, should a lot of effort go into investigating possible subversives in trade unions? Whatever answer one chooses to give to such questions, it is hard to believe that they are not just as important, and just as clearly political or policy questions, as questions about how social service department resources should be spent. While no one would believe that the Director of Social Services in a local authority should have uncontrolled discretion, the doctrine of operational autonomy gives the Chief Constable the sole responsibility for answering such questions.

The second area of discretion covered by operational autonomy is both more important and more unusual. Almost alone among western democracies, England and Wales entrust to the police the business of criminal prosecution in most, though not all, criminal cases. The usual pattern is to have an independent civilian officer either, as in Europe, a member of the judiciary or, as in North America, an elected politician, who decides when and whom to prosecute, and for what. With certain exceptions where the case must be referred to the Director of Public Prosecutions (DPP), the police themselves are the prosecuting authority in England and Wales, which means that discretion as to whether or not to bring an alleged offender to court lies with the Chief Constable. The occasions when the DPP or the Attorney-General must give permission for a prosecution are important in the sense that they cover major crimes – murder, cases involving the Official Secrets Act, etc. – but these are comparatively few in number and probably of little overall impact. It is noteworthy that this pattern is not found in Scotland, where a judicial officer, the Procurator Fiscal, acts as does the juge d'instruction in France or the District Attorney in America.

This discretion too is vital; it is no part of the law of England that all offenders must be prosecuted, so again the legal duties of policemen do not remove policy discretion. For it is policy discretion that matters here. Were we only talking about prosecuting decisions in individual cases, decisions about whether or not the evidence is strong enough to give a good chance of conviction, it might matter less. We are considering, however, whole policies on what sort of crimes and what sort of offenders should be prosecuted whenever possible, or when it might be better to make extensive use of cautions, or indeed to ignore some offences completely.

A real example concerns juveniles. Should the police try whenever possible not to prosecute juvenile offenders, should they prosecute only for a second or subsequent offence? Should they prosecute all juvenile offenders? In one police force in the mid-1970s four adjacent divisions systematically used different policies of this sort on juvenile offenders, according to the preferences of the divisional commanders to whom prosecution policy decisions were delegated by the Chief Constable.

It may be a good thing to have variety and experiment in prosecution policy, and varying circumstances may make it advisable to enforce laws differently even in contiguous neighbourhoods. But who should make such decisions? Elected local politicians, or independent policemen?

It is this sort of subject matter inside the label of operational autonomy that makes it clear that the English police service is *not* fully accountable in vital ways, but forms independent baronies each able to construct and apply its own policies. Naturally there are many other such areas of autonomy, some more obviously of political relevance. The power to ban marches of political extremists is shared, for example, between chief constables and Police Authorities and the Home Secretary, but no ban could be imposed without a chief constable asking for it. Then, clearly, it is an operational matter whether or not to provide police protection for a march, how to react to violence during a demonstration, and so on.

Police impartiality

If the police are constitutionally able to make policy in this way, if they are free from political control in carrying out their job to a degree greater than most of our institutions, how do they justify this? What major value in society is upheld by this autonomy?

An answer to this involves a discussion of three concepts: the policemen's notion of political impartiality; their understanding of the nature of the law; and their idea of the link between the police and the citizen. In short, we must come to grips with the typical police officer's view of the political role of the police.

It has always been a tradition in Britain, since the days when Peel persuaded a reluctant Parliament to let him set up the metropolitan constabulary, that the police should not be agents of the government, or even of the state as such, but should impartially uphold the law. Where conflicts have a clear political aspect it has always been seen to be of prime value that the police should not take the government's side, and should not be seen to do so. The contrast is often drawn with France, where the Minister of the Interior has frequently used the police to help his Government in a clash with some opposing sector of society. In contrast we have British examples like the Home Secretary during the General Strike of 1926 trying to prevent the use of the police in any way that might make them seem to be on the side of the government against the unions. It is ironic that political thinkers on the left and right naturally assume the police are an agent of the state which upholds the government against those challenging its authority, while the agent in question does not agree and seeks to avoid this role.

Senior police officers intensely dislike anything which involves them in such clashes. When the incoming Government in 1979 proposed to make secondary picketing illegal, chief constables and Home Office officials were desperately keen that the criminal law should not be used, because they did not want their officers involved in disputes with unionists and thus appearing to 'take sides'. The industrial disputes of the winter before that election were, it is argued by some, made worse by the unwillingness of the police to take any action against pickets who broke the then existing law, again because of the need to be seen as impartial.

But while police officers in command positions seek to avoid protecting the government *per se*, they have a totally different attitude to the idea of upholding the law. This they see as sacrosanct, however little they think of the politicians who create it. It is this notion of the law as an absolute which must be upheld and protected, which justifies the absence of political control. In this perspective, not only is there no need for detailed control (because no political decisions are seen as involved in upholding the law), but detailed control is unacceptable. The law is pure, politics dirty, and the police serve the pure law, not the potentially corrupt politicians. The image of impartiality in upholding the pure law that the police believe they have is of practical value to them. Police officers are well aware that they can only uphold the law with at least the passive acceptance of the population; and such acceptance, so the argument goes, is dependent on the image of impartiality.

The police as a pressure group

This argument, firmly believed by most senior policemen, is long-standing, and obviously has much truth in it. In the last decade, however, there has occurred a new development in the police image of themselves and of their relationship to politics. Increasingly senior policemen are becoming more vocal in public about policy matters; they are becoming public political actors and propagandists, though they would probably not accept that label. And, as part of the same development, they are beginning to assert a special relationship between themselves and the people and a special knowledge of the public needs. Sometimes, indeed, they claim what amounts to a superior role in interpreting what the public wants, compared with politicians.

Much of this development can be attributed to one man, Sir Robert Mark, the controversial Commissioner of the Metropolitan Police in the mid-1970s, whose book *In the office of constable* is the only serious and thoughtful work by a senior police officer on the role of the police. Until he took over the Met. and started appearing on television and writing in the papers, there had been an unspoken rule that, as a corollary of their political independence, senior police officers would never make public their beliefs and arguments on policy.

The beginning of this new openness in entering public controversy was Sir Robert's Dimbleby Lecture on BBC TV in 1973. This caused a furore because he attacked, amongst other targets, what he described as 'crooked lawyers', who fabricated alibis for criminals. It was all part of a general campaign to shift the balance in favour of the prosecution in criminal trials, a campaign that has been pushed hard by the police ever since. Afterwards many other chief constables entered the public arena, trying to move public opinion and to bring, in this way, pressure to bear on governments for reform. Now Sir Robert has retired the most constantly outspoken campaigner for strengthened police powers in many situations, but especially in public order, is the Chief Constable of Greater Manchester, James Anderton. But many more engage in public discussion, to the point that local politicians often complain bitterly at what they see as a usurped role.

It is not clear how effective such political involvement is; very little has been done by governments in response to police officers' demands, and the Royal Commission on Criminal Justice has now moved to abolish one vital area of police discretion with its recommendation that decisions on prosecution should be given to an independent civilian body. The police failed to prevent the passing of the 1976 Police Act, which set up an independent review board of laymen to investigate complaints against the police and to decide on disciplinary matters, a right previously exclusive to chief constables. Although this was the only controversial matter on which the Association of Chief Police Officers was unanimous for twenty years, and though it was opposed fiercely and publicly, it went through virtually unchanged, and Sir Robert Mark resigned rather than accept it in the Metropolitan. In his book, as in public and private comments by other chief constables, there is a feeling that the police are 'the people's police', that they owe a primary obligation to the interests and demands of 'the people' which transcends that of any duty to the government. This is accompanied by a firm belief that policemen, by virtue of their daily contact with the population, know better than the politicians what it is the electorate really want in matters of social control. This belief, coupled with a deep suspicion of politicians of all colours, both justifies what they regard as a basic constitutional principle of police independence, and makes it seem all the more important.

Whether there really is such a basic constitutional principle is doubtful. As a principle it is perhaps enshrined in the 1964 Act, but previous precedents are rare and odd. The oldest actual precedent, on which most of the argument for autonomy depends, is a 1903 case in which the courts ruled that a police officer cannot make a local authority responsible for his acts, as he is not a servant of the local authority. It is argued almost from this sole precedent that if the local authority is not liable in civil damages for an officer's acts, it cannot be in control of him either. The argument is particularly anomalous because for a long time the Crown could not be held liable for acts of public servants, but no one ever suggested that civil servants should be independent of the Crown in carrying out their duties. Of course, with the British constitution mere duration of a practice is enough to make it a constitutional convention, but in this case sustained debate on whether it really is a principle would be less odd than asking if the independence of the judiciary is a basic constitutional provision.

Police powers

This brings us to a final area of concern about policing in Britain. What are the powers of the police, and where do they come from? There is a well-known doctrine that a police officer has no special power, but is a uniformed citizen exercising professionally the common law powers we all have. The idea is not even technically correct any more, and in real terms it is absurd. Not only is it more or less impossible in practice for a private citizen to arrest, but his legal position is a good deal less safe in so doing. There are other powers, particularly in the increasingly vital area of public order, which only the police can use, as under the 1936 Public Order Act or the 1973 Suppression of Terrorism Act.

The problem about the powers of the police is that there exists no general authoritative statement at all about the matter, but instead myriads of court precedents, statutes and bye-laws. Police officers themselves often have grave doubts about what, for example, their legitimate powers are in arresting or searching premises. In other cases the powers do not stem from any rule, whether of precedent or statute, but from traditional Crown prerogative powers. Thus for a long time the right to open letters or tap phones was exercised by the police with the permission of the Home Secretary under the doctrine that, as the Post Office is the 'Royal Mail', the Crown's agents needed no special permission to open it. Very recently a High Court judge has suggested that the whole law on this matter is confused and uncertain.

Partly to remedy this general situation, and partly as a result of a political pressure for action against a perceived crime problem, police powers are currently being enhanced. The Police and Criminal Justice bill, which should be in operation by 1985 is a curious mixture, as a result of parliamentary ammendment, of greater powers and greater restrictions for the police. On the one hand it considerably increases the length of time they can hold suspects without charging them and allows suspects to be denied access to a solicitor for up to 36 hours. At the same time, much wider powers of search and seizure are permitted on suspicion.

However, as a result of ammendments in the House of Lords, a tighter restriction on the use of illegally gathered evidence in trials is to be imposed. The bill will also strengthen the suspect's rights by requiring the tape recording of all interogations. At this stage it is impossible to be sure how the act will work out, but most opinion would suggest that it is the strengthening of police powers, and not the safe guarding of rights that will be paramount.

One could multiply such examples for pages; one interesting point is police vetting of juries which, though defended as traditional, was not mentioned at all in the Juries Act 1974, although the Act took care to make statutory several restrictions on jury membership which had until then been purely traditional.

When police activity was almost entirely a matter of preventing or investigating ordinary crime it may have mattered less that their powers were inchoate and randomly derived, and that restrictions on their actions, like the 'judges' rules' governing interrogation of suspects, were purely conventional. The change in the last ten to fifteen years, a change the police themselves are sharply aware of, has been the vast increase in problems of public order. Now the police have to deal with masses of people who are breaking no law at all, as when the Special Branch keeps surveillance on what they think of as extremist agitators. Alternatively, when they have to control demonstrations they deal with masses of people who are breaking essentially minor common law rights of free access on the highway. Or in protecting demonstrators and the public, they are dealing with a situation where it is the risk of a breach of the peace by a few which makes the whole mass of demonstrators a potentially explosive police problem. In addition they have to deal with the very real danger of deliberate political crime by terrorists; there were in 1978, for example, sixteen serious terrorist events in London, most connected with the Middle East.

There are two aspects to this problem. One is that in such a situation rights and powers of the police which were never deliberately worked out with any clear policy in mind, and which are dubious in interpretation, are inadequate. The other is that the police must now find it more difficult to assert that they are impartially upholding a law devoid of political content in regard to public order. The industrial relations events of 1984 have been good examples of this. Police involvement in controlling picket lines in the miners strike has been made politically controversial, culminating in a demand by the Labour Party conference that police should never be involved in industrial relations. Whilst the demand is manifestly absurd, there has probably not been an industrial dispute for 50 years in which the police have been so unpopular with the left.

One example of how significantly this difficulty is taken by the government has been the insistence on making the legal penalties in recent industrial relations acts entirely a matter of civil law remedies to avoid direct police involvement in enforcing any order. Noticeably the legal prohibition on secondary picketing, which could only be enforced by police manpower has not been made use of in any serious case yet. Here the police appear much more clearly as agents and as defenders of the state; and their constitutional position, their powers, and their responsibilities need to be reworked with this in mind. Politics have changed, and the police cannot respond while both their perception of their role, and constitutional control over them, are based on a golden political past.

The political importance of the armed forces

As with the police, very little research has been done on the role of the military in British politics and government, although of course there is a large technical literature on defence policy and strategy. In part this may reflect a feeling that the military are just not important, because our defence forces are small and weak. This leads to a relatively minor and subsidiary role in NATO (the North Atlantic Treaty Organisation, the chief western alliance against Russia, which groups most West European military forces with some of the United States forces in a unified military command based at Brussels). As the military have never been important in British politics in the sense of intervening directly in government, an illusion continues that they are hardly worth serious study.

But for three reasons we do need to know more about them. First, Britain's foreign policy, and therefore its economic policy, is geared to our membership of NATO and the consequent alliances and enmities. The role and importance of the NATO commitment is thus vital for government decision-making. Secondly, Britain spends a very large amount of money on military defence, and the role and importance of the military establishment in guiding, influencing and pressurising politicians about defence expenditure is something we badly need to know about. Finally (and closely tied in with the changing role of the police), the military are increasingly important in maintaining internal law and order. Such 'aid to the civil power' occurs not only in the obvious case of Ulster but in mainland Britain, as social unrest and terrorism stretch civilian police beyond their capacities.

We shall start with a brief description of the constitutional and legal position of the British armed forces and a sketch of their size and resources, before discussing each of these three areas in greater detail.

The constitutional position

One reasons why the military have never interfered directly in British government in the last 300 years is that they have never been trusted not to. Since the 'Glorious Revolution' of 1688 Parliament has kept firm control over the army's right to exist at all. So strong was the fear of a standing army after the experience under Cromwell, and James II's raising of an all-volunteer standing army, that any such force was declared illegal except as provided for specifically by Parliament. Though clearly it was necessary to have a permanent army, the legal basis for recruiting, paying and disciplining such a body has always been provided on a temporary, year by year, basis. Up till 1879 this meant that each year a special Act, the Mutiny Act, had to be passed to keep the army in existence; and this continued, renamed the Army Act, from 1881 to 1936. Even now the principle remains. Every five years an Army and Air Force Act is passed which can last only for five years, and this Act requires an annual Order in Council to be made. That order is tabled in Parliament and requires an affirmative resolution by both Houses which could, hypothetically, be refused by members. The Navy, though it was never so feared in the past (it being harder to stage a coup with battleships than with infantry platoons), is now dealt with in a similar way.

Constitutionally, however, though the continued existence and funding of the military requires parliamentary approval, the control over and use of the military machine is a prerogative power of the Crown, exercised by the Cabinet or the Prime Minister, and does not depend much on statute law. Military officers and other ranks are much more directly under the control of the government than are the police, or arguably even the Civil Service, for they have virtually none of the rights of employment security and so on that the other workers have, and are subject to a separate and more draconian set of laws and courts in the form of military law and courts martial. As their working is so tightly covered by the Official Secrets Acts and similar measures, this all adds up to the military being a very powerful and, as it were, 'private' tool of the government, more or less beyond parliamentary control, and without even the claim to discretion and autonomy the police have.

Officers' political attitudes

There are two other historical points that help explain why the British army has so low a political profile and has been so little-involved in government and politics, compared with most European states.

For most of its existence it has been a small volunteer force, unlike say Germany and France which from the early nineteenth century have maintained huge conscript armies. Only in the two world wars, and for some years after 1945, has Britain had conscription. The army has always been a thing apart from public life, rather than being part of the experience of most male citizens or a microcosm of the political turmoil in the wider society. Indeed, for most of the period up to 1939 about half the army was always out of the country, controlling the Empire. Typically an infantry regiment of two battalions would have one posted to India for anything up to a dozen years at a time. Since 1945 a substantial force has always been posted in Germany, as the British Army of the Rhine (BAOR).

There has therefore been little chance of the military having either the capacity or the interest to be involved in political life. In addition, it was ensured, completely until 1870 and to a large extent until the Second World War, that the officer corps would not desire to intervene in politics because they all came, themselves, from the dominant stratum of British society. This was ensured by the simple practice of paying them so little (and indeed charging them a fixed price for their commission and each rank they gained) that only the wealthy could possibly become officers. Only the military fiasco of the Crimean War persuaded Parliament that professional competence might be worth the risk of letting only marginally affluent middle-class families send their sons into the army, and hence of abolishing the purchase system. Even then, officers were paid too badly for anyone without a private income to manage in any 'smart' regiment, and the general consensus of class ensured that nearly all commissions went to middle- or upper-class boys on graduation from public schools. Not until the 1939–45 war demanded the creation of a mass citizen army, retained until the early 1960s, did this process break down, but it is still the case that most officers come from a relatively privileged middle-class background.

Whatever we may feel about social privilege in the military profession, the consequence has been the highly desirable inculcation of an antipolitical, apolitical culture amongst the professional officer corps, of implicit unquestioning obedience to the civilian government and a disinclination to engage in any public political activity at all. This is reinforced by the close symbolic links between the army and the monarchy. As the latter remains neutral as between parties and governments, so is the army expected to be.

One would thus be very unlikely, for example, to find a British senior officer testifying before the new Defence Select Committee of the Commons and urging some new weapons programme in the way American generals represent the army before Congressional committees. As with the police, there are, however, signs that this may be changing. Service chiefs are now a little more willing to publicise their beliefs. The Chief of the Defence Staff in June 1979 was more than usually open in.endorsing Mrs Thatcher's new Government as likely to increase defence expenditure. And when an officer who had commanded a brigade in Belfast a few years ago published an allegedly controversial book on the use of the army in controlling civilian conflict he was promoted to be Commandant of the Infantry Training School rather than finding himself posted to the English military equivalent of Siberia.

The political authority structure

The armed forces were integrated in the 1960s as far as high level and political command goes, into one united Department of Defence with a junior minister for each of the services to aid the Secretary of State for Defence; a single civilian Permanent Secretary; and a Defence Council which includes the military commanders as well as the civilians. For each service there is a Chief of Staff, and together the three form the Chiefs of Staff Committee under a fourth senior officer, the Chief of the Defence Staff. Although in theory the 'super Ministry' of Defence serves to reconcile the competing demands of army, navy and air force, in practice intense inter-service rivalry exists which spills over into Cabinet discussions (for example, whether new seaborne missiles should be acquired at the cost of failing to replace existing tanks). Although it is rarely exercised, the four Chiefs of Staff have the right of direct access to the Prime Minister. A recent use of this was when they insisted on seeing Mr Callaghan during the 1976–79 Government to complain that low levels of service pay were adversely affecting recruitment. It is not so much the fact of this visit, but the fact that we know it was made because of deliberate military leaks, that is significant.

At the highest level, defence policy is made by a sub-committee of the Cabinet, the Defence and Foreign Affairs Committee, which the Chiefs of Staff are often invited to attend, and which consists principally of the Prime Minister, and the Foreign, Defence and Home Secretaries. No one can know very fully what role the full Cabinet plays in such policy deliberations, but appearances indicate that it is a very thin one. Journalistic comment, for example, suggests that the decision in 1980 to buy a highly expensive American missile system to replace Polaris missiles was not reached in full Cabinet. Certainly, various members of the 1974–79 Labour Cabinet were at pains to insist that they had never known of their Government's decision to continue with a £1,000 million upgrading project for the existing missiles, which had been initiated under the 1970–74 Heath administration.

In time of war or other actual operations there is naturally no question of the full Cabinet being very closely involved in the creation of military policy. To some extent this can be seen as a direct prime ministerial prerogative. But for reasons we shall examine it is unlikely that anyone but the service chiefs can play much of a role in any future war, except in the special case of the use of nuclear weapons.

NATO: defence policy and politics

The political message that came across most strongly in the late 1970s from the Conservatives was that NATO in general, and the British contribution in particular, was disastrously weak. From the Conservative Party and from the occasional military comments one gets the impression that the Labour Governments of the 1960s and 1970s ignored a pressing need for defence expenditure, and ran down British military capacity. It is never easy to assess such claims, both in the general sense of knowing whether or not the British contribution is as large as in some sense it ought to be, and the more specific suggestion that one party rather than another is better or worse at providing for military expenditure.

Table 8.1 Defence force comparisons, selected states, 1978

	France	United Kingdom	German Federal Republic	USA	USSR
Population	53,850,000	56,700,000	63,410,000	218,630,000	261,310,000
GNP 1977, estimated in $	374.8 billion	263.6 billion	508.6 billion	1,890 billion	516 billion roubles
Defence expenditure 1978	$17.52 billion* (Fr. 80.77 billion)	$13.04 billion* (£6.92 billion)	$17.26 billion*	$115.2 billion	17.2 billion roubles
Military service	12 months	Voluntary	15 months	Voluntary	2 years
Personnel: Total armed forces	493,000 (inc. 266,200 conscripts)	313,253	478,900 (inc. 236,000 conscripts)	1,877,300	2,713,000
Army	324,000 (inc. 209,000 conscripts)	160,837	336,200 (inc. 187,000 conscripts)	774,200	1,825,000
Navy	68,200 (inc. 18,400 conscripts)	67,770	36,500 (inc. 11,000 conscripts)	532,300	433,000
Air force	100,800 (inc. 38,800 conscripts)	84,646	106,200 (inc. 38,000 conscripts)	570,800	455,000
Paramilitary	76,400 gendarmes		20,000 border guard		450,000 KGB and MVD
Combat aircraft	471	511	484	3,400	4,650
Major surface combat vessels	46	72	33	172	243
Submarines	21	27	24 (coastal)	75	243

*approximate

Source: Compiled from *The Military Balance, 1978–1979*, London, International Institute for Strategic Studies, 1978

Certainly it would be hard to argue that Britain spends less than other major European nations, given the capacity of the economy. Although in 1978 Britain spent a little over $13 billion on defence compared to over $17 billion by both France and Germany, this actually represented a higher proportion of the gross national product. As Table 8.1 shows, the actual level of military force provided with that money is arguably higher, especially if one discounts the conscript element of the French and German forces, which are probably undertrained and of dubious utility in either a hot or internal war situation.

On the other hand, there has been a trend in Britain to decrease the share of government expenditure on military defence, a trend which does not exist elsewhere in the NATO alliance, at least to the same extent. In France, for example, the 1977–82 defence programme calls for defence expenditure to rise from being 17 per cent of the budget to 20 per cent. In Britain, military expenditure as a proportion of all government expenditure has, until recently, declined continually. The figures for 1978 show a military defence expenditure only 83 per cent of that in 1968, and which accounted for only 22 per cent of general government expenditure compared with 32 per cent in 1968. There was, therefore, an absolute as well as a relative decline in military expenditure. Most of this decline was probably accounted for by the 1974 Defence Review, which severely trimmed plans for military expansion.

The extent to which the running down of military expenditure is a partisan matter is hard to estimate; all governments tend to hold down this form of expenditure when in economic trouble because, although it may in abstract be publicly popular to have strong forces, the effects of cuts here are less dramatic in terms of government unpopularity than in, say, education and the social services. Nor, given the adoption by one government of a particular defence policy is it really very easy for a successor government to reverse it. The real cut in Britain's expenditure followed the abandonment of an 'East of Suez' policy by the 1964–70 Labour government. Although it may be argued that the Conservatives, had they won that election, would not have taken the same decision, it is clearly impossible for them now to decide that Britain should go back to having a worldwide defence force commitment.

In terms of party membership, and perhaps typical voters, defence matters are indeed partisan. In 1979 there was a much greater tendency for Conservative party voters to regret the run down in military capacity. Over 70 per cent of Conservative voters thought that such military reduction had gone at least 'a little too far', 25 per cent more than thought so amongst Labour voters. One has only to remember the periodic attacks by Labour party conferences and left-wing MPs on retention of a nuclear strike capacity to see this point more strongly. However, it must at the same time be remembered that the Wilson government in the 1960s did in fact keep up the Polaris programme, and the Callaghan Government in the 1970s helped to increase its capacity, pointing the conclusion that the actual decisions of governments have not obviously differed.

The nuclear strike capacity is of particular political importance in British defence politics in a way that makes it hard for Conservative and Labour governments to act very differently, because of a delicate problem about the

American and British role in NATO, which has been a source of quiet contention for some years. Briefly the problem is this. Most analysts would agree with General Sir John Hackett, a former commander of the British Army of the Rhine, who published in 1978, thinly disguised as science fiction, an estimate of the likely consequences of a war between NATO and the Eastern bloc. He and his fellow authors (including an Air Chief Marshal, a Brigadier and a Vice-Admiral) were convinced that the conventional force levels in NATO could not stand for long against an all-out attack by the Warsaw pact armies. It is inevitable, according to British military thinking, that some form of nuclear battlefield weapons, all of which are under American control, would have to be used, in some estimates within three days of the start of hostilities. What America would prefer is a considerable increase in the conventional troop levels provided by her European allies, who she feels are sheltering behind the American nuclear shield – both the low yield battlefield weapons possessed by the US forces in Europe, and even more the massive deterrent capacity of America's strategic nuclear arsenal. What worries British politicians is that the shield might not be available, because an American President might think twice before risking Russian nuclear strikes on continental USA as reprisals for American use of nuclear weapons to defend her European allies, were there no immediate threat to the USA itself.

Hence the importance in British nuclear defence policy of having an independent nuclear deterrent, however little credible. If the UK can launch a nuclear strike by itself, America is seen as having no option but to go along with the predominantly nuclear strategy of NATO, thus saving Britain from having to increase conventional forces massively and expensively. For conventional forces are much more expensive than strategic nuclear forces; in France, which has a rather bigger strategic nuclear force than the UK, each of the three conventional arms costs more per year than the nuclear capacity.

When one gets to arguments of such a highly complex (and macabre) degree it is unlikely that the typically marginal policy differences that exist between British political parties will yield a defence policy which is highly partisan. The only serious option for a major cut in Britain's defence expenditure would be to withdraw from NATO. While that is contemplated on the left of the Labour Party it is unlikely that it could be adopted as official policy without splitting the Party and rendering its prospects of government even more tenuous. While we stay in NATO it is doubtful whether anyone in Britain can be said to make defence policy other than the technical advisers, that is, the Chiefs of Staff. NATO is a highly organised single-purpose machine into which our troops are fully integrated, and apart from the nuclear option there are no major political decisions to be made. Or rather, there are, but they are decisions which will be made either by NATO itself, or by the American President.

Defence policy decisions are in fact nowadays equivalent to decisions about equipment – what tank, fighter, ship or missile to buy, and how much the government can make available for their purchase. In this area too, the demands of NATO, as well as the economic realities of the defence industry, are beginning (though too slowly for the generals, who complain bitterly about lack of standardisation of equipment) to remove autonomy from British policy-makers. Complex equipment like planes, and even slightly less complex machines like tanks, cannot any longer for reasons of cost be designed and built in one country. There is increasing investment in co-operative ventures where Britain joins with Germany and either France or Italy, with a resulting loss of autonomy and an increase in the relative importance of technical and military experts. Much is shrouded in secrecy, but a recent statement by someone well qualified to know provides an example of how effective power over defence procurement policy has shifted to the technical experts in the military, and even more in the defence research institutions.

In 1979 Sir Solly Zuckerman, for years scientific adviser to the British Cabinet, claimed that every chief scientific adviser either to the UK Prime Minister or to the President of the USA since 1945 has opposed and argued against each stage of the development of nuclear weapons. All have been convinced that an increase in nuclear capacity reduced rather than increased national security. Yet their unanimous advice (in which he joins) has been disregarded. Zuckerman claimed that politicians have always yielded to the advice of the military, but also pointed out that the generals and admirals are themselves dependent on advice from experts. The ultimate advisers are the experts working in the defence industries and the government-run research and development institutions, whose views cannot easily be gainsaid by politicians or civil servants.

Aid to the civil power

There has been no incident since the early years of the century in which British soldiers have been used against British civilians in mainland Britain. But there is a more or less regular army detachment at Heathrow Airport, the SAS (Special Air Service) were used to break the siege of the Iranian Embassy in London in 1980, which led to several deaths, and armed soldiers have been present at a series of other incidents. Even where violence does not occur, troops are indispensable to the government for internal duties. It was the army that provided fire-fighting services when the fire brigades went on strike in 1978, the army that cleared up refuse in Glasgow when a strike by dustmen caused a health and safety hazard. The army has either been called in for, or on call for, running services in transport, electricity and docking at various times in post-war Britain. Army officers are now regularly trained in crowd control, and soldiers exercised in how to deal with riots and urban terrorism. As mentioned earlier, Brigadier Frank Kitson, author of *Low intensity operations*, has risen far in the army hierarchy. And there is Northern Ireland, where British troops have been in a war situation since 1968, with numbers varying between ten and twenty thousand posted there at any one time. No one can join the British army without having to face the certainty of patrolling the streets of Belfast at some time, which will put him in risk of his own life, and leave him authorised to use deadly violence should an (entirely probable) situation so require it.

How important is the internal security role of our armed forces, and what is the legal framework for their use in such a role?

Table 8.1, which made force comparisons between France, Germany and Britain, contains a rather important point; under its military budget France fields 76,400 gendarmes, equivalent to 33 per cent of its non-conscript troops, while the German BundesGrenzPolitzei, again part of the military budget, is 20,000 strong. These parliamentary forces, trained and armed as soldiers, do not exist in Britain – which into the bargain has a police service with no great capacity, training or resources for the use of extreme violence in a systematic way. (Apart from the fact that all French police are armed, there is also the CRS (*Compagnies Republicaines de Securité*) which numbers nearly another 20,000.)

Nor are France and Germany unusual; most countries have some form of disciplined armed force they can call on to deal with major disturbances without having to go all the way to using regular military. But Britain, which traditionally does not trust the government to dispose of coercion (hence the localisation and autonomy of the ordinary police), has never had such a force. Consequently, when situations occur beyond the scope of the police, the army has to be used.

The legal situation when troops are used to control civilian events is confused in the extreme. Traditionally troops were only used in a riotous situation, under the control of a local magistrate, and after he had read a proclamation as required from the 1714 Riot Act (hence 'reading the riot act'), which had the effect of making those taking part guilty of a felony. This Act was repealed in 1967 when the old felony/misdemeanour distinction was abolished. Under section three of the Criminal Law Act 1967, which repealed the 1714 Riot Act, it is now lawful to use such force as is reasonable to suppress a riot.

The trouble is that no one knows exactly what this means. The presence of a magistrate, and his command to troops to fire on a crowd, for example, is required by military law, so that an officer who gave such an order off his own bat might be court-martialled. But it is *not* required by common or statute law; an officer in a position to use force to prevent a riot and who did not do so might be at fault under ordinary law and, more to the point, if a magistrate ordered firing, the officer complied, people were killed and later a court decided that the amount of force used was excessive, the fact that the officer was obeying the magistrate's order would probably *not* be a defence to a murder or manslaughter charge. The general doctrine in question is that where troops are giving aid to the civil power it may not be inaccurate to describe the legal rights and duties of a soldier as being no more than those of an ordinary citizen in uniform.

This all seems to mean that if the government uses troops to control civil disturbance it can rely on no special legal protection for them, and there is no way that they can transform the situation into one where anything but the most extreme caution needs to be used. Nor can they make life easy for the soldiers in question, who are accordingly always unwilling to be involved in such a situation. On the other hand, there is no constitutional restriction on when, how, where or why the government does use troops. As part of the Crown prerogative the Cabinet can order the troops to go into any situation whatsoever, and do anything – so long as what they do is to uphold the law and does not break the law.

That is the situation on mainland Britain, but not, it appears, in Northern Ireland, for both Parliament and the courts. In Northern Ireland different codes prevail which give more freedom to the military, stemming from a tradition of almost continual civil disturbances and buttressed by emergency powers granted not only by British governments but by the devolved Northern Irish Parliament (1922–72) and the nineteenth-century Irish Courts.

Police and military: fragmented professionalism

What all this adds up to is that police and army enjoy a surprising degree of autonomy within their own specialised areas of operation. There is very little accountability either to the public directly or to elected politicans. The government and the Civil Service can certainly call upon the army at will, but any actions undertaken under government command are liable to scrutiny by another body of autonomous professionals, the judges, who are prejudiced against damage to property or violence against persons. Such action might also provoke damaging reprisals from trade unions, which could not be prevented without further violence.

Under these constraints, army leaders are not anxious to get involved in politics, whether as agents of government or on their own account. Such an attitude is reinforced by tradition and the sheer institutional difficulties hindering direct involvement. The police are even more distrustful of involvement. Although in recent years their leaders have been taking on some attributes of a pressure group, their activities and statements are confined very much to their own area of law and order. They show no disposition whatever to take sides in major societal conflicts, such as those between government and trade unions – quite the reverse, in fact.

The self-regulation of police and military leaders represents a process very typical of the British system of government. Each area of society tends to be hived off to a semi-autonomous policy-making body whose operations are shrouded in considerable secrecy. The means of controlling such bodies are typically indirect, consisting of budgetary or manpower controls or retrospective enquiry and inspection. In operational matters it is difficult to enforce public accountability. What keeps them on the rails and prevents an undue assertion of power are their own internalised attitudes and professional ethics. The effectiveness of these in keeping autonomous decision-makers to their own area is shown at its most extreme in the police and military, the two forces which with their weapons monopoly could most easily assert their supremacy if they so wanted. The fact that it is the last thing they do want speaks volumes for the efficiency of British political arrangements in this respect. Loose-jointedness and limited accountability pose problems for economic planning, but in other ways can produce highly beneficial results.

Chapter 9
Characterising British politics

Since the last war, perceptions of British politics have changed radically. Until the early 1960s, conventional wisdom had it that Cabinet government, in conjunction with the two-party system, worked rather well. Over succeeding decades serious doubts developed about its efficacy and responsiveness. The gaps between the traditional picture of how things are done and the actual ways in which they are done – discussed at various points in earlier chapters – call for a new analysis of how the system now operates.

Economic decline has stimulated much rethinking of previously accepted assumptions. Rather than an absence of new ideas, the danger is one of confusion between the sheer numbers of reinterpretations and associated diagnoses on offer. Confusion is compounded because the different accounts highlight very diverse aspects of the situation and propose very different – and often conflicting – remedies for what they see as major political weaknesses.

A first aim of this chapter is therefore to compare and evaluate some of the more popular and influential of the new interpretations and to contrast these with evidence accumulated from our detailed analyses. After this review we will present our own conclusions, which provide a more complex and (we hope) more balanced account of the main trends in contemporary British politics.

The traditional view

Two distinctive political parties holding a virtual monopoly of electoral votes and exchanging governmental power smoothly and peacefully dominated British politics from 1945 to 1974. During the earlier part of this period, the two-party system did seem to guarantee good government. Party discipline in the Commons, Cabinet government, and the doctrines of individual and collective responsibility, together solved the problem of combining popular accountability with efficient administration. A permanent, incorruptible and able Civil Service imposed coherence on policy choices and supplied technical advice, while ensuring that the actual machinery of government ran smoothly.

Within this system interest groups were not disruptive since they enjoyed close working relationships with civil servants, trading support and technical information for concessions on the detailed administration of policies affecting them. No organised interest was totally ignored and a neutral Civil Service held the balance between them. Local/central relations took care of themselves, with limited and benevolent central direction matched by local compliance.

Public records now reveal that relationships were never as tidy or smoothly regulated as in the idealised picture. Uncertainty, confusion and downright chaos were present in all governments of the post-war period. Increasingly bold media coverage helped dent the myth of individual and collective responsibility so crucial to any claim that government is accountable for its actions.

By the mid 1960s the growing economic difficulties and failure of attempts to meet them had led to initial doubts about how well the system was functioning. By the early 1980s these had swollen to the extent that a new party emerged to 'break the mould of the old two-party system', as the Social Democrats put it. Even the traditional parties repudiated the 'consensus politics' of the 1950s and seemed anxious to disavow their previous record. Within twenty years, conventional wisdom had passed from almost complete acceptance of the old model to near-unanimous rejection.

As we have shown, the weaknesses of the system cannot be attributed to any one institutional feature, historical event or individual government – although critics have been quick to single out each of these for blame. An analysis of five of the most important accounts of what went wrong shows that each diagnosis has some validity. This should lead us to look deeper and search wider for weaknesses when attempting ourselves to characterise what could be called the 'new British political system', as we try to do at the end of the chapter.

The technocratic critique

The decade following 1960 was dominated by attempts to reform the machinery of government. The mood was predominantly technocratic. By implication, at least, little was wrong with the party and electoral system or with the actual policies of governments. It was assumed that the welfare state and Keynesian demand management were inviolable foundations upon which policy was based. What apparently was defective was the linkage between these and society at large. Thus the Civil Service was branded as old-fashioned and unresponsive. The Treasury, in particular, was considered unable to take the longer view which planning required. Local governments were too small to operate with necessary economies of scale and required amalgamation into larger units. Industry and the unions were basically sound but needed the aid and guidance of a reformed governmental system intent on economic growth. Such assumptions led successive governments to embark on a series of reforms and reorganisations (for details see Chapters 1, 2 and 5). Experience of these showed that reforms were often very difficult to achieve – even internally –

witness the weakening of the Fulton recommendations (1968–69) on reform of the Civil Service (Ch. 2) or the compromises forced on local government reorganisation (Ch. 5).

But more importantly, the reforms revealed the fundamental weakness of British governments when they attempted to influence, persuade, cajole or coerce the main economic and political actors in British society. Incomes policies foundered on the rocks of trade union resistance. Price controls were often opposed by industry. Individual firms shied away from anything but a voluntary or highly flexible industrial policy. The Treasury was constantly suspicious of long-term planning or any agency established to promote it. Many local governments showed a marked reluctance to accept central government's *diktats*.

Of course in theory British central governments could do virtually anything. Party discipline, Cabinet and unitary government should ensure this. Perhaps successive Governments' reliance on administrative reforms shows that they too believed the myth. More fundamental changes in polity and society were considered unnecessary. But as the individual chapters of this volume have shown, both British government and British society are much more fragmented than either the traditional view or the technocratic critique would have us believe. Administrative reform has been piecemeal at best and has certainly failed to make any discernible improvement in the quality of economic policy.

Although characteristic of the late 1960s and early 1970s under Wilson and Heath, the influence of the technocratic diagnosis has not entirely waned. As noted in Chapter 3, further tinkering with the 'machinery of government' was planned for the 1980s by all the main parties and a number of other bodies too. While some reforms may be useful (and any breach in official secrets is likely to promote accountability and responsiveness), it is not necessarily the case that these go hand in hand with enhanced efficiency. Change itself may be initially disruptive and is in any event likely to be less farreaching than planned, owing to the entrenched opposition it will provoke. The major obstacles to growth lie in the power relationships inside and outside government, rather than in the administrative structure itself.

The corporatist thesis

If the problem lies in the independent power of societal groups, which governments cannot effectively coerce, perhaps these should be drawn into the process of negotiation and consultation instead? As we have seen, in the traditional view this was already happening. All significant organised groups stood in a close relationship to civil servants, feeding in advice and offering support in return for sympathetic application of relevant programmes.

We have seen, however (Ch. 2), that this symbiotic relationship does not exist for all groups and that in particular the trade unions get pushed to the periphery of Civil Service consultations, besides having repugnant policies imposed on them by governments. This tendency to dictate to interest groups reflects the British tradition of strong, autonomous and rather aloof government, which knows better than anyone else what to do in the national interest.

As this fails to elicit the necessary compliance from organisations which are too strong to knuckle under, an obvious solution is to treat these as equals and buy or win their support. This would involve mutual concessions, on the part of government as well as of the other participants, but it would be worthwhile in return for effective and workable agreements. Obviously governments have been driven to such negotiations in recent years, the most notable case being the Labour Government's social contract with the trade unions in 1974–78, when the Government traded legal concessions and price restraint for limits on wage increases.

The corporatist thesis (strictly speaking the 'societal' or 'liberal' corporatist theses) sees such negotiations as becoming increasingly necessary and increasingly prevalent in modern societies. The independent power of labour and business organisations renders their agreement indispensable to any effective economic policy, so there is really no alternative to recognizing their autonomy and bidding for their support.

In the British case such mutual recognition is often described as 'tripartism', a form of 'societal corporatism' which emphasises the need for co-operation between government and the peak associations representing both sides of industry, the TUC and the CBI. This will be brought about by growing recognition of common interests (e.g. the benefits of greater prosperity). While some disagreements will remain, these can be limited to specific policy details. In particular the organisations involved in the negotiations have to set aside fundamental disagreements about ultimate goals in order to arrive at agreed solutions to individual problems. In this process of negotiation all three participants must have influence on the development of policy. The government cannot expect to dominate and coerce, since this would simply mean that the other groups would feel no obligation to recommend acceptance to their members. Such acceptance is of course a crucial part of the arrangements. There is no point in leaders making agreements if their members do not accept them. It is here that corporatism or tripartism as a description of what is actually going on reveals a fatal flaw. It is only too obvious in the British case that organisations cannot bind all their members and that 'peak associations' such as the TUC and the CBI are particularly weak in that respect.

To some extent, however, the weakness extends to all the functional groups representing economic interests. Even a powerful individual union such as the Transport and General Workers' finds it difficult to control its individual sections, while these in turn find it difficult to exact compliance from committees of shop stewards in individual factories. (Such committees in many cases were in fact promoted by Communists or other left-wingers to strengthen grass-roots representatives against the official union leadership.) On the other side, even the powerful financial interests of the City of London are divided by sharp conflicts of interest. So there is little chance of finding a set of generally supported top level representatives with whom to do business.

To the extent that corporatism identifies a growing tendency for societal interests to build themselves into organisations with a permanent bureaucracy and some kind of representative leadership, it is undoubtedly right. It is also correct in its recognition of the power of such groups. This is what has driven governments from time to time into seeking some accommodation with them. On the other hand, the diagnosis is surely over-optimistic in assuming that leaders can control their members more effectively than the government itself can, through legislation or other means. (Neither government nor group leaders are *very* effective.) Corporatism also assumes the existence of enough agreement on fundamentals to provide a basis for constructive negotiation, whereas it is the creation of such a consensus that is the root of the problem. If sufficient agreement existed in the first place, negotiations would probably be unnecessary, as what the government did would attract support in any case.

Government overload

One of the dangers of negotiating with interest groups is the tendency for governments to trade permanent concessions – enhanced legal privileges in the case of unions, subsidies in the case of business – for temporary support for an incomes or prices policy lasting only a year. Further longterm concessions are then exacted when the agreement comes up for renewal.

The trade-off is even worse for government if the rank and file refuse to keep the agreement. In any case the attempt to placate societal interests has been seen by some political scientists as a major cause of government weakness. The government, they feel, has become increasingly 'overloaded' with demands from all sections of society from unions to motorway protesters, from local governments to Welsh Nationalists. Faced with this barrage from a society holding unrealistic expectations of government, politicians have attempted to please everybody but have really succeeded in pleasing no one. In taking on an inflated set of responsibilities to meet or head off popular demands they have outpaced their financial and manpower resources. An over-extended administration is necessarily less efficient, and its failings add up to an impression that government is in perpetual minor crisis. More public services are delivered but their quality has declined. Higher civil servants are so strained by their extended responsibilities that the increased numbers of policies are less well co-ordinated and it becomes difficult to distinguish between matters of higher and lower priority. The government, in its efforts to accommodate competing claims, constantly changes its mind, modifies programmes or even completely reverses its general strategy. Fundamental to the overload thesis is the assumption that British society is too pluralistic – that there are too many channels of influence exploited by interests with independent bases of political power. By implication, it is not the political institutions or machinery of government that are primarily at fault, although they may be less adequate as a result of strain.

There are points at which this interpretation fits our earlier analysis. As the 1960s and 1970s wore on, so governments appeared increasingly under siege and unable to produce satisfactory policies. The Conservative Governments of both Heath and Thatcher hived off a number of trading activities and abolished some quangos without noticeably reducing government responsibilities.

On the other hand, there is little to indicate that popular or group demands in Britain *are* particularly voracious. Indeed, all the evidence is that ordinary electors have very modest expectations and simply look to the government to stop things getting much worse rather than taking on vast new commitments (Ch. 4). There is also no evidence that government has been particularly accommodating or responsive to organised groups, except for limited and exceptional periods (notably 1974–78).

The case of the lobby against motorway extensions and the administrative handling of its objections is instructive. There has been statutory provision for public inquiries into the line of new roads since the Trunk Roads Act of 1936. Until the late 1960s there were relatively few inquiries, and these were peaceful; the need for new roads were generally accepted. As the basic network was completed, however, and environmental concerns came to the fore, there was an increase in the number of inquiries into new schemes, many of which became extremely acrimonious. The Ministry of Transport responded to this development by restricting the scope of inquiries and giving only grudging and limited concessions to the objectors. For example, they tried to exclude discussion of the need for a road, and restrict arguments to whether it should take the proposed line. In general the Ministry was as obstructive as possible. At the inquiry of 1976 into the widening of the Al at Archway in North London, an objector was first promised a line-by-line derivation of a cost benefit table, then told that such calculations did not exist, then offered information which would enable him to do the calculations himself – information which was never in the end supplied.

This hardly looks like government bending over backwards to meet group demands and overloading itself with new programmes in the process! Rather the situation is the familiar one of a ministry fighting to preserve existing responsibilities in accordance with a fixed departmental view. The example is particularly piquant as the pressure group demand in this case was for government to disengage rather than to expand, and the representatives of government rejected the opportunity.

All the stresses and strains which the government machine increasingly experiences can be more convincingly attributed to its own difficulties in making and implementing effective policies rather than to having external demands imposed upon it. As pointed out in Chapter 2, British central government lacks any central co-ordinating body. The main decisionmaking body, the Cabinet, has little control over other institutions, which as a result tend to pursue their own policies and interests without regard to overall priorities. In an increasingly complex modern society, this is bound to show up in inconsistencies and policy muddles. The cause lies not in the range of government responsibilities but in the way they are handled.

Adversary politics

One aspect of this is the constant switches in economic policy characteristic of the period since 1964, and associated with changes in party control of the government. As a result some observers have asserted that the major weakness of British politics is its adversarial nature. Strong party discipline in combination with periodic elections ensures dramatic changes in policies every four or five years. In such an environment the sort of longer-term structural adjustment needed to adapt the British economy to technological and trading changes is impossible. Related arguments posit the existence of a 'political/business cycle' – or the tendency for governments to reflate the economy before elections to enhance their popularity. This school of thought stresses the extent to which the particular nature of British two-party politics aggravates the tendency towards party division found in all democracies. For in Britain the two major parties provide stark ideological contrasts and once in power they feel obliged to carry out the sometimes radical promises contained in party manifestoes. The fact that electoral considerations oblige governments to reverse or modify these policies in the period preceding general elections only serves to add more confusion.

No doubt there is something to this general thesis and we have referred both to party reversals of policy and adversary politics several times during this book. Clearly the SDP are persuaded that the argument is valid, their major rallying cry being the alleged capriciousness of the old two-party system together with the 'unfair' electoral system which polarises Labour and Conservatives and heavily penalises moderate third parties. However, on its own the adversary thesis is simply not sufficient to explain the trials and tribulations of British governments. Failure in policy implementation cannot be related to electoral calculations or to the rigidity of a first-past-the-post two-party system. Party competition as such has little to do with the machinery of central government, where the failures in policy implementation have their origin.

The radical alternative

Perhaps party programmes *should* translate more effectively into government actions – thereby guaranteeing responsiveness, at any rate, and possibly improving the prospects for implementation?

A final diagnosis of the British political predicament, which stresses the potential of party as a co-ordinating and driving force, emanates from the radical Left – particularly from the Bennite and allied sections of the Labour movement. Simply stated, this dismisses the constraints imposed by societal pluralism, the nature of the party system, or the complexity of administration. Instead, the blame for social and economic malaise is placed squarely on the shoulders of unresponsive and weak Labour governments.

The Left take it for granted that non-Labour governments, the Civil Service as at present constituted, and capitalism, will in combination always guarantee economic decline and deepening inequality. Financial interests are maximised under a regime which allows free investment abroad, and they have an ultimate influence over the other institutions by threatening a run on the pound.

Only Labour can save British industry from stagnation through lack of investment, by forcing fundamental reforms based on a planned and directed economy.

The Labour Governments of 1964–79 and 1974–79 failed because they vacillated in face of the City, the Civil Service and international financial pressures. A revamped party supporting a Labour Government committed to radical change, and held steadily on course by intra-party democracy, is the only hope for the economy, and for Socialism. This critique is interesting because its very existence testifies to the breakdown of any earlier liberal consensus. To a greater extent than earlier interpretations, it combines a clearcut programme for action with an (unflattering) description of the present situation.

The success of the programme, if it is ever tried, will rest heavily on the validity of the description. A first assumption is that Labour could be elected on such commitments. This is problematical. As we have seen (Ch. 4), electors are repelled by the prospect of change unless it confers immediate benefits. Extensions of government control, rather than guaranteeing these benefits, tend to disadvantage Labour when they become foremost in a campaign. Hence a programme of full-blooded Socialism, far from catapulting Labour to power, would result in a further loss of Labour support, probably to Social Democrats and Liberals.

The radical reply to this is first, that electors would react differently if given a real choice rather than the marginally contrasting alternatives which are all they have been offered before; secondly, left-wingers argue that electors are misled about their real interests through the biased presentation and comments of the media (radio, television and newspapers).

This is ground already covered in Chapter 4. Media commentators and reporters are undoubtedly more sympathetic to moderate and widely agreed policies, involving limited change, than they are to sweeping proposals for radical action. Hence they have given a better hearing to Social Democrats – within the Labour Party and outside it – than to the Bennites or other representatives of the Left. Of course this tendency cuts both ways: support for moderation has also resulted in less sympathetic treatment for free marketeers, monetarists and extreme nationalists within the Conservative Party.

Nonetheless, neither Socialists nor extreme Conservatives have been denied a hearing and the former particularly have succeeded in establishing themselves as newsworthy. So their statements and policies have been relayed to the audience in no more distorted a form than happens with other political groups. Given a necessary minimum of information, electors are quite capable of relating policies to their own concerns and evaluating them in the way described in Chapter 4. Since evaluation is based on policy emphases made by the parties at a very broad level, subtleties like the tone of surrounding media comment will simply get lost. The existing situation does offer electors a chance to evaluate all the major alternatives. Given their suspicion of change, they *are* likely to vote against extreme left-wing policy, but this reflects their own preferences rather than any media bias.

Quite apart from its unrealistic view of electors, the radical diagnosis also discounts constraints on government action identified earlier, and in particular those stemming from the autonomy and considerable power of extra-governmental institutions – from pressure groups (Ch. 2) and courts (Ch. 7), to 'other governments' (Ch. 5 and 6). These cannot simply be swept away. Possibly Britain could leave the EC, but the government would have to go through a complicated disaffiliation procedure first, and would still have to face internal bodies with substantial delaying powers and obstructive potential in various areas. There is no reason for considering a Left-wing government better equipped to deal with failures of implementation due to internal and societal opposition, than any other kind of government. Indeed, the inference is that obstruction at all levels would be greater under a government trying to put through radical Socialist policies. Whatever the innate merits of a Socialist programme, one thing that would count against it is precisely the long period of delay and uncertainty before it would be implemented and the consequent effects on the currency and economy. This assumes, of course, that the programme *is* practicable, given the existence of multiple power centres in British politics and society.

Constraints on government decision-making

It is the existence of diverse groups and institutions, all with independent standing of some sort, which we have identified as the most striking feature of British politics. It is their obstructiveness which subverts the traditional picture of British government as centred on a supremely authoritative body, the Cabinet, able through its command of Parliament and the Civil Service to do practically anything. Similarly their presence casts doubt on technocratic solutions which simply create new co-ordinating or planning procedures. Without effectively subordinating the separate ministries and 'other'governments, new procedures cannot of themselves ensure effective implementation. Corporatism and tripartism similarly fail to reckon with the inability of central representation to guarantee membership compliance.

Given the spread of responsibilities among a variety of institutions, the overload thesis appears simply misplaced. There *is* no tightly organised government structure taking on increasing tasks which in the end overstrain it. Responsibilities are accumulated by separate departments and quangos without much reference to each other or to popular demands. Overlap between departmental responsibilities, and failures to resolve them, cause confusion and delays, but these are due to the inability of the centre to assert itself sufficiently, not to central overload. This is a weakness which remains unaffected by the presence or absence of adversarial parties.

All the accounts we have examined fail, crucially, to take cognisance of the loose-jointedness of the political system as a whole, the autonomy of its component parts, and the external and internal constraints these impose on decisionmaking. In this section we examine the constraints revealed by earlier analyses before attempting our own overall characterisation.

Internal constraints

We have already detailed the existence of independent 'departmental views' of government policy, and the freedom which 'advocacy politics' give ministries and other government institutions to advance their own goals within the administration. As noted in Chapter 2, clashes also occur between civil servants and ministers within departments. If the minister agrees with Cabinet policy he may find himself fighting his own civil servants to get it accepted. At the same time, opposition will mount from other departments on joint working committees. The Cabinet itself may not be particularly united, and factions may form along ideological lines which spill over into the parliamentary parties. If the policies affect quangos and nationalised industries, other centres of criticism and obstruction may form.

As central government lacks an extended local administration of its own, it depends on councils and authorities for the implementation of most programmes. Hence the attitudes of local officials and their national associations, perhaps even more than those of elected councillors, become crucial to effective promotion of policies. As Chapter 5 amply demonstrated, local representatives are only formally subservient to the government. In practice they can deploy many resources of expertise, information, control of manpower, etc. against their legal masters. They are often motivated to do so by belonging to a party opposed to the one(s) controlling government.

Local governments do not impinge only at the level of field administration. Collectively they account for about a third of total public expenditure. As targets for such expenditure form the main reference point and instrument for the whole of the government's macro-economic policy, local bodies are inevitably drawn into argument about priorities. If cuts are made they must be imposed against strenuous opposition. Although their power is essentially one of reaction against government policy, rather than the creation of a line of their own, their ability to delay or modify centrally imposed policies can be considerable.

Such power also belongs to judges – partly by default as we saw in Chapter 7. Their ability to assess the propriety of ministerial actions under various statutes adds another element of uncertainty to the general political situation and opens up another course of action to those opposing government policy. The judges favour the *status quo* and so tend to rule against 'other governments' taking on more powers. The *status quo*, however, also covers the existing rights and privileges of bodies like the trade unions, which have been upheld by courts in recent years in contradistinction to government attempts to restrict them.

Under stress of economic crisis it is unlikely that any central government can rest content with existing relationships. It is bound to try to change them in some way to promote greater efficiency. Hence judges' attachment to established rights and disinclination to challenge any powerful existing group by no means favour, and may actually hamper, government plans. The same to a lesser extent can be said of the police and army, whose overpowering aim is to avoid being branded as agents of the government.

It is, of course, usually the interest groups, and particularly trade unions, which are popularly regarded as the main challenge to government. The trade unions can exercise considerable constraints over policy. The TUC prevented legislation based on the Labour Government's White Paper on industrial relations, *In Place of strife*, being enacted in 1969 and turned the Conservative's 1971 Industrial Relations Act into a virtual dead letter by refusing to co-operate with its administration. Subsequently, under the social contract, they won the repeal of the Industrial Relations Act (and its replacement by the Trade Union and Labour Relations Act of 1974, and the Trade Union and Labour Relations (Amendment) Act of 1976), the passage of the Employment Protection Act 1975 and the Health and Safety at Work Act 1974. At the same time, certain individual trade unions in key strategic industries, notably the miners in the winter of 1973/4 and transport and public sector workers in the winter of 1978/9, have managed to restrict the effectiveness of governments' voluntary or statutory incomes policies. This hardly means that the trade unions are the dominant force in British politics. After the election of a Conservative Government committed to market mechanisms in 1979, the trade unions were consulted much less often and the Government pushed through new Acts to restrict picketing and limit their other immunities. Nevertheless, trade unions can certainly inhibit government action, although the extent of their influence depends partly on the party in power and, probably more significantly, the level of unemployment. It also depends crucially on the state of unity among trade unionists themselves; as we have seen, they are often internally divided between powerful individual unions and between the official leadership and 'unofficial' shopfloor committees inside unions.

The influence of industry and commerce is at least as strong in Britain as that of labour, although the way it is exerted is less obvious. Within business there are also divisions. The interests of finance and industry, manufacturing and retail, nationally based and multinational firms, and large and small companies, often diverge. This prevents unanimous representations being made to government. On the manufacturing side the CBI has close contacts with the Civil Service and has had one or two notable successes in influencing policy. For example, the 1975 Industry Act, based on a very radical Labour Party policy document, was almost totally emasculated due to a large extent to pressure from the CBI in particular and business in general. Much of the manufacturing sector's power, however, is less direct. Here the top one hundred UK companies account for 40 per cent of sales, capital expenditure and exports; over a third of employment; and 75 per cent of outward investment. This concentration means that the decisions of these companies are vital for the future performance of the British economy and, therefore, for the prospects of the government in power. In a very different sense the government must take account of these companies' views and interests because they play such a crucial role. In other words, the constraint they exercise is largely, although not exclusively, structural.

The power of financial interests – that is, of the City, the banks, insurance companies and pension funds – is even less direct, although it is becoming better documented. Insurance companies and pension funds have increasingly large equity holdings in British industry, while the merchant banks often control the voting rights attaching to such shares. At the same time the important position of the City of London in world financial markets means that their activity has a crucial influence on the British balance of payments through the so called 'invisible exports' – made up of insurance premiums, broking commission, etc. All this imposes another structural constraint on government which can be very restrictive, as in the period between 1974 and 1977 when the Government's freedom of manoeuvre in economic areas was effectively lost through a near-permanent 'run on the pound' in the money markets. As a somewhat jaundiced Jim Callaghan said, with only limited exaggeration, at the 1976 Labour Party Conference: 'An unwise resolution, an ill-judged statement can knock £200 million off the reserves in a minute or add 20p to the price of goods in your shopping basket.' No government can ignore the political implications of such power. In addition, the finance sector has now evolved direct contacts with the Treasury through the Bank of England and more recently through its developing trade associations. Such representations ensure that in some cases the influence of 'the City' is overt and direct. Though again we have noted the internal divisions which prevent financial representatives, unlike those of industry, even joining together in the same peak organisations.

None of this should imply that the power of business is overwhelming, although there is a tendency to ignore its influence, a development which is not dissociated from the very visible activities of trade unions in recent years. All we are arguing here is that industrial and financial interests act as a constraint on government, and like the trade unions, restrict its autonomy. At the same time we must not ignore examples of other interest groups constraining government in other fields of policy-making – for example, the National Farmers' Union in agriculture, the British Road Federation in transport and the British Medical Association in health and welfare. Governments do not make policy in a vacuum; they are influenced and restricted in their decisions by many societal forces.

External constraints

Most analyses of the British political system treat it as though it were a discrete system and not part of an international political and economic order. There are, however, obvious external constraints on government action which are worth considering briefly at this point.

As we saw in Chapter 6, the relationship between the EC and British government is not a simple one. The Commission is vested with authority which is independent of the national governments but it is still tied by decisions taken by the Council of Ministers. In the Council of Ministers the British, in common with all other members, can veto decisions. Nevertheless, membership of the EC has restricted the autonomy of British governments in a number of ways.

Our earlier analysis indicated that Britain has become deeply enmeshed in the EC although the extent of involvement differs in various policy areas. As the EC is a political organisation, decisions taken by the Council of Ministers inevitably involve compromise and concessions. So, for example, the British may have to make concessions on farm prices in order to protect the interests of their fishermen. At the same time, the British government and its legislation is subject to rulings of the European Court. Indeed, the Court has the power to determine the constitutionality of British Acts of Parliament. In both these ways the autonomy of the British government has been reduced by membership. Whether or not it remains a member (Labour Party policy is ambiguous), Britain will still have to reckon with the fact that trade with the Community is increasing and its economic success will still depend heavily on tariff decisions made by the Commission and Council of Ministers.

Perhaps the greatest constraint on central government stems from the structural reality that Britain is a trading nation dependent on exports and imports for its economic survival. Like all advanced industrial countries, Britain has been buffeted by the instability and unpredictability of the world economic system over the last fifteen years. Oil price increases, fluctuations in world interest rates and in the general level of trading in the world economy, have had profound effects on British domestic policies. Until the advent of North Sea oil, Britain was in a particularly vulnerable position. Low productivity and growth constantly exposed the economy to balance of payments and currency crises.

These reached their apotheosis during the life of the 1974–79 Labour Governments when the major factor shaping economic policy was the falling value of the pound on the world's money markets. The continuing crises led eventually to the International Monetary Fund requiring the Government to pursue even more cautious fiscal and monetary policies which had widespread repercussions for public expenditure and thus a wide range of social programmes. Unfortunately, Britain remains in a poor, even deteriorating, position as an international trader, and from 1979 serious crises were averted only because of the cushioning effect of North Sea oil revenues and the adoption of deflationary policies by the Thatcher government.

Fragmentation – a jigsaw without a picture?

The evidence points to a variety of groups, interests and organisations all exerting considerable influence over policies but divided internally and externally. Government decision-making is severely circumscribed by their activities. Most exercise a negative or veto power: they can constrain the alternatives considered by governments or open for them to pursue. They can even prevent a government carrying out a policy to which it is committed. But they cannot substitute their own policies. On the whole they can only react to central suggestions or policy imposition.

All this limits the scope for real change. Governments whose policies are often thwarted appear as decreasingly in control of events. Decision-makers in general seem both to themselves and to others as merely responding to political and economic forces they can do little about.

This situation, of course, is hardly confined to the United Kingdom. All modern industrial states face problems of adaptation and control, and at least two of the interpretations discussed earlier (corporatism and overload) have been applied to a number of other governmental systems. However, Britain seems to be experiencing especially difficult problems – in part because of secular economic decline, but also (and relatedly) because of the particular nature of its political system.

Briefly the British state (i.e. British governments in general) seems weak in comparison to governments in comparable countries. As a result it is poorly equipped to engage in the kind of highly positive intervention which the vast changes wrought by economic and technological developments have made necessary in recent years. The large number of goods and services provided by government and public utilities (over 40 per cent of gross domestic product) does not contradict this point. Public spending patterns are only one indicator of the extent of government influence and power. Others include the extent to which, historically, the agents of central government have managed, controlled, coerced and influenced economic and social forces. Developments in Britain which seem to have limited their role drastically can be summarised as follows:

1. The eighteenth and nineteenth centuries saw the emergence of a set of institutions: a strong executive, a unitary system of government and highly centralised political parties dominated by London-based élites. The strength of these institutions, and the unity of the élites, produced the impression of a strong centralised state, especially as for most of this period economic liberalism was proving so successful and the society was unusually homogeneous and secure from outside threats. Crucially, élites found it unnecessary to establish strong linkages with economic and other groups in society, either to speed industrialisation or to maintain order (in contrast with post-Tokugawa Japan, Bismarck's Germany, or even the Third Republic in France). And when linkages were established it was on an *ad hoc*, functionally fragmented, basis, lacking co-ordination or general policy direction.

2. The relative independence (or autonomy) of local government, unions, business, police, courts and so on, can be traced to this period. As can the assumption in British political culture that 'governments know best' or that professional civil servants and London-based politicians and parties can solve society's problems. And so they could and did during the nineteenth century – usually by delegating power to lower level authorities. When industrialisation produced a more reformist Liberal Party and a new socialist party, they too took on the attitudes to governing of the established élites. Hence neither the politicians (old or new), nor the civil servants, perceived any need to move into society to negotiate support, to build a consensus, to create hierarchical relationships incorporating economic interests (in particular) into decision-making structures.

3. The advent of total war, the emergence of a powerful labour movement and serious economic dislocation in an increasingly changing and unpredictable world, did of course force governments to intervene more and more

in economics and social life. Chapters 2 and 5 especially have documented the extensive nature of such intervention, involving close contacts between affected interests, lower authorities and central government. However, intervention seems to have taken on particular forms which limits its effectiveness:

(a) It often consists of *ad hoc*, unco-ordinated action inspired by a particular problem or policy.

(b) Intervention is also functionally differentiated and fragmented, i.e. individual firms have access to the Ministries of Trade or Industry on a piecemeal rather than a systematic basis.

(c) Individual local government departments often have strong links with Whitehall, but few horizontal links at the grass roots. Corresponding horizontal links at the central level are (historically) also weak. Home Office/police relations are similarly fragmented. A corollary here is that peak associations and their equivalents have developed similarly. Peak associations have always had a very generalised representative role but few close working relationships with individual members.

(d) Underlying this particular form of contact and strengthened by it is an active distaste of governments and administrators for systematic and detailed intervention. Hence great discretion is accorded lower level authorities – whether they be police, army, judges, local authorities, quangos, various organised interests, or corporations – to implement policy in functionally distinct areas.

(e) The distaste for detailed intervention has both produced and been justified by an adherence to simple, general solutions to economic and social problems. Such solutions have been patterned on the free trade and non-interventionist policies which worked so successfully in the nineteenth century. The most obvious successor was Keynesian macroeconomic planning. Precisely because this rested on central manipulation of finances without any detailed follow-up, it was universally accepted for thirty years. Contemporary successors are monetarism (restriction of public expenditures without detailed follow-up) or block import controls. Adoption of such 'unitary' panaceas which will transform problems through generalised central action, are understandable given the formidable political problems involved in strengthening vertical and horizontal linkage. But they are not really a substitute.

(f) Hence as pressures have increased, successive Governments have found themselves obliged to confront individual lower level groups and authorities, often in ways leading to serious conflict, especially as the political Opposition tends to back those resisting central direction. Examples are the confrontations with both unions and local governments in the early 1980s. Governments lack both the central co-ordinating structures and institutions and the vertical authority structures which strong peak associations disciplining their members could provide. The result is a continuing sense of political crisis and confrontation.

(g) This accepted, new corporatist arrangements have been tried (NEDC, planning agreements in industrial policy), if not always successfully.

And peak associations are constantly exhorted by government to exert greater influence on members. The London-based media play an important part in this process, always favouring consensus-building options to ones involving confrontation.

Developments in the post-war period

Against this background post-war developments fall into an entirely understandable pattern. With the first limited attempts by governments to manage aspects of social change on a permanent basis, during the 1930s and 1940s a fragile consensus with the leading economic and political actors of society was established. The Labour triumph of 1945 precipitated a flood of social and economic reform which led to a greatly enhanced role for government at all levels.

Crucially, however, amid the frenzy of activity associated with the Second World War and its aftermath, little in the way of permanent or fundamental changes in the role of the state occurred. The machinery of government remained virtually unchanged. Vertical linkages between central officials and the leading economic and social groups in society remained weak. And when new linkages were forged they tended to be between central government and business and labour élites who, as we have noted, often had little contact with or control over their own members. The institutions of the state itself remained fragmented. The judiciary was fiercely independent; the police remained largely under local control. Local governments, in spite of being given vast new responsibilities, were controlled indirectly by statute and through the purse-strings. Central government did not impose its own agents (such as prefects in France) on the system. Finally, important divisions within central government, and particularly between the Treasury and the spending departments, persisted.

So, in spite of greatly increased public expenditures (and the higher public expectations of government which they brought), British politicians continued to depend on remarkably undeveloped institutions of co-ordination and control. It was almost as if the pulling of levers in Whitehall and Westminster was all that was needed to operate the new system. Keynesian demand management with its emphasis on macro-economic policy almost certainly reinforced such views. To reform the economy, detailed, micro-intervention was unnecessary. All that was needed was a change in public expenditure or in fiscal and monetary policy and all would be well.

The workings of this type of attitude can be illustrated by an example from the late 1970s when it was increasingly obvious that general fiscal manipulation was inadequate, partly because the collapse of large enterprises like British Shipbuilders and British Leyland (cars) with vast social consequences had to be averted by direct subsidy. At this point one of the larger British car-hire firms – like most large institutions a traditional purchaser of British cars – passed under the control of foreign interests. No particular notice of this was taken either in Whitehall or in the media. Yet it was highly likely that foreign control would be quietly followed by purchase of cheaper cars abroad after a year or so. Where French administrators would have been concerned to ensure that French control and purchasing policy remained, the British apparently did not even consider the loss of a small but steady market share for their manufacturing industry.

Similarly, when the government invested close to £100 million to set up a car manufacturing firm in Belfast in the early 1980s, they apparently left total operational control in the hands of the American founder and were taken by surprise by his bankruptcy in 1982. The firm had not been monitored even to the extent that administrators knew of its month by month economic prospects.

Perhaps surprisingly, at least until the 1960s, Labour Governments were as prone to see the world in general terms as were Conservative. In the context of relative economic prosperity and a broad acceptance of the traditional view of the constitution and party system, it is perhaps not surprising that politicians of all shades broadly agreed that the system worked. Why, after all propose a stronger state, more planning, co-ordination and control when Britain was widely recognised as stable, efficient and politically mature?

When, during the ever-intensifying crises of the 1960s and 1970s, governments did attempt reforms and greater control, the fragile consensus with interest group leaders quickly evaporated. To their great consternation governments discovered that unions, local governments, industrial corporations and others could act independently. Nothing better illustrates the structural problems of British governments than the continuing struggle to control public expenditure. In this area successive governments have fallen foul of both internal weakness and external constraints. The absence of success eventually led the Thatcher Government to impose draconian solutions such as 'fining' recalcitrant local governments, which have themselves yet to prove effective.

British policy in Northern Ireland can also be partly understood within this general argument. Until the beginning of the present troubles British administrations virtually ignored the internal government of the province. Certainly the Whitehall/Stormont linkages were tenuous; what Stormont did was an Irish affair. Following the assemblies' demise, London had no alternative but to govern direct, but in a context of virtually no historically established linkages with Northern Irish society. The devolved administration of Northern Ireland, Scotland, and increasingly Wales, reflects the absence of such links.

A fragmented British political system?

If the British state is fragmented and weak, so too it might be claimed are the administrative and governmental arrangements of most states, especially under the stresses to which they are subjected in an increasingly interdependent and unpredictable world. The difference lies in the long-standing recognition of such weaknesses elsewhere, in contrast to the traditional characterisation of Britain as politically stable and efficient. This view, which we examined at the outset of the chapter, saw the two-party system in conjunction with Cabinet government as a uniquely effective method of governing. Clearly such a claim is not appropriate for the 1980s. Indeed in functional terms a number of other countries appear to operate political systems better suited to the modern world than the British. Most of these – France, Germany, Sweden, Japan, the Netherlands – are 'democracies'. But each has political arrangements considered alien to the British way of governing. It is testimony to the present bankrupt state of the British system that there are serious proposals to incorporate some of these alien features, including proportional representation; multi-party and coalition governments; federalism and regionalism; open government; and corporatist arrangements in industrial and economic policy. It is also significant that many of Britain's more successful competitors do have relatively strong central state institutions or (equally important) decision-making structures built more on consensus and co-operation than on conflict and confrontation.

We should not infer from this some blueprint for the reform of British government. It is one of the merits of the explanation in terms of fragmented centres of power, and lack of central co-ordination, that simple one-factor solutions to British problems are ruled out. Any attempt at change will in any case be undermined by the opposition it provokes from various interests and groups. Even such a minor institutional adjustment as Welsh and Scottish devolution was defeated in the late 1970s, despite the fact that the country had lived with a much more thoroughgoing devolution of power to Northern Ireland for half a century. When the central government could not get its solution accepted in this case, it is unlikely to muster enough support for more serious changes in power relationships, especially if it tries to impose them unilaterally.

The most likely outcome in the near future is an uneasy, shifting equilibrium as governments experiment with institutional changes, negotiate with societal interests, and try to back this up by imposing key policies. Some such combination may work if it is accompanied by a willingness to establish permanent administrative relationships with individual organisations in particular sectors. The breakdown of class barriers noted in Chapter 4 may aid an attempt to build up consensual working relationships. The attitudes of the general population are positive and encouraging. In the end, however, the traditional aloofness of government may well prevent this happening; and whatever the means of general form of economic management happens to be in force when the world recession breaks could serve as a fresh justification for avoiding detailed intervention.

There is certainly some merit in avoiding ill-advised and hasty institutional changes. It may be that some of the alternative arrangements we have reviewed are inappropriate for Britain. Some may even constitute threats to long-established individual freedoms, for greater administrative and economic efficiency is unlikely to be achieved without sacrifices in terms of other societal values. A fragmented system does after all have some beneficial effects, as we saw at the end of the last chapter. Centralised police and military coercion is difficult to achieve with a fragmented structure. And the relative independence of lower level governments and policy networks does provide a bulwark against the emergence of a centralised, strong and unresponsive élite.

But, as was pointed out earlier, fragmentation does not guarantee effective popular control. Instead, it puts a great premium on the *negative* or *reactive* power of various organisations. Unfortunately there is no magic formula which can produce both popular control with participation, and efficient and responsive government.

What is important, however, is that British élites and public recognise the fragmented and often inefficient nature of the present political system. The serious problems that have plagued successive governments since the 1960s – poor economic performance, sour industrial relations, racial unrest and a state of near civil war in Northern Ireland – remain with us and are unlikely to be resolved in the foreseeable future. Reforms are, therefore, urgently needed. Moves in the direction of greater accountability and participation may actually increase fragmentation, while moves towards centralisation or a corporatist consensus may undermine popular control. This is the central and possibly irresolvable problem of British politics over the next decade.

References and Bibliography

As each chapter summarises a variety of findings and discussions, and also reports original research, we have not deemed it necessary to clutter the text with detailed references on each point. Generally these have been given only when another author was directly quoted, where a table was based upon particular references, or where a whole section of the discussion was based on one book. The purpose of this note is to give detailed references for the main sources for each chapter. Generally these divide between broad treatments which provide a good overview of a particular topic, and detailed studies on which we have relied for supporting evidence. Books with broader coverage are listed first under each heading.

Place of publication is London except where otherwise stated.

Economic difficulties and central decision-making (Chapters 1 and 2)

S. H. Beer, (1965) *Modern British politics*, Faber, is a good general background to policy-making in British central government, though inevitably dated by now.

A. H. Birch (1964) *Representative and responsible government*, Allen & Unwin, deals with many of the problems of accountability and answerability that crop up throughout the discussion, again from an earlier perspective. A more up-to-date account is **J. J. Richardson** and **A. G. Jordan** (1979) *Governing under pressure: the policy process in a post-parliamentary democracry*, Oxford, Martin Robertson.

On 'Whitehall' specifically is **G. K. Fry**, (1981) *The administrative revolution in Whitehall*, Croom Helm. See also **V. M. Herman** and **J. Alt** (1975) *Cabinet studies*, Macmillan.

Budgetary processes are reviewed in **A. Wildavsky** and **H. Heclo** (1974) *The private government of public money*, Macmillan.

The amorphous ground occupied by officially sponsored 'non-departmental organisations' is covered most recently in **A. Barker**, ed. (1982) *Quangos in Britain: government and the networks of public policy-making*, Macmillan.

Views from the inside, based on personal experience, are given in **R. Cross-**

man (1979) *The Crossman diaries: selections from the diaries of a Cabinet minister*, ed. **A. Howard**, Magnum, **G. Kaufman** (1980) *How to be a minister*, Sidgwick & Jackson; **W. Rodgers** *et al.* (1980) *Policy and practice: the experience of government*, Royal Institute of Public Administration, London.

General surveys of pressure groups are **R. Taylor** (1980) *The fifth estate: Britain's unions in the modern world*, Pan; **R. Undy, V. Ellis, W. E. J. McCarthy** and **A. M. Halmos** (1981) *Change in trade unions: the development of UK Unions since the 1960s*, Hutchinson; **W. Grant** and **D. Marsh** (1977) *The Confederation of British Industry*, Hodder & Stoughton; **G. K. Wilson** (1977) *Special interests and policy-making*, Wiley. On the role of the City see **M. Moran** (1984) *The Politics of Banking*, Macmillan.

On 'planning' see **A. Budd** (1978) *The politics of economic planning*, Glasgow, Fontana, **D. Foley** (1963), *Controlling London's growth*, Los Angeles, University of California Press; **J. Leruez** (1975) *Economic planning and politics in Britain*, Martin Robertson; **M. Shanks** (1977) *Planning and politics*, Allen & Unwin.

Government and Parliament (Chapter 3)

A useful coverage of both Parliament itself and its relationship with other institutions is **R. M. Punnett** (1980) *British government and politics*, Heinemann. See also **R. Leonard** and **V. M. Herman** eds (1972) *The backbencher and Parliament*, Macmillan; **S. A. Walkland** and **M. Ryle**, eds (1977) *The Commons in the seventies*, Fontana.

J. A. G. Griffiths (1974) *Parliamentary scrutiny of government Bills*, Allen & Unwin, is illuminating on the extent of Parliament's legislative powers.

The major work on dissent in the parliamentary parties during the 1970s is **P. Norton** (1980) *Dissension in the House of Commons 1974–9*, Oxford University Press; this also summarises earlier work and gives more extended references.

For divisions on moral legislation see **D. Marsh** and **J. Chambers** (1981) *Abortion Politics*, Junction Books.

Ideological lines of dissent over the post-war period are traced by **S. E. Finer** and **H. Berrington** with their associates (1961 and subsequent dates) *Backbench opinion in the House of Commons*, Oxford, Pergamon.

The major work on Select Committees is **A. Robinson** (1978) *Parliament and public spending*, Heinemann.

On the structure of the press and its effects on political reporting see **J. Tunstall** (1970) *The Westminster lobby correspondents*, Routledge, and (1971) *Journalists at work*, Constable; and **C. Seymour-Ure** (1974) *The political impact of the mass media*, Constable.

Political parties and voting (Chapter 4)

A book which integrates most of the field is **J. Blondel** (1980) *Voters, parties and leaders*, Penguin Books.

A critical treatment of the British parties is **S. E. Finer** (1980) *The changing British party system 1945–79*, American Enterprise Institute, Washington, D.C.

For an analysis of the impact of parties on policy see **D. H. McKay** and **A. Cox** (1979) *The politics of urban change*, Croom Helm.

Party relationships and the internal balance within the major parties themselves have changed so rapidly since 1981 that the best guide to the current situation are reports in *The Times, The Guardian, The Sunday Times, The Observer* and *The Economist*.

Election issues and party strategies are systematically reviewed in **I. Budge** and **D. J. Farlie** (1983) *Explaining and predicting elections*, Allen & Unwin. A detailed account of party activity in each campaign is provided by **D. E. Butler** and associates (various dates), *The Nuffield general election series*, Macmillan (the latest is with **D. Kavanagh** (1980) *The British general election of 1979*, Macmillan.

Detailed analyses of party election manifestoes are **D. Robertson** (1976) *A theory of party competition*, Wiley and **I. Budge** and **D. J. Farlie** (1977) *Voting and party competition*, Wiley, ch. 11. The latter also measures the effects of issues, class, religion and region on individual voting for elections up to 1974.

The authoritative account of national voting in the 1970s is **I. Crewe** and **B. Sarlvik** (1983) *Why the Conservatives won: voting in the 1979 general election*, Cambridge University Press; this traces the declining influence of party loyalty and class affiliation on voting.

A specific comparison of class and area influence is **W. L. Miller** (1978) 'Social class and party choice in England: a new analysis', *British journal of political science 8*: 257–84. The major study of class structure and class mobility in contemporary Britain is **J. Goldthorpe** *et al.* (1980) *Social mobility and class structure in modern Britain*, Oxford University Press.

Regional variations in class structure are explored in **I. Budge** and **C. O'Leary** (1973) *Belfast: approach to crisis*, Macmillan, ch. 8. Regional influences as a whole are assessed in **I. Budge** and **D. W. Urwin** (1966) *Scottish political behaviour*, Longman; **W. L. Miller** (1980) *The end of British politics? Scots and English political behaviour in the seventies*, Oxford University Press; **I. Budge** and **C. O'Leary** (1977) 'Permanent supremacy and perpetual opposition in Northern Ireland', in **A. Eldridge**, ed., *Legislatures in plural societies*, Durham, N.C., Duke University Press; **K. Morgan** (1970) *Wales in British politics*, Cardiff, University of Wales Press.

For electors' values see **I. Budge** (1970) *Agreement and the stability of democracy*, Chicago, Rand McNally; **L. Moss** (1980) 'Some attitudes towards government', Birkbeck College, London, and various surveys reported in *The Times* (London) 26–28 June 1980; **J. Dennis** *et al* (1971) 'Support for nation and government among English children', *British journal of political science* **1**: 254–8.

For electors' reactions to the economic situation the best source is **J. Alt** (1979) *The politics of economic decline*, Cambridge University Press. *Family expenditure survey* and *Social trends*, both published annually by the H. M. Stationery Office, give valuable information on living standards.

Local and other governments of Britain (Chapter 5)

An extensive bibliography on central–local relationships can be found in **R. A. W. Rhodes** (1981) *Control and power in central-local government relationships*, Farnborough, Gower. An extensive bibliography on the peripheral regions is **L. Pollock** and **I. McAllister** (1980) *A bibliography of United Kingdom politics: Scotland, Wales and Northern Ireland*, Glasgow University of Strathclyde, Centre for the Study of Public Policy.

The following list covers the more important contributions to the study of inter-governmental relations in Britain.

The peripheral regions

A. H. Birch (1977) *Political integration and disintegration in the British Isles*, Allen & Unwin.
D. Birrell and **A. Murie** (1980) *Policy and government in Northern Ireland*, Dublin, Gill & Macmillan.
J. G. Kellas (1975) *The Scottish political system*, 2nd edn, Cambridge University Press.
D. G. Kermode (1979) *Devolution at work: a case study of the Isle of Man*, Farnborough, Saxon House.
P. J. Madgwick and **M. James** (1980) 'The network of consultative government in Wales', in **G. W. Jones**, ed *New approaches to the study of central-local government relationships*, Gower, Farnborough.

Non-departmental organisations

D. C. Hague, **W. J. M. Mackenzie** and **A. Barker** eds (1973) *Public policy and private interests*, Macmillan.
C. C. Hood (1978) 'Keeping the centre small: explanations of agency type', *Political studies* **26**: 30–46.
A. Barker (ed), (1982) *Quangos in Britain: government and the networks of public policy-making*, Macmillan.

Central–local relations

Committee of Inquiry into local government finance (Layfield) (1976) *Report* Cmnd 6453, H.M.S.O., London.
J. A. G. Griffith (1966) *Central departments and local authorities*, Allen & Unwin.
G. W. Jones (1980) *New approaches to the study of central-local government relationships*, Farnborough, Gower.
R. A. W. Rhodes (1981) *Control and power in central-local government relationships*, Gower and (1984) *The National World of Local Government*, Allen & Unwin.

Local political systems

J. Dearlove (1973) *The politics of policy in local government*, Cambridge University Press.

G. W. Jones (1969) *Borough politics*, Macmillan.

J. M. Lee (1963) *Social leaders and public persons*, Oxford, Clarendon Press.

K. Newton (1976) *Second city politics*, Oxford, Clarendon Press.

L. J. Sharpe ed. (1967) *Voting in cities*, Macmillan.

Financial relationships

C. D. Foster, **R. Jackman** and **M. Perlman** (1980) *Local government finance in a unitary state*, Allen & Unwin.

N. P. Hepworth (1980) *The finance of local government*, 4th edn, Allen & Unwin.

Local government – general

R. Greenwood, **K. Walsh**, **C. R. Hinings** and **S. Ranson** (1980) *Patterns of management in local government*, Oxford, Martin Robertson.

B. Keith-Lucas and **P. G. Richards** (1978) *A history of local government in the twentieth century*, Allen & Unwin.

J. Lagroye and **V. Wright**, eds (1979) *Local government in Britain and France*, Allen & Unwin.

D. Regan (1977) *Local government and education*, Allen & Unwin.

The European Community and British government (Chapter 6)

Considering the importance of relationships here academic coverage has been slight. The most up-to-date review is **D. Kavanagh** (1977) 'New bottles for new wines', *Parliamentary affairs* **31**: 6–21. The most comprehensive is **W. Wallace**, **H. Wallace** and **K. Webb** (1977) *Policy-making in the European Community*, Wiley.

Earlier studies are: **H. Wallace** (1973) *National governments and the European communities*, London, Chatham House; **H. Wallace** (1974) 'The European Community and British government', in *The European Economic Community: national and international impact*, Milton Keynes, Open University Press; **R. J. Lieber** (1970) *British politics and European unity*, Berkeley, Calif., Berkeley University Press.

Courts and legal decision-making (Chapter 7)

The general structure is covered in **R. M. Jackson** (1977) *The machinery of justice in England*, Cambridge University Press; **D. Walker** (1976) *The Scottish legal system* Edinburgh, Green; **H. Calvert** (1968) *Constitutional law in Northern Ireland*, Stevens.

B. Abel-Smith and **R. Stevens** (1970) *Lawyers and the courts*, Stevens, covers the legal profession.

J. A. G. Griffith (1981) *The politics of the English judiciary*, Fontana, is a controversial treatment of judges, their background and decisions.

D. Robertson (1982) 'Judicial ideology in the House of Lords: a jurimetric analysis', *British journal of political science* **12**: 1–25 is a first attempt at uncovering voting patterns in the highest court.

G. Drury (1975) *Law, justice and politics*, Longman; **T. C. Hartley** and **J. A. G. Griffith** (1975) *Government and law*, Weidenfeld & Nicolson, examine the political significance of court decisions.

The police and military (Chapter 8)

R. Mark (1978) *In the office of constable*, Allen & Unwin, examines the system from a policy viewpoint, as does **J. Alderson** (1979) *Policing freedom*, Macdonald & Evans. **G. Marshall** (1965) *Police and government*, Methuen, covers similar ground from outside. **R. M. Jackson** (1972) *Enforcing the law*, Penguin Books, is a helpful survey, now overtaken by events.

J. Lambert (1970) *Crime, police and race relations*, Oxford University Press, foreshadows some questions of great relevance to the 1980s.

There is very little on the internal role of the military, a point which is significant in itself. Some references are made in **R. Clutterbuck** (1975) *Living with terrorism*, Faber.

On future strategy see **Sir J. Hackett** (1978) *The third world war*, Sidgwick & Jackson.

Characterising British politics (Chapter 9)

The traditional view is given in textbooks of the 1960s such as the concise book by **G. Moodie** (1963) *British government and politics*, Methuen. Their criticisms point the way to the 'technocratic' reforms of the late 1960 and early 1970.

Corporatism is discussed generally in **P. Schmitter** and **G. Lehmbruch**, eds (1979) *Trends towards corporatist intermediation*, Beverley Hills, Sage. For Britain see **T. Smith** (1979) *Politics of corporate economy*, Oxford, Martin Robertson; **K. Middlemass** (1979) *Politics of industrial society*, Deutsch; **N. Harris** (1972) *Competition and the corporate society: British conservatism, the state and industry*, Methuen; **R. Taylor** (1978) *Labour and the social contract*, Fabian Society Tract **458**.

On 'overload' see **A. King** ed. (1976) *Why is Britain becoming harder to govern?*, BBC Publications; **S. Brittan** (1975) 'The economic contradictions of democracy', *British journal of political science* **5**: 129–59.

Adversary politics are most powerfully condemned in **S. E. Finer** (1975) *Adversary politics and electoral reform*, A. Wigram. **A. Wedgwood Benn** (1980) *Arguments for socialism*, Penguin Books, is the radical alternative by one of its proponents.

A comparison with the industrial–institutional development of other countries is implicitly provided in **C. Trebilcock** (1981) *The industrialisation of the continental powers 1780–1914*, Longman. See also **M. Stewart** (1977) *The Jekyll and Hyde years*, Dent; **W. Keegan** and **R. P. Rea** (1979) *Who runs the economy?* Temple Smith.

Notes on contributors

Ian Budge: Professor at the Department of Politics at the European University Institute at Florence and at the University of Essex. He is the author of numerous books and articles including *Agreement and stability of democracy* (1970) and *Voting and party competition* (1977, with D. Farlie).

David McKay: Senior Lecturer in Government and Director of the European Consortium for Political Research at the University of Essex. His most recent publications include *Planning and politics in Western Europe* (ed. 1982) and *American politics and society* (1983).

David Marsh: Lecturer in Government at the University of Essex. Among his many publications are *The Confederation of British Industries* (1977, with Wyn Grant), *Abortion politics*, (1982, with Joanne Chambers), and has edited *Pressure politics* (1983).

Edward Page: Lecturer in Politics at the University of Hull. Has edited with Richard Rose *Fiscal stress in cities* (1982). Has worked generally on local fiscal problems and central/local relations.

Roderick Rhodes: Lecturer in Government at the University of Essex and a former editor of *Public administration bulletin*. Among his many publications are *Control and power in central local relations* (1981), *Public administration and policy analysis* (1979).

David Robertson: A Fellow of St Hugh's College and a Lecturer in the sub-faculties of Politics and Sociology at the University of Oxford. His major publications include *A theory of party competition* (1976) and *Class and the British electorate* (1983).

Martin Slater: Lecturer in Government at the University of Essex. He has published articles on French and Italian politics, focusing particularly on trade union politics and labour migration issues.

Graham Wilson: Professor of Political Science at the University of Wisconsin. His publications include *Special interests and policy making* (1977), *Unions in American national politics* (1979) and *Interest groups in the United States* (1981).

Index